Daniel
Prophet of
Integrity

A COMMENTARY ON THE
BOOK OF DANIEL

Douglas Williams

BookVenture Publishing LLC
1000 Country Lane Ste 300
Ishpeming MI 49849
www.bookventure.com
Hotline: 1(877) 276-9751
Fax: 1(877) 864-1686

Ordering Information:
Quantity sales. Special discounts are available on quantity purchases by corporations, associations, and others. For details, contact the publisher at the address above.

Printed in the United States of America.

Library of Congress Control Number	2018951727
ISBN-13:	
Softcover	978-1-64069-697-6
Hardcover	978-1-64069-698-3
Pdf	978-1-64069-699-0
ePub	978-1-64069-700-3
Kindle	978-1-64069-701-0

Rev. date: 03/27/2018

CONTENTS

Answers to test

1. b	19. g, e	37. c	54. d	72. b	90. d
2. c	20. b	38. d	55. b	73. a	91. a
3. d	21. d	39. a	56. b	74. c	92. c
4. c	22. d	40. d	57. b	75. b	93. c
5. d	23. d	41. d	58. c	76. a	94. b
6. a	24. b	42. a	59. d	77. b	95. b
7. a	25. a	43. e	60. b	78. b	
8. c	26. b	44. c	61. d	79. b	
9. b	27. a	45. b	62. d	80. b	
10. b	28. d	46. e,c	63. c	81. a	
11. b	29. c	47. d	64. a	82. d	
12. b	30. p,b,e	48. f,a	65. a	83. d	
13. c	31. s,c,.h	49. a	66. b	84. d	
14. b	32. r,d,.g	50. a	67. c	85. d	
15. c	33. t,a,f	51. a	68. e	86. c	
16. b	34. w,m	52. b	69. a	87. e	
17. b	35. n,j,k	53. d	70. a	88. d	
18. e	36. b	54. d	71. d	89. c	

FOREWORD

The Purpose for this book on Daniel

There are many very good commentaries on Daniel and so I am asked, "Why are you writing another one on Daniel?" There are 6 reasons for this book.

1. Several students at Seoul Jangsin University in Gwangju, Gyeonggido, Korea asked me to explain the message of Daniel. I hope this book helps to fulfill their request. I seek to make the message as clear and simple as possible so that the basic message of Daniel can be easily understood. John Calvin's 1,000-page commentary and Albert Barnes' 600-page commentary on Daniel are very good but too exhaustive for the average reader. I use over 50 sources to help me to accurately and completely cover the subject but also be as brief and concise as possible.

2. Daniel is the skeleton and foundation of all Biblical prophecy. A correct understanding of Daniel will greatly help all of us to understand all the other Biblical prophecies concerning Christ's first and second coming and protect us from many false teachings.

3. Daniel 9:24-27 is the backbone of the skeleton of all prophecy. It's the only Old Testament passage where the Hebrew term, *Moshiakh* (Messiah, anointed one) is used in prophecy concerning Jesus Christ. It also gives the exact day when Israel's messiah is revealed. Over 25% of this book covers this all-important passage. A proper understanding of Daniel, especially 9:24-27, will virtually guarantee us protection from the many false teachings that are prevalent today.

I received excellent instruction on the book of Daniel at Toccoa Falls Bible College, Toccoa, Ga. 30577 USA. Soon after graduating in 1971, a pastor of a strange church showed me his church's erroneous interpretation of Daniel 9:24-27. After asking him some questions he replied, "I don't have the answer. You were better prepared than I was." He never brought up the subject again and resigned as pastor and became a dentist.

4. The theme of Daniel is the absolute sovereignty of God in all individuals and all the nations all the time (Dan. 4:17; 34-35, Dt. 32:39, IChron. 29:10-16, Ps. 47:2-9; 103:19; 115:3; 135:6, Pr. 21:1, Isa. 14:27; 43:13, Rev. 1:5) King Nebuchadnezzar thought he was the sovereign ruler and therefore could do whatever he wanted but he learned that Yahweh God alone is sovereign (4:17, 34-35). Modern rulers like Nebuchadnezzar think they rule their countries but they will also learn that Yahweh alone rules over the affairs of man.

5. Since all of Daniel's prophecies concerning Christ's first coming have been literally and completely fulfilled we can be absolutely confident that the prophecies concerning Christ's 2nd coming will also be literally and completely fulfilled. This is tremendous encouragement to all of us who have faith in Jesus Christ as we eagerly look forward to our bright future (John 14:1-3).

6. The most important reason for writing this book is the same reason that Apostle John wrote his gospel. "These things have been written so that you may believe that Jesus is the Christ, the Son of God and that believing you may have life in His name" (John 20:31). Throughout this book I continually fervently encourage all readers to trust this Sovereign God of the universe and receive His generous gift of eternal life through His Son, the Lord Jesus Christ as personal savior.

Unless otherwise noted, the New American Standard Version Bible (NASV) is used when I quote Scripture because in most cases this version gives the most literal and accurate English translation from the original biblical languages.

Even though there is no "J" sound in Hebrew many Hebrew words are spelled with "J" in English Bibles. The 1611 King James translation of the Bible is very good and in some cases superior to modern translations but I smiled when I learned that King James required the translators to put his name in the translation and so the apostle Ya'akov (generally translated as Jacob) is called James.

I spell the Hebrew word Halleluyah (Praise to Yah, LORD) with "y' instead of "j". The English letters Y, H, W, and H spell the name of our heavenly Father and therefore *Yahweh* (Hebrew, the eternal self-existing one) not Jehovah is the personal name of God, our heavenly Father. *Yehoshua* (Yahweh's salvation) or *Yeshua* is our savior's name but since most English readers know Him as Jesus Christ I usually refer to Him this way.

Even though the Apocrypha is not a part of Scripture the history recorded in 1st Maccabees and part of 2nd Maccabees is considered accurate. I therefore quote from these books as recorded in Barns' commentary on Daniel.

BACKGROUND AND INTRODUCTION TO DANIEL

1. The beginning

In the popular musical, *Sound of Music*, Julie Andrews sings, "Let's start from the very beginning, a very good place to start" as she teaches music to the children. We also do this as we study Daniel.

John 1:1-3 clearly teaches that Jesus Christ did not start His life in Bethlehem a little over 2,000 years ago but has always existed from eternity past along with His Father and the Holy Spirit. Verses 3 and 10 teach us that the world and all things were created by Him (Col. 1:16-20; Heb. 1:2). Yahweh, our heavenly Father is the architect and Jesus Christ the Son implemented the architect's plan and did the actual creating. The Holy Spirit empowered the creation (Gen. 1:2, Rom. 8:11; 15:13, Eph. 3:16, 2 Tim. 1:7).

Genesis 1:1-2:7 gives details of the creation. After it was completed God declared that all of it was "very good" (Genesis 1:31).

In Genesis 1-2:3 we see God's rich, marvelous grace to mankind in the beginning. Since God created man on the 6th day of the week, man's first full day of life is the Sabbath, a day of rest with rich fellowship with his maker. God sanctified and declared holy the 7th day as a day of rest for all mankind (Gen. 2:1-3, Mk. 2:27-28). God first gives man rest and then man works 6 days (Ex. 20:8-11; 31:12-18). Israel received great grace as she was freed from 400 years of cruel Egyptian bondage on the Sabbath day (Dt. 5:12-15).

Today we see that the creation obviously did not remain "very good." There are no perfect pairs living in perfect peace in perfect places and therefore we ask "Why? What happened?" Please read the following.

2. The origin of the evil prince (Satan)

Genesis 2:1 and Exodus 20:11 teach that the heavens, the earth, and the entire *host* were created during the creation week. The Hebrew word for host is *sava* meaning army and in this case, God's army; the angels. All the angels were created during the creation week in order to exalt, glorify and praise Yahweh God, their creator.

God asks Job in 38:4-7 (paraphrase) "Where were you when I created the earth and all the morning stars sang together and all the sons of God (angels) shouted for joy?" The angels were created early on the first day of creation week to be on hand to shout, sing, and celebrate the creation of the earth. Light was created later that day (Gen. 1:1-3). Over 4,000 years later Christ, the light of the world (Jn. 8:12) boldly defied and defeated death as He came back to life on resurrection day (John 20).

Lucifer (brilliant and morning star) bore the light for Christ but instead of humbly and graciously receiving his high position he attempted to exalt himself by demanding a higher position. He envied Yahweh and Christ's position and rebelled against God and demanded that he himself be worshiped as God (Isaiah 14:12-15, Ezekiel 28:11-19). He seduced one-third of the angels to join the rebellion (Rev. 12:4) but were greatly humiliated as they were cast out of Heaven (Isaiah 14:15, Ezekiel 28:17, Jude 1:6). Lucifer, the bright, shining star, bearing the light of God became Satan (Hebrew, accuser, slanderer, and adversary) and the devil. Satan hates God but knows he cannot hurt Him directly so he attacked God indirectly by seeking to destroy the supreme object of God's love and the crown of His creation: Mankind.

3. Trouble in the garden

God made man in His own image and thus became the crown of God's creation (Ps. 8; 103:4). He placed Adam and Eve in a perfect paradise: A perfect place of perpetual perfect peace where they could freely eat from all the trees of the garden except one: The tree of the knowledge of good and evil because, "in the day you eat of it you will surely die" (Genesis 2:17).

Since misery loves company Satan freely shared his misery with mankind: The supreme object of God's love (Ps. 8:4-9) as he seduced them to sin (Ge. 3:6). Not only did Adam deliberately and willfully rebel and commit high treason against his creator (I Timothy 2:14) he also refused to take responsibility for his actions as he blamed his wife, Eve and indirectly blamed God (Gen. 3:12, Pr. 19:3). Eve followed her husband's very sorry, corrupt and irresponsible example and blamed the snake (3:13). Cain followed his parents' example as he refused to take responsibility for the cruel murder of his brother Abel (4:9).

Like Adam and Eve mankind willfully and continually rebels against God and refuses to take responsibility for his obstinate sinful behavior (Ps. 51:5, 95:10; Pr. 19:3, Isaiah 53:6; 56:11; 57:11). The good news of Freud, Jung, Rogers, and modern psychology is that no one needs to take responsibility for his actions. He simply blames someone else, bad circumstances, impatient potty training, poverty, or any other excuse that can be found. Pastor Erwin Lutzer in his book, *How to Say No to a Stubborn Habit* (Victor Books, Wheaton, Ill. USA, 1979, p.26) states,

> We cannot exaggerate the harm that has come to individuals from the teachings of Sigmund Freud, that those who misbehave are sick. We don't hold people responsible for catching the flu, measles or having cancer. We have hospitals, not prisons for the physically sick, simply because they bear no moral blame for their illness. The reprehensible Freudian implication is clear; if we are not responsible for physical illness, why should we be blamed for crime, a symptom of moral illness?

The following humorous quote from Jay Adams' *Competent to Counsel* (p.8) is a great illustration of this.

I went to my psychiatrist to be psychoanalyzed
To find out why I killed the cat and blacked my husband's eyes.
He laid me on a downy couch to see what he could find
And here's what he dredged up from my subconscious mind
When I was one my mommy hid my dolly in a trunk,
And it follows naturally that I'm always drunk.
When I was 2 I saw my father kiss the maid one day.
And that's why I suffer from kleptomania
At 3, I had the feeling of ambivolence toward my brothers
And so it follows naturally I poison all my lovers.
But I am happy; now I've learned the lesson this has taught.
That everything I do that's wrong is someone else's fault

Adam was the first psychologist. He taught Eve, his children and all mankind to live irresponsibly if desired and blame others if confronted with its consequences.

There's no record of Adam or Eve's repentance. If they did repent and asked for forgiveness they like all who repent will be warmly welcomed into the kingdom (I Jn. 1:7) but if they continued to reject responsibility for their rebellion as they boldly did in Genesis 3 they also perish in the lake of fire (Rev. 20:15).

The 18th century Prussian King Frederick II visited a prison and learned that, "no one deserved to be there because they were all innocent, framed, wrongly incarcerated, and victimized." All proclaimed their innocence except one who freely confessed his irresponsible, sinful behavior against the state and asked the king for forgiveness. The king was surprised and with rich sarcasm said, "Everyone else here is innocent and you're the only guilty one. I've got to get you out of here before you corrupt all these innocent people in prison." The king set the prisoner free (Turning Point radio broadcast, August 23, 2017).

In the early 1990s romance fiction author Janet Daley (5-21-1944 to 12-22-2013) callously plagiarized Nora Roberts' romance novel, *Sweet Revenge*, as she wrote *Notorious* and *Aspen Gold*. Mrs. Dailey has written 93 books which were translated into 19 languages and sold in 98 countries (Over 300,000,000 in print). After being exposed she explained, "I had a psychological disorder. Emotional stress made me plagiarize."

Mrs. Dailey was not guilty of deliberately, callously, and cruelly stealing from Ms. Roberts' work but was an "innocent victim of a psychological disorder that she couldn't help." SIC!

John C. Hinckley Jr. (born 1955) came very close to murdering President Reagan on March 30, 1981 but since he also had a "psychological disorder" he was not guilty of his cold-blood murder intent and now he is a free man. Adolf Hitler and Josef Stalin were severely abused by their fathers while they were growing up and so these "severely mentally disturbed men" should not be held responsible for the 100,000,000 plus deaths they caused. Right?

Ted Bundy (11/24/46-1/24/89) was one of America's cruelest serial killers. According to his testimony he murdered over 30 women after seducing them. His parents habitually took him to Sunday School and church but he enjoyed pornography. Did he have a psychological disorder too? The state of Florida did the world a great favor by putting this severely demonized man to death (Gen. 9:6, Rom. 13:4)!

All who follow Adam and Eve's very irresponsible example of trying to hide their sins like Mrs. Dailey are doomed to failure (Ps. 66:18, Pr. 28:13) but all who follow King David's example of freely acknowledging and confessing their sins receive mercy, forgiveness, reconciliation, and restoration (Ps. 51),

The fall of man was indeed very severe as man became depraved in sin (Rom. 1:18-32; 3:23, Isaiah 64:6). The literal Hebrew translation of Genesis 2:27 is, *in your dying you will die.* Adam immediately died spiritually as death entered him the very moment he rebelled against God and continued to dwell in him until 930 years later he physically died (Gen. 5:5). Adam's rebellion produced a sinful rebellious nature for all mankind resulting in death (Rom. 5:12-21, Ps. 51:5, I Cor. 15:21-22).

Vladimir Lenin, (1870-1924, Russian Communist leader) told his followers, "You are all dead people on furlough." Though definitely NOT one I normally quote, I quote him here because he accurately portrays all mankind's situation. Because of Adam's sin all mankind is conceived and born in sin and though temporarily alive we're all destined to death (Gen. 2:17, 3:17-19, Job 15:14, Ps. 51:5, 58:3, ICor. 15:21-22). Therefore we all are "dead people on furlough."

Despite the severity of the fall, God still earnestly desired to redeem man, restore fellowship with him, and make it possible for him to return to the high calling of reflecting God's holy character. God is sovereign and omniscient (Psalm 44:21; 139:1-6; 115:3; 135:6) and therefore was not surprised with the events of the garden. In eternity past it was decided that Jesus Christ, the self-existing, eternal Son of God would be the sacrifice for the sins of mankind (Rev. 13:8, I Peter 1:20).

God gives us the first promise of the redeemer in Genesis 3:15. The seed of a woman (Isa. 7:14) will mortally bruise the snake's head but the redeemer will not be unscathed as the snake will strike His heel: A perfect illustration of the crucifixion, resurrection, and return of Christ.

Many other prophecies are given in the Hebrew Scriptures concerning the promised redeemer, the messiah who will deliver mankind from the curse of sin. Jacob predicted that Messiah would be a descendant of Judah (Gen. 49:8-10). Moses said that Messiah would be a prophet like himself (Dt. 18:15-18, Jn. 5:46). Micah 5:2 tells us Messiah's birthplace and David and Isaiah tell of Messiah's humiliation and suffering (Ps. 22, Isa. 52:13-53:12). Psalm 2, 24, Isaiah 9:6-7 and 11:1-10 tell us of a mighty conquering messiah; the Lion of Judah (Rev. 5:5). Daniel 2:36-45 gives us Yahweh's sovereign plan for the ages and Gabriel gives us the exact day for the revelation of Israel's messiah (Daniel 9:24-27). It is therefore so important to understand Daniel the skeleton, key, and foundation of prophecy.

4. History in a nutshell

About 1600 years after the creation, the earth was filled with violence and evil as all of man's thoughts were only evil all the time (Gen. 6:5). God regretted creating man and decided to wipe man off the face of the earth (6:7) but Noah, "found grace in the eyes of the LORD" (6:8). The world was destroyed as everyone perished except Noah and his family (2 Peter 2:5). Thus God started over again with Noah and the other 7 members of his family (2Pe. 2:5).

About 400 years later God called Abraham to leave his family and follow Him to a new location. He promised him that a great nation (Israel) would come out of his loins (Gen. 12:2) and all the nations would be blessed through him and that nation (v. 3). Israel spent 430 years in Egypt (Ex. 12:40-41) and was liberated through Moses to the land of Canaan. Joshua led Israel into Canaan where Israel demanded a king in order to be "like the other nations" (I Samuel 8:5). The first king was a severe disaster (15:22-29) and therefore Samuel anointed David, a man after God's own heart as king of Israel (13:13-14).

Israel had its golden age under King David who expanded its territory from 6,000 to 60,000 square miles. His son Solomon started off well as he requested wisdom from God (I Kings 3:5-15) but we learn in chapter 11 that King Solomon, though considered the wisest man who ever lived became very foolish and irresponsible as he gathered to himself 700 wives and 300 concubines who seduced him into idolatry. He and Israel therefore received God's wrath instead of His blessings (1Kings 11:9-11, Dt. 28, Lev. 26).

The kingdom was divided into the northern kingdom of Ephraim or Israel; containing 10 tribes and the southern kingdom of Judah with the tribe of Benjamin. All of Israel's kings and most of Judah's kings were evil. Prophets earnestly continually pleaded with both nations to repent as they warned them of the consequences of their sinful, rebellious behavior. Tragically the people rejected the warnings and reaped severe consequences. (Hosea 13:16, Isa. 30:1, 9; 65:2, Jer. 5:6, 23-29, Ez. 2:3-5; 20:8, 13, Hab. 1:5-11, Neh. 9:17). God used pagan nations to discipline them. Assyria conquered Israel in 722 BC (Isa. 10:5) and Babylon conquered Judah in 605 BC.

Jeremiah, known as the weeping prophet because of his extreme anguish of spirit (4:19; 9:1; 10:19-20; 23:9), repeatedly warned Judah of the severe consequences of judgment if the nation continued to rebel against the Lord (16:12-13; 20:4-6; 21:5-8; 25:8-11; 36:29; 46:1-12). Tragically Judah ignored the warnings and therefore God gave her to Babylon (Jer. 13:8-27, 2 Chron. 36:15-21; 44:17-30, Dan. 1:2).

Jeremiah's deep personal anguish over the situation of his people is recorded in Lamentations; the only book in the Bible containing only laments but it still focuses on the goodness of God. Yahweh is the Lord of hope, (3:24-25), love (3:22), faithfulness (3:23), and salvation (3:26). Yahweh's "loving kindnesses indeed never cease, for His compassion never fails for they are new every morning. Great is your faithfulness." (3:22-23).

In 605 BC a decisive battle took place between 2 ancient superpowers: Egypt and Babylon. The Babylonian crown prince, Nebuchadnezzar attacked and soundly defeated Egypt in this battle forcing Egypt to retreat south and therefore made Judah ripe for Babylonian control. King Nabopolassar, Nebuchadnezzar's father died in August that year and Nebuchadnezzar rushed home to claim the throne. On his way home he carried with him the sacred vessels of the Jerusalem temple and placed them in the temple of the chief Babylonian god, Marduk. He also kidnapped and exiled many youths including Daniel, Hananiah, Mishael, and Azariah. Babylon invaded Judah again in 597 and 586 BC. In the last invasion the temple and Jerusalem were destroyed and the people at large were exiled to Babylon (Psalm 137).

5. Introduction to the book of Daniel

The theme in Daniel is the absolute sovereignty of Yahweh, the God of Israel in *all* the affairs of *all* men and *all* nations *all* the time (Ps. 103:19; 115:3; 135:6, Pr. 21:1, Isaiah 14:27; 40:15; 43:13; 47:2-8, Acts 17:24-26, Rom. 13:1, Rev.1:5). Babylon conquered Judah, destroyed the temple, and made the situation seem hopeless. Even though the pagan gods and evil were winning, Yahweh God demonstrated that He is quite capable of accomplishing His sovereign purposes despite the extreme determined opposition of the fiercest and mightiest kings on earth. He was pleased to use Daniel and his 3 friends to demonstrate His awesome sovereign omnipotent power to the pagan kings who learn who really is in charge.

The message of Daniel is as relevant today as it was when it was written over 2500 years ago. We should not be discouraged when we see evil winning but rest in the truth of God's sovereignty over everything. Today we need people like Daniel, Hananiah, Mishael, and Azariah who will stand strong and firm for Yahweh and His righteousness and holiness regardless of the immediate consequences. We need to remember that the ultimate consequences for standing for righteousness are "out of this world" (Revelation 21:7, John 14:2-3). God promises to strengthen everyone whose heart is fully committed to Him (2 Chronicles 16:9) and Christ promises to confess before the Father everyone who confesses Him before men (Mt. 10:32). Hebrews 13:5b-6 is a great comfort also.

He Himself has said, "I will never desert you, nor will I ever forsake you" so that we confidently say, "The Lord is my helper, I will not be afraid. What can man do to me?"

Soon after Martin Luther posted his 95 thesis on his church in 1517 the Protestant Reformation got under way and the Roman Catholic Church started persecuting the Protestants. Many were driven from their homes and thus made exiles as they fled to Switzerland. One of these exiles was John Calvin who wrote a passionate 1,000-page commentary on Daniel. It proved to be a great comfort to the Protestants because they could easily identify with Daniel and the Jewish exiles.

We believers in Jesus Christ are also exiles here on earth as our home is in Heaven (John 14:3, Philippians 1:21-23). I therefore pray that this study will greatly comfort, strengthen, and encourage you as you sojourn in this strange land.

The Book of Daniel

1

Nebuchadnezzar's Reorientation (Brainwashing) Program

After the Japanese surrender ending World War II General Douglas MacArthur wisely hired Japanese officials to carry out his policies. He knew it would be much easier to rule over Japan through these Japanese nationals who knew the Japanese culture and customs. An English teacher in Shimonoseki told me that the Japanese people are thankful for his benevolent rule. This resulted in continual good relations between Japan and the US.

Nebuchadnezzar also knew it would be much easier to rule over Judah through Jewish people. Daniel and his 3 friends were about 14 years old when they were callously kidnapped from their families and brought to the strange land of Babylon. In accordance with ancient custom, they were involuntarily castrated (Isa. 39:6-7, Swindoll, *Daniel*, p. 14). Though callously and cruelly robbed of their manhood, they showed no bitterness and proved to be the only real men in the book of Daniel.

King Nebuchadnezzar, Yahweh's servant (Jer. 25:9) instructed Ashpenaz, the master of the eunuchs to bring the Israeli youths into the king's service. They needed to be handsome and teachable with no physical blemish. The youths were to learn the Babylonian language, religion, and culture and hopefully forget their own. The king wanted the men to forget their identities and therefore he gave them new Babylonian pagan names in place of their Hebrew ones.

Daniel: *God is my judge, deliverer* changed to **Belteshazzar**, *Bel's Prince*

Hananiah: *Yahweh's favored one; Yahweh is my grace* changed to **<u>Shadrach</u>**: *One inspired by the sun god.*

Mishael: *One like God* is changed to **Meshach,** *One like the Babylonian goddess.*

Azariah: *Yahweh is my helper* is changed to **Abednego,** *a servant and worshipper of Nego. The servant of the shining fire; Lucifer.*

The king also wanted the men to forget their "strange" diet taught in Leviticus 3:17; 7:22-27; 11:1-47; 17:10-14; 19:26, Deuteronomy 12:16, Isaiah 65:3-4; and 66:15-17. He therefore generously offered them the best Babylonian pork generously seasoned with blood, and fat from the king's table. The men obeyed Proverbs 23:1-3 which instructed them to put a knife to their throats and reject the king's delicious but deceptive food. The king's food had been sacrificed to the pagan gods and was therefore forbidden to be eaten by Jews (Exodus 34:14-15). The Babylonians understood that eating food sacrificed to idols is the same as worshiping them.

The 4 men were determined not to be defiled with the king's food (v.8) and therefore respectfully yet firmly rejected the king's diet and opted for a vegetarian one (v.12 Hebrew: That which grows from the ground). Though living in an unclean world, the men were determined to remain clean. They were in the world but not of the world (John 17:14-20). Understandably Ashpenaz was shocked, worried, and very scared because he knew he would lose his head if these men became unhealthy (v.10). Instead of grandstanding Daniel proposed a simple 10-day test to demonstrate the superiority of the biblical diet. The test proved that God's diet was superior to the Babylonian diet (v. 15). The 4 men were 10 times better than the Babylonian wise men (v.20) and so they were allowed to continue their diet. The king rewarded them with good government jobs (19).

The ancient biblical diet these 4 brave men obeyed in the Babylonian pagan culture is also good today. Elmer Josephson, an ordained Baptist minister, was dying of cancer and as a last resort opted for the Levitical diet which resulted in his healing. He shares his testimony in his book, *God's Key to Health and Happiness.*

Dr. Jordan Rubin was afflicted with Crohn's disease; a severe digestive disorder. Even though Dr. Rubin's father spent over $150,000 sending him all over the world seeking help, this dreaded disease continued to cause Dr. Rubin's health to deteriorate until he weighed 85 lbs. and was near death. He was cured after he opted for the diet in Leviticus (3Jn 2). He testifies of God's healing is in his book *The Maker's Diet* with a foreword by Dr. Charles Stanley, best selling author of over 60 books with sales of more than 10,000,000 copies. He has been the senior pastor of the First Baptist Church, Atlanta, Georgia, USA since 1971. Dr. Stanley's messages are translated into over 100 languages.

Rex Russell, MD authored the book, *What the Bible Says about Healthy Living.* He strongly recommends the Levitical diet and documents the fact that the early Christian Church observed the Levitical diet at least until 70 AD (p. 138, 254). Dale Thomson, pastor of the First Baptist Church of Fort Smith, Arkansas; Elmer Towns, Dean of the Liberty University School of Religion, Lynchburg, Va.; Dr. John Morris, president of the Institute for Creation research; and many other Christian leaders strongly recommend this book.

Apostle John joyfully proclaims that Jesus' life was so saturated with miracles that it would be impossible to document all of them (Jn. 20:30; 21:25). All 4 gospels record many of Christ's miracles but only 1 is recorded in all 4 gospels: The feeding of the 5,000 with 5 loaves and 2 fish (Mt. 14:13-21, Mk. 6:32-44, Lk. 9:10-17, Jn. 6:1-13). After the people were filled and satisfied Christ instructs the disciples to, "gather up the leftover fragments so that nothing will be lost" (Jn. 6:12). This clearly shows that Christ disapproves of wasting food.

In Mark 5:1-13 Christ delivered a man from 6,000 demons who requested to inhabit some pigs. Christ granted their request and 2,000 pigs killed themselves. Christ rejected wasting food but obviously saw nothing wasteful in allowing the demons to cause 2,000 pigs to commit suicide (or pigacide?). Christ showed His support for the biblical diet as He rejected pigs as food and knew they were created only as scavengers (garbage collectors). Christ also rejects snakes and scorpions as food but teaches that fish and eggs are healthy and good (Luke 11:11-12).

God tells Peter in a vision to, "Get up Peter, kill and eat" unclean animals and is rebuked when he refuses (Acts 10:9-16). Peter clearly states that the purpose of the vision was to "call no man unclean" (v.28).

We do not use God's command to Abraham to sacrifice his son Isaac (Ge. 22:2) to justify killing our children nor do we use God's command to Hosea to marry a harlot (Hos. 1:2) to encourage Christian men to marry harlots. God commanded Prophet Isaiah (20:3) to walk naked in public for 3 years. Prophet Micah (1:8) also walked naked in Jerusalem. Can we therefore use these examples to justify public nudity or pornography? Can we use Joseph and Mary's very unique situation (Mt. 1:18-25) to encourage a young man to marry a pregnant woman? God gave many wives to David (ISam.12:8) and so polygamy is permitted; Right?

These were obviously unique, special one-time events that were used to illustrate a special teaching but never meant to be repeated or practiced in normal Christian life. Let's apply this same principle to Acts 10. Apostle Peter continued to consider pigs to be unclean 30-35 years after the vision (2Pe. 2:22). Don't forget that the church honored the Levitical diet at least until 70 AD (Dr. Rex Russell, *What the Bible teaches about Healthy Living*, p. 138, 254).

In Mark 16:17-18 Christ promises special grace and protection for believers who drink poison or handle vipers. This promise is fulfilled in Acts 28:3-5 but in Christian services today we do not handle snakes or drink poison because of Christ's warning (Dt. 6:16, Lk. 4:12). God can indeed protect His children from the ill-effects of vipers, poison and the consumption of pigs, lobsters, crabs, shrimp, rats or mice but let us not presume upon God but reject the consumption of scavengers as well as drinking poison or handling snakes.

The Jerusalem council declared that new Gentile converts were not required to follow the law of Moses but were still required to reject the consumption of blood (Acts 15:19-21, Lev. 17;11, 14, Dt.12:16).

Dr. S. I. McMillen, a medical missionary wrote a book called *None of These Diseases* (Ex. 15:26). In his book he tells us how following the simple health and hygiene principles of Leviticus can save us from many dreaded diseases and give us good health. US Presidents George Washington and William Harrison were bled to death by "modern enlightened physicians" who rejected the clear and plain truth of Leviticus 17:11 and 14 which proclaims that the life of all flesh is in the blood. These physicians believed that the remedy for disease was bleeding. Today medical science recognizes this truth taught in Leviticus and blood is never taken from one who is ill but in many cases is given to the ill. If the same medical treatment given to Presidents Washington and Harrison were given to anyone today it would be homicide.

In the 20th century doctors freely cut out tonsils, adenoids, and the appendix for any problem they may cause. Did God give us these in order to create business for modern MDs? Thank God they have corrected this erroneous corrupt behavior. Let us pray that modern MDs understand the awesome truth of Psalm 139:14. We are "fearfully and wonderfully made."

In the Friday-Sunday, June 14-16, 2013 edition of the Wall Street Journal there is a very interesting book review on page 11: *Stumbling Toward Greatness* by Samuel Arbesman (author of "The half-Life of Facts: Why Everything We Know Has an Expiration Date"). His professor delivered a lecture on ecology and after reading a newspaper article which invalidated his teaching he told the students, "Remember what I told you on Tuesday? It's wrong. And if that worries you, you need to get out of science." Arbesman stated that even though Linas Paulding won the Nobel Prize in chemistry, it was later learned that his DNA structure was in error. Einstein introduced the constant and withdrew it which gave science problems. He also writes about Mario Livio's "Brilliant Blunders" which explores the slip-ups of 5 of the most famous scientists since the scientific revolution.

It's quite obvious that science regularly changes and sometimes is an outright deliberate fraud. Between 1908 and 1912 parts of a human skull and a chimpanzee jawbone were found at Piltdown in Sussex, England; about 40 miles from London. Teeth were filed down to make them look human and iron salt was applied to make them appear old. Over 500 doctoral thesises were written as "scientists joyfully proclaimed the discovery of the missing link of human evolution." In 1953 the hoax was exposed and again God's Word triumphed (WBE, vol. 15, p.417, D. Jeremiah, Radio Broadcast).

Indeed science changes but God's Word NEVER changes! "Forever, O LORD, Your Word is settled in Heaven" (Ps. 119:89, Isa. 40:8, Mt. 24:35, Lk. 16:17, 1Pe.1:25). Let us rejoice that we can always trust the divine instructions in God's eternal unchanging Word! Don't worry if science contradicts God's Word. Since science is constantly changing let us patiently wait for science to catch up with the Bible just as it did with Leviticus 17:11, 14 and Deuteronomy 12:16.

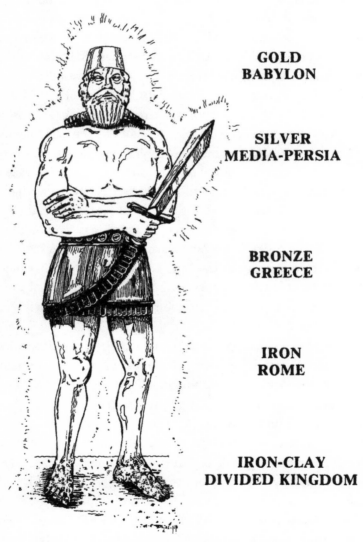

**GOLD
BABYLON**

**SILVER
MEDIA-PERSIA**

**BRONZE
GREECE**

**IRON
ROME**

**IRON-CLAY
DIVIDED KINGDOM**

From *The Most High God* by Renald Showers
p. 27

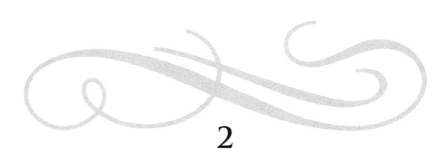

2

Nebuchadnezzar's Distress
In his Forgotten Dream

God states that He would reveal His will to His people through a prophet with dreams and visions (Nu. 12:6). He used dreams and visions to communicate with Jacob (Gen. 28:12-17; 32:24-30; 35:1-9), Joseph (Gen.37:5-9), Pharaoh (41:1-7), and Solomon (I Kings 3:5). Here He reveals this very important message through one of the world's cruelest and fiercest dictators. It would be almost like God showing His future plans to Mao, Stalin or Hitler.

King Nebuchadnezzar had a very disturbing dream that he could not remember. He demanded that his Babylonian wise men not only interpret it but also tell him the dream itself. A very strange demand but he reasoned that since his Babylonian wise men had a special supernatural intimate relationship with supernatural beings who enabled them to interpret dreams, these same gods would have no problem revealing the dream itself. His wise men stated that they could not fulfill the king's unusual and unreasonable request. Nebuchadnezzar therefore required death for these fake wise men and Arioch began to execute the order.

When he came to Daniel's place, Daniel informed him that he had not heard about the king's order and requested time. Even though Nebuchadnezzar rejected his wise men's request for more time (2:8) he freely granted Daniel's request. Daniel remembered Proverbs 3:5-6 and prayed with his 3 friends for Yahweh's answer and the LORD revealed to Daniel the dream and interpretation (vs. 17-19).

Daniel took no personal credit nor did he rush to the king with the answer but first overflowed with praise and thanksgiving to God for this supernatural, wonderful answer to his prayer (v. 20-24). He obviously did not know Hebrews 13:15 but he perfectly obeyed it as he offered a sacrifice of praise to Yahweh for His gracious answer to his prayer. What a great model prayer Daniel has given us! The Apostle Paul must have remembered this story when he instructed us in Philippians 4:6-7 to;

> Be anxious for nothing but in everything by prayer and supplication with thanksgiving let your requests be known to God. And the peace of God which surpasses all comprehension will guard your hearts and minds in Christ Jesus.

Hananiah, Mishael, Azariah, and Daniel never read Philippians 4:6-7 but knew this truth and applied it to their lives.

Daniel informed Arioch that he had the answer and interceded for the lives of Babylonian pagan wise men (24). Daniel is brought before the king and says (author's paraphrase);

> "Your Babylonian wise men can't help you and neither can I in my own strength or wisdom. I'm not any wiser than any of them but I do have an intimate relationship with an eternal infinite all wise God who knows everything and can easily reveal to me not only the meaning of your dream but the dream itself" (Pr. 1:7; 9:10, Job 28:28, Ps. 111:10; 139:1-4; 94:11, Pr. 24:12, Isa. 46:10).

The world's future is explained in this dream. The great statue the king saw represents the 4 major kingdoms that would rule the world. The head of gold represents Babylon. The silver shoulders, arms, and chest represent Medo-Persia. The bronze abdomen and thighs represent Greece; and the iron legs represent Rome. The feet with a mixture of iron and clay represent the deterioration of the Roman Empire. The stone, supernaturally cut out without hands represents the glorious 1,000-year kingdom of Jesus Christ (Rev. 20:4).

Gold is a very fitting metal to represent Babylon. The chief god, Marduk is the god of gold. Babylonian shrines, buildings, and walls were generously overlaid with gold. The Greek historian Herodotus was amazed to see the extravagant amount of gold in the temple 100 years after Nebuchadnezzar's reign. (D. Jeremiah, *Agents of Babylon*, from Herodotus, *The History of Herodotus*, book 1.183). Isaiah declared (14:4), "How the oppressor has ceased. The golden city ceased!" Jeremiah 51:7 states, "Babylon is the golden cup in the LORD's hand."

Silver is the most fitting metal to represent the Medo-Persian Empire. In ancient times silver signified money. Medo-Persia required tribute in silver coins through its extensive tax system (Ezra 4:13, Daniel 11:2, Boutflower, p. 29-30 from Showers, p. 18). The 2 arms and chest are an excellent representation of Media and Persia which came together in 550 BC to form one political entity (Leupold, p. 117 from Showers, p.18).

Bronze is an excellent representation of the third kingdom. Greece developed it highly. Her soldiers were clothed with its bronze shields, helmets, breastplates, and swords (D. Jeremiah, *The Handwrititng on the Wall*, p.59). The bronze belly was subdivided into 2 thighs symbolizing Egypt and Syria; 2 of the 4 divisions of the empire that have a direct bearing on Israel. (Leupold, p.118 from Showers, p.19).

Iron is used 14 times to describe the 4th kingdom. The 2 iron legs perfectly represent Rome and its extensive western and eastern domination. In chapter 7 it has iron teeth. Known for its extensive use of iron weapons, Rome cruelly crushed the ancient empires of gold, silver, and bronze.

The iron and clay feet represent the deterioration of the Roman Empire. Unlike the earlier kingdoms, the Roman Empire was never conquered nor did it disappear. Germans, Slavs, and others invaded and intermingled with Rome but Rome continued but without domination. The western empire lasted till 731 and the eastern one lasted till 1453. The 10 toes represent the 10-nation division of the revived Roman Empire that will be in effect when the stone, Jesus Christ crushes the image to powder at His second coming (Daniel 7:13-14, Rev. 11:15; 17:12; 19:6).

The fifth kingdom will be established supernaturally after the stone supernaturally cut out without human hands crushes the image to fine powder and is blown away with the wind (Is. 40:15). Christ is identified as the stone over 14 times in the Scriptures (I Peter 2:4-8, Ps. 118:22, Ex. 17:5-7, ICor. 10:3-4, Rom. 9:33, Isa. 8:14; 28:16). It suddenly and violently crushes the image and fills the whole earth (v. 35). The fifth kingdom of

Christ crushes the image to powder after the fourth kingdom deteriorates into the feet of mixed iron and clay. This represents Christ's second coming in His power and glory to rule the world (Rev. 11:15; 19:6b). In Romans 9:33 Paul quotes Isaiah 8:14 and 28:16:

"See, I lay in Zion a stone that causes men to stumble, and a rock that makes them fall, and the one who trusts in Him will never be put to shame."

The 4 kingdoms in the dream were built on one another and were gradual in the making. The fifth kingdom of Christ will not be built on the world's kingdoms but will come suddenly with a violent, catastrophic, and decisive blow that fills the whole earth. Christ's kingdom will be supernatural, sudden, severe, sovereign, successful, sure, and hopefully soon! (D. Jeremiah, *The Handwriting on the Wall*, p.66-67). Dr. Showers states it so well on page 21 in his book.

The Babylonians called their chief god, Marduk, "The Great Mountain." They believed that their gods came from the sacred mountain of the earth- the mountain they called, "The Mountain of the Lands" The temples of Babylon were intended to be imitations of mountains. (The Babylonians considered mountains to be associated with the supernatural). Because of this Babylonian mindset, God purposefully portrayed his future kingdom first as a stone cut out of a mountain and second as a stone that becomes a great mountain (v. 35). This helped Nebuchadnezzar to understand that the fifth kingdom would not be of human origin but would be supernaturally established (Boutflower, p. 45-46).

Marduk was also called, "Lord of the wind" (Boutflower, p. 46-47 from Showers, p. 22). Yahweh is making it clear that He alone is the divine wind that will blow away the powder from all traces of man's kingdoms as He sets up His 1,000-year kingdom (Rev. 20:4). After this comes the eternal kingdom (Rev. 21-22).

The stone cannot represent Christ's first coming since the Roman Empire was in its zenith of power and glory during the time of Christ. Its borders began to shrink in 117 AD and began to rapidly deteriorate about 300 years later (Most historians teach that Rome fell in 476).

The metals decrease in value but increase in strength. The specific gravity of gold is 19.3, silver is 10.5, bronze is 8.5, iron is 7.6, and clay is 1.9. The absolute despotism of Nebuchadnezzar (5:19) descended to the democratic system of checks and balances that characterized the Roman senates and assemblies. Each successive empire was larger and lasted longer than the previous one.

Babylon had lots of religion (over 50 temples) but without God. Persia had law without God. Their laws were made by "infallible monarchs" and therefore never needed to be changed (So they thought! Dan. 6:15, Esther 8:8).

Greece had wisdom without God (Socrates, Aristotle, Plato, etc. Ps. 111:10, Pr. 1:7; 9:10; 11:2, Isa. 29:14, ICor. 1:24-25; 3:19-21). The theory of evolution originated not in science but in Greek pagan wisdom (Rom. 1:22).

Rome had power without God. After very callously and sadistically torturing Christ to death on a cruel Roman cross, Rome sealed the tomb and guarded it with 16 elite soldiers; the ancient equivalent of navy seals or green berets. Rome and Israel with fierce determination very diligently worked hard together to make sure that Christ stayed in the tomb but 3 days later we see how effective Roman power was. God and the host of Heaven were laughing (Psalm 2:4).

The fifth kingdom will be supernaturally established and have everything with God but without Satan (Rev. 20:1-3, 10).

When Nebuchadnezzar had his dream Persia was a Babylonian vessell state, Greek cities were at war with each other, and Rome was a small village on the Tiber River. There was no way that Daniel could have known the future except through the supernatural revelation from God.

In chapter 6 we read that Daniel bowed before Yahweh, the king of the universe as he prayed 3 times a day (Ps. 55:17) but here he boldly stood before the king of Babylon and confidently told him the message from God. King Nebuchadnezzar prostrated himself before Daniel and praised Daniel's God, Yahweh as the "God of gods and Lord of kings and revealer of mysteries." (2:46-47). He rewarded Daniel with many valuable gifts, made him governor over Babylon, and head of all the Babylonian wise men (v.48). Daniel did not forget the help he received from his 3 friends and therefore requested that they also be promoted in government service. The request was granted as the 3 men served as local administrators under Daniel (v. 49).

3

Resisting Peer Pressure

Psychologist Dr. Ruth Berenda did an experiment on peer pressure. Teens and children were placed in groups of 10 and were instructed to vote for the longest line on a chart. The students being tested did not know that each one of them would be placed with 9 others who were instructed previously to always vote for the second longest line. The test would determine if the tested student would vote for what was obviously the longest line or fearing to be different, vote with the other 9 peers. Dr. Berenda learned that 75% of the time the tested student would want to vote for the longest line but after noticing no other hands going up he sheepishly put his hand back down and lifted it when the other nine voted for the second longest line. 75% succumbed to peer-pressure. Praise God for the 25% who did not! (Swindoll, *Ultimate Book of Illustrations & Quotes,* p. 434). In this chapter we learn of 3 very courageous young Hebrews who refused to yield to peer-pressure as they boldly and confidently stood alone for Yahweh and righteousness in a very corrupt pagan society.

The Septuagint teaches that the events of chapter 3 happened in the 18th year of Nebuchadnezzar's reign. Thus the king had 16 years after his dream to marvel at the greatness of Babylon. He saw no indication of its deterioration or decay and so despite the clear teaching of his dream he decided that Babylon would never be conquered but would last forever. He therefore built the image he dreamed about but made it all of gold, the metal that represents Babylon. It was 60 cubits high, (about 28 meters) 6 cubits wide (about 3 meters) and had 6 musical instruments for his musical service (The first mention of 666, the mark of the beast in Revelation

13:18). Everyone was required to fall down and worship the image with the sound of music or else be thrown into the fiery furnace.

3 Hebrews successfully resist peer-pressure

About 300,000 bowed to the idol (D. Jeremiah, *Agents of Babylon*, p.98) but 3 brave Hebrews stood as they boldly resisted peer-pressure. The accusers, the same Chaldean officials who were spared death after Daniel revealed the king's dream and interpretation showed their appreciation by demanding their death because they were "disloyal and very ungrateful for the king's favor and kindness generously given to them." They said (author's paraphrase);

> "Even though you have greatly honored these foreigners with lucrative high-paying government jobs they have boldly disdained with contempt and scorn the king's command and therefore deserve to be severely punished!"

Nebuchadnezzar in typical pagan thinking thought he conquered Judah because his god, Marduk was stronger and superior to Judah's God, Yahweh. He did not understand that Yahweh had given him Judah because of Judah's continual willful obstinate rebellion (Dan. 1:2; 2:37-38, Isa.42:24, Jer. 17:21-27; 20:4-6; 21:3-7; 27:7; 32:25-36; 38:3, 44:3-6; 17-30, 2 Chron. 36:11-21). Instead of immediately putting them in the furnace, Nebuchadnezzar, very much out of character tried to reason with them about the importance of obeying the king's command. He probably told them (author's paraphrase):

> "We have a very high respect for you and your god, Yahweh, but you must also respect ours and obey my command. Just don't stand so straight but kneel a little and make the people think you are honoring and worshiping our god. Your God, Yahweh is a good God and certainly deserves respect and you are free to worship Him but honor our god Marduk by bowing down to and worshiping him too. Don't you understand that I really like you or I certainly would have never given you another chance so please co-operate for the sake of unity and

peace. Don't forget that Babylon conquered Judah because our god Marduk is stronger and superior than your God, Yahweh."

Nebuchadnezzar obviously had not read the previous Scriptures which clearly state that Nebuchadnezzar conquered Judah *only* because God had given him Judah because of her idolatry. The 3 Hebrews knew that Yahweh, the holy sovereign God of Israel was also the sovereign God of Babylon and the whole world. They therefore preferred physical death to spiritual death as they knew their lives would be worthless if they yielded to idolatry. "The fear of man brings a snare but he who trusts in the LORD will be exalted." (Pr. 29:25). They probably prayed the Psalmist's prayer of 119:134, "Redeem me from the oppression of man that I may keep your precepts." They knew the Scriptures well; including Exodus 20:3; 34:14, Deuteronomy 6:4-14, and Psalm 34:1-3. The righteous have afflictions but Yahweh is more than able to deliver them (Ps. 33:18-19; 34:19). They also read and rejoiced with the promise of Isaiah 43:2-3,

> Do not fear, for I have redeemed you; I have called you by name; you are Mine. When you pass through the waters, I will be with you. And through the rivers, they will not overflow you. When you walk through the fire, you will not be scorched. Nor will the flame burn you. For I am the LORD your God: The holy one of Israel, your Savior.

They remained totally unintimidated even though they knew that Babylonian kings roasted alive disobedient subjects (Jer. 29:22). They were consistent in their absolute unconditional commitment to Yahweh with absolute confidence and courage (3:18) and conscious of His presence. Unlike Martin Luther, who needed an extra day to consider his answer to those who wanted him to recant, they replied immediately (3:16-18, (author's paraphrase).

> "You're wasting your time trying to reason with us! We have already made up our minds and have firmly determined in our hearts to worship only Yahweh, the holy sovereign God of Israel and the only true God of the whole earth. He is all powerful and is more than able to save us from the fiery furnace but no matter what He does, we absolutely refuse to worship or bow

down before any god except Yahweh, the only true God, the Almighty, the Holy Sovereign God of Israel and the whole world!"

They had not read Romans 14:8, Philippians 1:21, 2 Timothy 1:7 or 12 but they obviously knew the truth of these New Testament Scriptures. Peter, James, and John followed in their footsteps as they also refused to yield to human authority when it contradicted divine authority. They boldly declared, "We must obey God rather than man" (Acts 5:29).

In H.C. Leupold's Exposition of Daniel p. 153, he states;

> The quiet, modest, yet… positive attitude of faith that these 3 men display is one of the noblest examples in the Scripture of faithfully resigned to the will of God. These men ask for no miracle, and they expect none. There's is the faith that says, "Though He slay me yet I will trust in Him.' (Job 13:15 KJV)."

World War I Chaplain Studdert Kennedy wrote his young son this letter (*The Hardest Part*, p.110-111 quoted from D. Jeremiah, *Agents of Babylon*, p. 102)).

> The first prayer I want my son to say for me is not "God keep Daddy safe" but "God make daddy brave, and if he has hard things to do make him strong to do them. Life and death don't matter… right and wrong do. Daddy dead is daddy still but daddy dishonored before God is something awful, too bad for words…"

Nebuchadnezzar's extreme anger and surprise

In ancient times people were usually stripped naked when executed but in his extreme anger Nebuchadnezzar ordered them to be immediately cast into the fiery furnace fully clothed; burning 7 times hotter than usual (v. 19). The king was surprised (understatement) as he saw the 3 men thrive in the fire along with the Son of God. The men were unbent, unbowed, and unburned. The fire burned only the ropes that bound them and the king's high ranking officials who threw them in the fire (22-26).

It's far better to be in the fiery furnace with Christ than to be a high ranking favored official of a king without Christ. The pagan king then exalted the God of the 3 Hebrews and issued another death threat: This time to anyone who showed disrespect for Yahweh, the "God of Shadrach, Meshach, and Abednego" (v. 29). The king then caused the 3 men to prosper in government service (v. 30).

Genesis 9:6, Romans 13:1-7, and I Peter 2:13-17 make it clear that God has ordained governments to rule over mankind. We are required to submit ourselves to the authority of government except when government abuses its power and requires worship which belongs to God alone! If this happens we as believers in Jesus Christ are to respectfully but firmly reject the government's decree and obey God instead of the government.

Even though they were unjustly accused and punished the 3 Hebrews continued to be loyal to the king and faithfully served him. We need to follow their example!

Dr. Jeremiah (*The Handwriting on the Wall,* p.84) tells the story of a 4th century hero of the faith, John Chrysostom (347-407) who followed the brave Hebrews' example. The emperor told him that he must reject Christ or he would be banished from the land. This bold believer replied,

> "You cannot, for the whole world is my father's land. You cannot banish me."
> The emperor said, "Then I will take away all your property"
> He replied, "You cannot. My treasures are in Heaven."
> The emperor then threatened him with isolation with no one to speak to. Chrysostom replied, "You cannot. I have a friend who is closer than a brother. I shall have Jesus Christ forever."
> The emperor then threatened to take his life and Chrysostom answered,
> "You cannot. My life is hid with God in Christ."
> The very frustrated emperor said, "What do you do with a man like that?"

Contemporary heroes of the faith

Doris Sanford, daughter of missionaries in China, relates how the Chinese Communists were preparing to murder her, her brother, and mother while her father was away (*Unsolved Miracles*, p. 69). The communists offered to spare their lives if they simply renounced their foreign western God. Her mother boldly declared:

"We cannot deny the one true God. He is more powerful than your guns and if He chooses He can speak the word and we will be safe from your guns. Or if He chooses, we will go to heaven to live with Him forever, beginning today."

The leader raised his gun and the others followed. At that moment the sky suddenly darkened and crashed with thunder and lightening! My mother said that in the northern interior of China, thunder and lightening were unheard of. Snow and ice, yes, but torrential downpours along with flashes of light and deafening thunder, never!

The men trampled themselves in their eagerness to escape, convinced that the God of the missionaries had spoken. My mother smiled and wiggled out of the wet ropes to take her two young children back to the house for a cup of hot tea.

Mrs. Sanford obviously knew Hebrews 13:5-6:

… He Himself has said, "I will never desert you, nor I will I ever forsake you." so that we confidently say, "The Lord is my helper. I will not be afraid. What will man do to me?"

Korean Pastor Ju Ki-cheol was a martyr for Christ during the cruel Japanese occupation of Korea (1910-1945). On page 9 of his biography, *More Than Conquerors,* it reads,

In the darkest hour of the history of Korean church, he practiced true discipleship, adamantly resisting the worship of the Shinto sun-goddess of Japan. In a period of great national suffering, he did not compromise with Japan's imperialistic militarism and confirmed that to die with the Lord is to live with Him forever.

Pastor Ju and his family were tortured for their faith and they have a great reward in Heaven (Matthew 5:10-12). Many faithful believers in Jesus Christ were tortured and martyred for their faith when Kim Ilsung and North Korea invaded South Korea.

Romanian Pastor Richard Wurmbrand refused to obey his country's command to refrain from sharing the gospel and was tortured for his faith for 14 years in prison when Communism ruled his country. After his release he came to the US in 1967 and founded the *Voice of the Martyrs* (www.persecution.com). In his book, *Tortured for Christ* he shares his testimony and the following story.

> "We were forbidden to preach the gospel in prison. If we did we were beaten. We were happy preaching the gospel and they were happy beating us. So everyone was happy."

On page 46 of Boice's book on Daniel we read about another Romanian pastor who also freely preached the gospel under Godless communism. When the authorities threatened Dr Joseph Tson he replied,

> "I have to tell you first that I am ready to die. I have put my affairs in order. Your supreme weapon is killing. My supreme weapon is dying, because when you kill me people all over Romania will read my books and believe on the God I preach-even more than they do now."

The authorities let him go and people listen as he preaches the gospel.

In 1982 Israel invaded Lebanon to clean out Yasser Arafat's PLO terrorists who were determined to destroy Israel. A US State Department official said, "We need to bring Israeli Prime Minister Menachem Begin to his knees!" He boldly replied, "We Jews bow to no one but God!" I pray that all believers in Jesus Christ will have the same strong attitude and spirit of Israeli Prime Minister Begin and boldly proclaim, "We believers in Christ bow to no one but God"

Many like these previously described have followed the excellent example of Hananiah, Mishael, and Azariah and have been honored by God. They knew the truth of Hebrews 13:6 and Matthew 10:28 when Jesus said "Do not fear him who can only kill the body but rather fear him who can destroy both body and soul in Hell." "Be faithful until death and I will give you a crown of life." (Revelation 2:10). We will share in His glory as we share in His suffering (Rom. 8:17). Let us all therefore purpose in our hearts to worship only Yahweh our heavenly Father all the time through His Son Jesus Christ regardless of the consequences. Reject peer pressure and boldly confess with Israel's greatest leader, King David in Psalm 34:1,

> "I will bless the LORD (Yahweh) at *all* times: His praise shall continually be in my mouth."

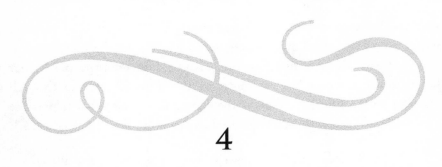

4

Nebuchadnezzar's Irresponsible Arrogant Behavior: Insomnia, Insanity, Insight, and Inspiration

"Pride is the only disease known to man that makes everyone sick but the one who has it." (Robinson, *Swindoll's Ultimate Book Of Illustrations &Quotes,* p. 465).

Franklin Graham, son of Evangelist Billy Graham in his autobiography, *Rebel with a Cause* (p. 56-58) gives testimony of his arrogant, irresponsible, immature behavior and freely humbling himself as he yielded to correction.

While driving his Triumph-Spitfire Franklin noticed Montreat, NC Police Officer Pete Post with his red-flashing bubble signaling Franklin to pull over. He raced to his home and closed the gate behind him after entering his residence.

"I laughed as I imagined the look on Pete's face as he sat in front of the locked gate at the bottom of the hill.

"I screeched to a halt, slammed the car door, and ran up to my room, and locked the door. My heart was pounding with excitement,.., a new thrill for me.

"My exhilaration didn't last long. Within minutes my father's voice rang out to me. 'Franklin, come down here!'"

The evangelist informed Franklin that Officer Pete Post would come in to lecture him on the importance of safety. Officer Post informed Franklin that if he saw that irresponsible behavior again he would take away his driver's license, handcuff him and put him in jail. His father nodded his head in full approval. He learned that he could NOT count on his father's support if he was wrong.

Franklin humbled himself when he was confronted and rebuked for his irresponsible and arrogant behavior. Today he faithfully continues the gospel ministry of his father with the Billy Graham Evangelistic Ministry (BGEA). In 2016 he led prayer rallies in all 50 state capitals for the Lord's guidance and will in the fall elections. The Lord graciously answered Franklin's prayer and millions of Americans in the election.

When the famous American boxer Muhammad Ali (1942-2016) boarded an aircraft the flight attendant instructed the passengers to, "Fasten your seat belts." Ali responded, "Superman don't need seat belt." The flight attendant responded, "Superman don't need airplane. Fasten your seat belt." Ali also proudly boasted, "It's hard to be humble when you are as great as I am. I am not the greatest, I'm the double greatest" (Moses and Muhammad, *Jewish World Review*. June 29, 2016).

In this chapter we learn about an ancient king who like Ali thought he was superman and the double greatest but goes insane as he lives like a wild animal for 7 years. He recovers when he like Franklin humbles himself before Yahweh, the sovereign God of the universe (4:34-35).

Pentecost believes that Nebuchadnezzar was about 50 (570 BC) when the events of this chapter happened. This is about 30 years after the fiery furnace episode (Swindoll, *Daniel,* p. 111) and the building of Babylon was finished. Nebuchadnezzar authors this chapter as he gives personal testimony of God's dealings with pride. He and Job are the only non-Hebrew authors of the Old Testament Scriptures.

In this chapter Nebuchadnezzar has another dream. Instead of going to the reliable and proven source he again contacts his phony Babylonian wise men who again are powerless to help him (4:7). In 2:4 these charlatans tell the king, "Tell us the dream and we will give you the interpretation." Unlike the chapter 2 dream the king here fulfills their request and tells them the dream but these inept phonies are still totally helpless and unable to give any interpretation. Daniel again comes to his rescue and interprets the dream.

Trees are used regularly in Scripture for symbolic purposes (2K 14:9, Ps. 1:3; 37:35; 52:8; 92:12; Ez. 17, Mk. 11:13-21, Rom. 11:17). The tree here in chapter 4 has a very significant meaning.

Nebuchadnezzar is the high tree that is cut down leaving only the roots and stump. He will spend 7 years in the wilderness living with and like the wild animals.

The king had greatly mistreated his subjects, especially during his great building projects (Hab. 2:11-13) and so he was ripe for judgment. Knowing the teaching of Jonah, Joel 1:14; 2:17-18, Amos 5:15, Jeremiah 18, 26:3, and 42:10, Daniel warns and earnestly pleads with Nebuchadnezzar to repent of his arrogance and humble himself before Almighty God. Perhaps God will show him mercy and relent (I Peter 5:6).

Tragically Nebuchadnezzar ignores the warning and lets his head swell with pride as he is consumed with his own vanity and glory. He still had not learned that Yahweh, the God of Israel is not the God of Israel only but also the Sovereign God of the whole earth; including Babylon.

Nebuchadnezzar thought he had every right to boast since he was probably the greatest ancient builder (Leupold, p.118 from Showers, p.45).

> "Forty-nine building inscriptions of this king have been uncovered thus far (Boutflower, p. 29-30). Most of the bricks recovered from ancient Babylon bear this inscription: 'I am Nebuchadnezzar, king of Babylon' (Schultz, p. 248 from Showers, p. 45). He himself declared that his heart impelled him to build." (Walvoord, p.73 from Showers, p.45).

> Nebuchadnezzar rebuilt the palace of his father and then built two more palaces and seventeen religious temples in Babylon... He completed the two great walls that surrounded the city... The king installed great fortifications to protect the city and had canals dug from one end of the city to another to facilitate commerce. (Boutflower, p.25, 31-32, 45-48 from Showers, p.46).

Over 90 miles of walls surrounded the city. They were 375 feet high and 60 feet wide, enough room for 4 chariots to ride abreast. A wide and deep moat also surrounded the city (Herodotus, p. 97 from Swindoll, *Daniel*, p. 38). The walls around the Ishtar gate were filled with brightly colored tiles and vivid detailed carvings of animals. (Boutflower, p. 76 from Showers, p. 46).

The king's greatest feat was the hanging gardens of Babylon. Mountains were placed on top of the royal palace complex and trees and plants were planted there. "An ingenious hydraulic machine was devised to lift water from the Euphrates River to water the elevated gardens." The Greeks were so impressed that they declared them one of the 7 wonders of the world (Boutflower, 66-68, from Showers, p. 46).

Indeed the hanging gardens, the Ishtar gate, the walls, etc. are very impressive to Nebuchadnezzar and man but not to God! Nebuchadnezzar utterly failed to understand that the only reason he could accomplish these things is because Yahweh gave him the ability and power to do so.

Apostle Paul says in Acts 17:28, "In <u>Him</u> (God) we live, move and exist." Psalms 103:14-16 reminds us that man is only dust. Job 12:10 teaches that God holds the breath and life of every living being and mankind are in His hands. Lester Maddox (1915-2003), former governor of Georgia (1967-1971) reiterated this truth as he declared, "Every breath and heartbeat is a gift from God."

Nebuchadnezzar did not realize these truths but continued to live in his arrogant pride. "Superman" refused to heed Daniel's warning to humble himself and give glory to God.

> Nebuchadnezzar's sin wasn't that he knew he was talented. His problem was that he considered himself the source of his talent. He wanted the whole world to acknowledge his abilities and did not give credit to the thousands of talented laborers and craftsmen who actually built the city of Babylon, much less to God (Dr. Jeremiah, *Agents of Babylon*, p.121).

One year after receiving the dream and interpretation his head swells with his glory as he reminds himself of his "tremendous, wonderful greatness." He arrogantly boasts (Author's paraphrase),

> "Is not this the great Babylon I have built by my wonderful mighty power for the glory of my majesty?" (4:30). "Look at all the wonderful things that I have done for my much deserved personal splendor, majesty, and glory because I am so great!"

The words were barely out of his mouth when God told him that his dream would be fulfilled. Nebuchadnezzar would be afflicted with lycanthropy (Greek: *wolf man*), a mental disease that will cause him to spend 7 years living with and like wild animals. He will eat grass with the oxen; grow hair like eagle's feathers and nails like bird's claws (4:33).

> For thus says the high and exalted One who lives forever whose name is Holy, "I dwell on a high and holy place, and also with the contrite and lowly of spirit in order to revive the spirit of the lowly and to revive the heart of the contrite" (Isa 57:15).

God Himself loves to humble Himself and comfort the lowly but He doesn't tolerate pride as He shares His glory with no one (Isa. 42:8).

"Pride goes before destruction and a haughty spirit before the fall." (Pr. 16:18). "Everyone who is proud in heart is an abomination to the LORD" (Pr. 16:5). "I hate pride, arrogance, evil behavior and perverse speech." (Pr. 8:13 NKJV). "A man's pride will bring him low but a humble spirit will obtain honor" (Pr. 29:23). Pride brings disgrace but humility brings wisdom. (11:2).

Nebuchadnezzar learned the hard way the truth of these Scriptures. The instruction from I Peter 5:5b-6 is so clear!

> Clothe yourselves with humility toward one another for GOD IS OPPOSED TO THE PROUD BUT GIVES GRACE TO THE HUMBLE. Therefore humble yourselves under the mighty hand of God that He may exalt you at the proper time.

Jesus said in Luke 18:14, "He who exalts himself shall be humbled and he who humbles himself will be exalted."

God cut Nebuchadnezzar down in his pride as he became insane and beastlike for 7 years. He was in worse shape than the beasts because beasts are expected to act like beasts but humans are not. A fitting punishment for anyone who takes glory that belongs only to God (Boice, p. 52). When man is beast like he lives far below his divine calling to reflect the image of God as he was made a little lower than angels. He is to rule over the beasts (Psalm 8:4-9) not with or like the beasts.

John Gerstner spoke at a Philadelphia conference and compared mankind to rats. Someone was offended and asked for an apology. He said, "I apologize profusely, the comparison was terribly unfair...to the rats." (Boice, p.53).

Humans do far worse things than rats! Romans 1:21-32 gives details of what happens when man in his arrogant pride refuses to be thankful and give God His deserved glory. Human pride is always insane but humility and praise to God is always sober and sensible.

Nebuchadnezzar's Sanity Restored

David Jeremiah states, "Humility isn't thinking less of yourself but thinking of yourself less." (*Agents of Babylon* p. 134). After living like a wild beast for 7 years his sanity was restored as he looked up and humbled himself before God.

> "I, Nebuchadnezzar raised my eyes toward heaven and my sanity was restored. Then I praised the most high; I honored and glorified Him who lives forever. His dominion is eternal. His kingdom endures from generation to generation. All the peoples of the earth are regarded as nothing" (4:24).

Amazing! Perfect theology coming from a fierce pagan ruler! Nebuchadnezzar finally understands the sovereignty of Yahweh and boldly proclaims it. In chapter 1 he sees that Daniel, Hananiah, Mishael, and Azariah are 10 times wiser than his wise men and therefore gets a hint that their God Yahweh deserves some honor and respect.

In chapter 2 he learns that the God of Daniel is wiser than the gods of Babylon as Nebuchadnezzar declares in 2:47, "Surely your God is the God of gods, the Lord of kings and revealer of mysteries."

In 3:28-30 he declared that the "God of Shadrach. Meshach, and Abednego can rescue his people much better than other gods," but in Chapter 4 he finally understands and fully recognizes the sovereignty of Yahweh, the God of Israel as he proclaims Him to be *most high God* and *most high* (vs. 2, 17, 24, 25, 32, and 34).

The first time this phrase is used is in Genesis 14:18-22 when Melchizedec, priest of *God most high* blessed Abraham with these words, "Blessed be Abram of *God Most High*, possessor (ruler) of heaven and earth." Abram said in verse 22, "I have sworn to the LORD God most high, possessor (ruler) of heaven and earth." The name *Most High God* obviously refers to the sovereignty of God as He is creator, possessor, and ruler of heaven and earth.

In Isaiah 14:12-15, Lucifer arrogantly boasts, "I will make myself like *the Most High*." In his arrogance Lucifer (bright, shining light) becomes Satan (accuser, slanderer) as he declares his determination to be sovereign like God.

My Sunday school teacher told us that we should be like God and yet Lucifer, the devil is punished because he wants to be like God. Is there a difference? Yes! Absolutely! We need to be like God in His tender mercies, kindness, goodness, peacefulness, wisdom, compassion, love, care, and humility (Eph.5:1). Did Lucifer want to be like God in His tender mercies, kindness, goodness, peacefulness, wisdom, compassion, love, care, and humility? Absolutely not!!! Overflowing with arrogance he wanted to be like the Most High God *only* in His sovereignty and power (Isa. 14:14). Lucifer told God, "Move over Yahweh as I take your place as the sovereign ruler of the universe." Lucifer who became Satan was thus cast out of Heaven and will be "tormented day and night forever and ever" in the lake of fire (Rev. 20:10)

Nebuchadnezzar's sanity was restored when he humbled himself. In Matthew 8:12 Jesus teaches that those who reject Him will be cast into "outer darkness with wailing and gnashing of teeth:" A perfect description of an insane asylum. It's always insane and beastlike to exalt one's self in pride and arrogance and rebel against God but it's always very sane to humble one's self before God and walk humbly with God (Micah 6:8). The prodigal son regained his sanity and was restored after he humbled himself and returned to his father (Luke 15:22-26).

While speaking to the inmates of the Federal Correction Institute in Memphis, Tennessee, on May, 1978, Evangelist Billy Graham quoted the director of a mental institute in London who said, "100% of the inmates could leave if they only knew they were forgiven." The director thus declared that the inmates are too arrogant to humble themselves by asking for and freely receiving forgiveness and therefore remain insane.

100% of humanity can be free of the future insane asylum of Matthew 8:12 by simply receiving the forgiveness that Christ freely offers to all (John 3:16, Romans 5:8; 2 Peter 3:9). Let us all therefore determine to fully reject, detest, abhor, and hate pride and, "walk humbly with our God" (Micah 6:8) and then we will be assured of peace and sanity in our lives (Philippians 4:7, John 14:27).

While working in Chaingrai, Thailand with a ministry that was helping to deliver members of the Akha tribe from drug abuse we were blessed with success. Jesus Christ graciously delivered many Akhas from drug abuse. At the graduation ceremony a local government official was very pleased and shared his appreciation as he addressed the group. He said,

"Your God is superior to our god. Your God can deliver people from drugs but our god can't. May your God continue to deliver people from drugs."

The Thai official saw and knew that Yahweh, the living God had delivered people from drugs but as far as I know he did not surrender his life to the living God but continued to honor and worship Buddha. We hope that Nebuchadnezzar had a genuine conversion to Yahweh, the holy, sovereign God of Israel and will rise on the first resurrection. We'll all know on resurrection day.

5

The Ball, Hall, Wall and the Great Fall (Belshazzar's Titanic)

This chapter is about a great debauchery **Ball,** (an undisciplined, frivolous, silly party) held in the great **Hall** with handwriting on the **Wall** prophesying of the great **Fall** of Babylon

Yahweh declares in Jeremiah 51:24 that He will repay Babylon for the wrong done to Zion. Jeremiah 27:4-7 declares that Yahweh gives lands to Nebuchadnezzar, his son, and grandson and then will make the king of Babylon a servant to other nations: A clear prediction that Babylon will last only through the reign of Nebuchadnezzar's grandson, Belshazzar. Isaiah 13:17-22 predicts Babylon's fall 150 years earlier.

The "Unsinkable" Titanic

The worst peacetime sea disaster happened on the night of April 14-15, 1912 with the sinking of the "unsinkable ship", *Titanic*. It was the largest vessel of its time; 4 city blocks long and weighing over 46,000 tons. The structure was seriously compromised as inferior iron was used for the rivets and the bulkheads of the watertight compartments did not have optimal height. The designer wanted 48 lifeboats but was overruled by Bruce Ismay, the chairman of the White Star line because, "people don't buy tickets to look at lifeboats: They clutter up the deck." Life boats weren't really needed since it was "unsinkable" but Ismay accepted 16 anyway: Enough room for about half of the people on Titanic.

The wireless operators received ice warnings even before the maiden voyage started on April 10 from Southampton, England. 1912 had one of the mildest winters in 30 years which helped to produce 70 miles of north-to-south ice in the shipping lanes. 10 ice warnings were issued on Friday and 12 on Saturday from more than 20 ships (Lee Merideth, *1912 Facts about Titanic,* p. 121).

The weather was perfect (55F) on Sunday, April 14 as they sailed on a sea of glass. The White Star Line required all liners to conduct lifeboat drills Sunday morning after worship services but Captain Smith decided not to do them. The 1st ice warning arrived at 9 AM and 4 more came but most were not taken seriously and some ignored. (Lee Merideth, *1912 Facts about Titanic* p.121-124). Captain Smith received only the 2nd one.

Senior Marconi wireless telegraph operator John Phillips earned money sending and receiving messages for the passengers but earned no money receiving and delivering iceberg warnings. While busy earning money with the wireless, a strong overriding signal interrupted him from *Californian,* a ship less than 10 miles away. The *Californian* wireless operator issued strong warnings of the many icebergs in the area and informed Phillips that *Californian* would remain still for the night because of the abundance of icebergs. Phillips angrily replied, "Shut up you bloody idiots! I'm working Cape Race." Phillips was too busy earning money sending messages to Cape Race, Newfoundland to be bothered with iceberg warnings. After this very arrogant, rude reply, the *Californian* wireless operator shut off its wireless and rested for the night (National Geographic DVD).

Just before the voyage started, Captain Smith dismissed 2nd Officer Blair who accidentally took the keys to the safe containing the binoculars. The watchmen in the crow's nest therefore had no binoculars on that moonless night when at 11:39 PM *Titanic* struck the iceberg. The frantic desire to avoid the iceberg caused *Titanic* to scrape the iceberg on its side, causing a puncture which allowed 400 tons of water to enter every minute. At 2:20 AM Titanic sank with 1513 dead and 723 survivors. Had Titanic struck the iceberg head on it would have survived just as the USS Arizona did in 1879 after striking an iceberg head on. (National Geographic DVD).

On page 119 of Lee Merideth's book a very chilling, frightening conversation is recorded.

Second Class passenger Mrs. Albert Caldwell asked a deck hand, "Is this ship really non-sinkable?" His reply was, "Yes lady, God himself could not sink this ship."

This is one of the greatest examples of modern arrogance.

Belshazzar's "Unsinkable Ship of State"

He who trusts in his own heart is a fool but he who walks wisely will be delivered." (Pr. 28:26). 25 years had passed since the chapter 4 events and so King Belshazzar had plenty of time to think about the lesson of chapter 4 and the teaching of Proverbs 28:26. But tragically he very boldly rejected these truths and placed himself under a divine curse as he declared that Babylon, an ancient version of *Titanic* to be unsinkable (Jer. 17:5-8). He basically said, "Even God can't sink my great Babylonian ship of state." Belshazzar learns that God can sink any ship or destroy any empire He desires (ISam. 2:7, Ps. 22:28; 75:7; 103:19; 147:6).

King Nebuchadnezzar died on October 7, 562 BC (Olmstead, p.35). After three other men ruled and passed on, Nabonidus, the son-in-law of Nebuchadnezzar became king of Babylon in 556 BC (Young, p. 298) and was king when the events of Daniel 5 took place (Showers, p.49).

If Nabonidus is the king why is Belshazzar called the king here in chapter 5? Belshazzar is the son of Nabonidus and served as king while his father conquered those who rebelled against Babylonian rule after Nebuchadnezzar's death. Nabonidus set up his palace in central Arabia and was content to let his son rule in Babylon as king (Olmstead, p. 37 from Showers, p. 50).

King Nebuchadnezzar made Babylon the world's mightiest fortress as described in Chapter 4. The outer wall (375 feet high) was so thick that 4 chariots could easily pass each other. It would be utterly useless to use a battering ram or any increment of war to tear down the wall. "The presence of an inner wall and numerous fortress towers and ramparts made any attempt to scale the walls suicidal." (Olmstead p.39 from Showers, p.52). The Euphrates River flowed freely under the walls through the city and there was enough food to feed the people in the city for 20 years. The people scornfully laughed at any siege the Medo-Persians planned for them (Boutflower p.22, 124 from Showers, p. 52).

The Medo-Persians had conquered large areas around Babylon about 4 months before Belshazzar's feast. High ranking government officials were fleeing before the advance of the invaders and found refuge inside the city (Boutflower, p. 121-132 from Showers, p. 52). Belshazzar and his high officials were therefore "safe and secure behind these impregnable walls with an everlasting water supply and a 20-year supply of food." (So they thought!)

In Hebrew there is no word for grandson or grandfather and so father is used to describe one's ancestor and son used for one's descendant. That's why Daniel calls Nebuchadnezzar "your father" (5:18). Belshazzar was 14 when his grandfather Nebuchadnezzar died (Boutflower, p. 114-115 from Showers p. 51) and so he had plenty of time to learn of God's dealings with Nebuchadnezzar (v. 22).

The temple of Marduk contained the vessels of other nations that Babylon conquered and so we wonder why did Belshazzar bring only the vessels from the Jerusalem temple? He wanted to boldly defy and insult Yahweh, the Holy one of Israel. Belshazzar showed his strong contempt toward Yahweh by drinking from the gold and silver goblets that King Nebuchadnezzar had taken from the Jerusalem temple and leading the guests in drunken praise to the gods of gold, silver, bronze, iron, wood and stone. He boldly ignored the teaching of Proverbs 31:4-5

> It is not for kings.... to drink wine, nor for princes intoxicating drink; lest they drink and forget the law. And pervert the justice of all the afflicted.

He gave the party in a hall about the size of the main section of the White House (172 feet by 60) with over 1,000 guests plus wives and concubines. In ancient Middle East culture it was extremely unusual to have women at such gatherings and so it must have been a very sensual party. Since Yahweh hates sexual immorality, idolatry, and drunk behavior, Belshazzar could not have chosen a more degrading way to show his utter contempt, scorn, and disdain for Yahweh, the Holy God of Israel.

Belshazzar, like his grandfather Nebuchadnezzar was proud, haughty, and arrogant but unlike Nebuchadnezzar, Belshazzar most boldly and openly insulted Yahweh. He refused to humble himself even though he knew the result of Nebuchadnezzar's pride and his dream predicting Babylon's fall. In his super arrogant pride he decided that he could thwart Yahweh's will and ensure that Babylon would last forever.

> The king was so confident of Babylon's defenses that he decided to challenge this God. His defiling of the vessels was his way of shaking his fist at God and saying: "You have said that Babylon will fall to the Medo-Persians who are now encamped outside our gates. I am declaring to you that Babylon will not fall. Its defenses are impregnable. No one will be able to take it. My actions show you what I think of you and your prophecy." (Showers, p.53).

"Even God can't sink my great Babylonian Titanic!" In his own arrogant ignorance Belshazzar joyfully celebrated his own funeral.

The Handwriting on the Wall

Suddenly the atmosphere changed 180 degrees as an unseen hand started writing on the wall. No longer proud and boastful, Belshazzar got scared and asked for help from the Babylonian enchanters, diviners, soothsayers, astrologers, etc. As usual these charlatans were helpless in explaining the meaning and so Daniel was summoned and he immediately knew the meaning and explained it to the king.

Mene literally means "numbered" or "reckoned." God had previously determined the length of the Babylon Empire and the time of the empire was over. It was stated twice to emphasize the termination of the Babylonian Empire.

Tekel means "weighed". Belshazzar was weighed on scales and he does not measure up to God's standards. He was too light and morally deficient.

Upharsin or *peres* means broken or divided. Both words have the same meaning. *Pharsin* is the plural of *peres*. The "U" means "and" in Hebrew. *Peres* is similar to the word "Persia". The kingdom is divided among the Medes and Persians (Showers, p. 57).

In chapter 4 Daniel liked Nebuchadnezzar and pleaded with him to repent after interpreting his dream and possibly be spared the judgment pronounced against him but he had no feeling for this super arrogant spoiled brat. The meaning is basically,

> "It's all over Bel! Even though you knew what happened to your grandfather after his arrogant behavior you have decided to boldly insult and defy God and therefore your goose is cooked. Prepare to meet your God for you are now history! Your unsinkable Babylonian ship of state has sunk!"

He therefore reaped severe consequences as he full of frivolity most boldly and arrogantly defied, mocked, taunted, blasphemed, and insulted Yahweh, the Holy One of Israel.

Belshazzar offered a gold chain, purple robe, and the 3rd highest position in the kingdom to the one who would explain the handwriting. Daniel was not seeking personal gain and therefore initially rejected them. What good is it to be promoted in a bankrupt company? After pronouncing Babylon's doom, he accepted them lest he be considered an ungrateful coward or even guilty of treason (p. 409 JFB).

The purple robe signified royalty and the gold chain could be worn in Babylon only if it were given to one by a king (Young p.121 from Showers p.54). The gold chain signified Daniel's co-regency with Belshazzar and Nabonidus. It's a witness to the world of God's faithfulness in deciphering the message on the wall. All of this would benefit Daniel and his people in the new Persian Empire.

> Today there are cuneiform letters on walls describing the exploits and victories of kings in order for visitors to see the splendor of the kingdom. It's interesting that on this same wall where the king was used to reading flattering legends of the greatness of his empire, he sees the inscription of his fall (JFB, vol. 2. p. 408).

In Acts 12:21-23 we read of another very arrogant king. Herod freely accepted the worship and adulation of the people as they proclaimed, "It's the voice of God and not of man." He did not give God the glory and was stricken by an angel.

In the 1960s the rock music band, Beatles took the US by storm as millions flocked to hear them. In an interview with the American teen magazine, *Datebook,* John Lennon (1940-1980) very arrogantly mocked God as he boasted,

Christianity will go. It will vanish and shrink. I needn't argue about that. I'm right and will be proved right. We're more popular than Jesus now.

On December 8, 1980, John Lennon was murdered. He like Belshazzar learned the hard truth that the warning of Galatians 6:7 should always be taken seriously.

Persia Conquers Babylon

Prophet Jeremiah predicted the fall of Babylon in 50:2-3, 51:11, 28-29, and v.57.

"Declare and proclaim among the nations...Babylon has been captured. Bel has been put to shame. Marduk has been shattered. Her images have been put to shame. Her idols have been shattered. For a nation has come against her out of the north. It will make her land an object of horror and there will be no inhabitant in it."

Sharpen the arrows, fill the quivers! The LORD has aroused the spirit of the kings of the Medes because His purpose is against Babylon to destroy it. For it is the vengeance of the Lord, vengeance for His temple (51:11).

In 51:36-37 Jeremiah predicts the way Persia would conquer Babylon.

".. (I will) exact full vengeance for you; And I will dry up her sea and make her fountain dry."

In verse 57 we learn that the Babylonian officials will be drunk while being conquered.

The Persian king knew that it was impossible to conquer Babylon using conventional means. The walls and fortifications were too great. He devised a way to divert the Euphrates River away from the city. When it became shallow enough his army simply marched under the walls into the city and conquered Babylon without a major battle or destruction (*The Wycliffe Bible Commentary*, p. 785). Security is only in God! (Psalm 20:7; 27; 46; 91, Jer. 17:5-8, Pr. 26:12).

"That very night Belshazzar...was slain and Darius the Mede took over the kingdom." (5:30). Darius is the title of the new ruler meaning, *holder of the scepter.* Gubaru, (Gobryas), born in 601 BC, was 62 years old when Babylon was conquered in October 13, 539 BC and was appointed by the Medo-Persian leader King Cyrus as the new king of Babylon (Wood, p. 155 from Showers, p. 60-61).

While fleeing from Muslims in Algeria a Christian found a cave and entered it for refuge. He knew he would eventually be found but he would enjoy temporary respite there. To his surprise he saw a spider build a web over the mouth of the cave. When his pursuers saw the web they knew it was impossible for their victim to be in the cave without breaking the web, so they left. God made the web into a wall. Belshazzar saw the fortified walls around Babylon made into a web.

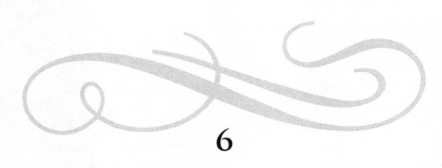

6

Daniel's Difficulty, Decision, And Deliverance from Disaster

In the conclusion of the greatest sermon ever preached (Matthew 5-7) Jesus gives the story of a wise and foolish builder. Both built houses that faced strong winds and severe rain storms. The house built on the rock stood strong and firm but the one on sand fell. Jesus instructs us to build the house of our lives on the rock by obeying His instructions so that we will stand strong through the storms of life. I Peter 4:12-13 tells us not to be surprised but be prepared to face the storms of life.

Sometimes God sends difficulty and storms in our lives in order to correct our sinful and irresponsible behavior (Jonah 1:4-17, Ps. 119:66-72). However many times people face difficulty and storms because they are obedient to the LORD. Abel, Noah, Joseph, Moses, the Hebrew prophets, Christ's disciples, Apostle Paul, and Jesus Christ's lives were full of difficulty because they were obedient to God.

Jesus told His disciples, "Let us go to the other side." While crossing the Sea of Galilee a terrific storm arose that scared the disciples to death (Mk. 4:35-41). The disciples faced this storm because they were obedient to Christ's instructions to "go to the other side." Jesus promised a safe landing but not smooth sailing.

Joseph like Daniel showed flawless impeccable character as he fully and diligently obeyed his father's instructions. This resulted in his being sold into slavery (Gen. 37:12-36). His refusal to be seduced into adultery resulted in his imprisonment. In this chapter Daniel also had a storm because he was obedient to God. He faced **difficulty,** made the right

decision, and received **deliverance.** His accusers received the **disaster** planned for Daniel.

When Daniel interpreted Nebuchadnezzar's dream in chapter 2 he told the king that another kingdom would arise that would be inferior to Babylon (2:39). The Persian Empire was larger than the Babylonian Empire and lasted almost 3 times longer (538 BC-331 BC) but is still called inferior. Why? This story gives us the answer. Nebuchadnezzar had absolute authority as the Babylonian king. He could put to death and spare anyone he chose (5:19). He could change any law at any time for any reason. The Persian monarch is declared inferior to the Babylonian monarch because he did not have this authority. Persian laws could never be changed nor needed to be changed because they were "infallible laws made by infallible monarchs." (So they thought! Dan. 6:15, Esther 8:8).

King Darius knew of the spotless, pure, impeccable integrity of Daniel and therefore made him the head of the 2 other fellow commissioners in charge of the 120 local governors of the empire. Darius knew the locals were ripping him off as they used taxes for their personal benefit. It's therefore no wonder that the 2 other commissioners and 120 satraps desperately wanted to get rid of Daniel. He greatly frustrated their desire to enjoy a privileged, pompous, penthouse lifestyle of luxury with their Rolls Royce Chariots, Kentucky derby horses, and exotic Hawaii vacations through their extortion of the tax payers. Daniel required integrity from these crooked governors and so they had to get rid of him but how could they? They exhaustably probed deeply into Daniel's life but were completely frustrated as they found nothing but pure, spotless, impeccable perfect integrity (Pr. 29:10, 27, Ps. 69:4). They knew that the only way to eliminate Daniel was to find something wrong with his religion.

The officials, filled with envy and wrath (Pr.27:4), hatched a plot to catch the king off guard with flattery and trap him in his vanity. They start with a lie by stating that *all* the officials have agreed that the king should be the Sovereign God for a month. It is now illegal to request anything from anyone except the king for a month. Daniel was *not* consulted and obviously would have never agreed to such a ridiculous and blasphemous law.

The very naive king's head swelled with his vanity as he freely fell into the trap and signed the law. This is difficulty for Daniel and Darius.

Flattery and cruelty usually go together (Ps. 5:9; 55:21, Pr. 26:24-28; 29:5, Jer. 9:8). James 1:19 tells us to be swift to hear and slow to speak. The king was swift to speak as he gave his approval but very slow to hear and understand the situation. He therefore reaped a very difficult time. (Ecc. 5:2-6), He loved the honor that comes from man (John 5:44).

Ezekiel 14:14 and Daniel 10:11 tell us that Daniel's prayers are highly valued in Heaven. Daniel read I Kings 8:46-53, 2 Chronicles 6:36-39; 7:14, Psalm 16:7-9; 27; 91; 46:1-10; 34:7; 20:7, and applied the instructions to his heart. No doubt he knew Psalm 55:17: "Evening, morning, and noon I cry out in distress and he hears my voice." His prayer life was far more important to him than the favor of the king or even his life. Daniel knew that he could not even last a day without prayer and so when he heard about the law he remained fully steadfast, totally unmoved, and consistent as he continued to do what he always did: Praying 3 times a day facing Jerusalem with his windows open (6:10).

Dr. Jeremiah (The Handwriting on the Wall p.123) quotes Shakespeare's famous line, "Cowards die many times before their deaths: The valiant taste death but once." Daniel knew the penalty for disobeying the king's decree but like his 3 friends in chapter 3, he far preferred physical death over spiritual death. Daniel was no grandstander. He did not flaunt or parade his heroics before others but neither was he ashamed of his faith. He simply continued to do what was right (James 1:27, Matthew 5:16; 6:5-13). Daniel boldly stood alone as he remained pure, strong, and unscathed in this pagan culture.

The word used in verse 6 and 11 is the same one used in Psalm 2:1, "Why are the nations in an *uproar* and why do the people imagine a vain thing?" These men assembled in uproar together and exasperated the king to enforce the law by punishing Daniel for his "willful rebellion against the king's command."

Darius felt terrible as he learned that he very naively fell into the accusers' trap. He knew he had been tricked and seduced by his very corrupt, unscrupulous, arrogant, self-seeking satraps who were jealous of Daniel's status. They couldn't stand Daniel's integrity and hated his demand for them to also have integrity, but what could the king do? Like an animal trapped he did his utmost best to free himself and deliver Daniel but since he was hopelessly bound and gagged by his own law (6:15) he was forced to put Daniel in the lion's den. Like the very naïve young man in Proverbs 7 who was flattered by a harlot, Darius goes like an ox to the slaughter (Pr. 7:22).

Daniel sleeps with the lions

Daniel slept well with the lions (Ps. 4:8; 22:21, Pr. 1:33; 3:24) but like King Nebuchadnezzar in 2:1 and King Ahasuerus in Esther 6:1, the king did not. When morning came the king ran to the den and was so very relieved to see that Daniel suffered no harm. Daniel did not rebuke the king for treating him unfairly but with courtesy showed proper respect to the king (v. 21, I Peter 2:20-24). Darius never heard any sweeter music than Daniel's voice that morning (6:22-23). Like King Nebuchadnezzar after the miraculous deliverance of the 3 Hebrews in chapter 3, King Darius exalts and glorifies Yahweh God and commands everyone to honor Him. Like King Nebuchadnezzar in chapter 4 this pagan Persian king also proclaims excellent theology (26-27). England's Charles Haddon Spurgeon said that the lions did not eat Daniel because he was 50% grit and 50% backbone.

David Jeremiah told a story of a plane going through a very severe storm. A pastor noticed that many were very nervous and some wailing in fear. All including the pastor were a little nervous but the pastor noticed an 8-year old girl who was totally undisturbed and calmly read and colored her books through the flight. After landing the pastor asked her how she could be so calm through such turbulent weather. She answered, "My daddy is the pilot and he will make sure that I safely arrive home to see my mother."

No doubt Daniel knew that even though God never promised smooth sailing through life he trusted his "daddy in Heaven" for a safe arrival.

Disaster for Daniel's enemies

Psalm 7:15-16 says that he who digs a pit will himself fall into it. His mischief and violence will return to him (Pr. 11:8). Like Haman (Esther

7:10) the conspirators suffered the consequences they planned for Daniel (Dt. 19:18-19). The lions rejected the tough 90-year old Jew but freely consumed the tender spineless Persians before they hit the ground (v 24).

Deuteronomy 24:16 forbids capital punishment for relatives of the guilty. It seems so unfair and cruel for the Persians to feed the lions with the accusers' families but they reasoned that it was necessary in order to prevent future assassination attempts by disgruntled relatives.

God's Will is always best!

The 3 men in chapter 3 were standing when everyone else was kneeling. Daniel kneeled when everyone else was standing. He who kneels before God will always be able to stand before man. God did not deliver them from the pressure of death but accompanied them through "the valley of the shadow of death" (Psalm 23:4). The lessons of Daniel 3 and 6 are very clear and strong! It's far better to be in a den of raving, savage, fierce, and hungry lions with the angel of the Lord than to be a comfortable accuser outside without the angel. It's far better to be in a fiery furnace with the Son of God than to be one of the king's favored officials executing his orders.

Always remember! The safest place for the believer in Jesus Christ is in the center of God's will; even if it's in a fiery furnace or a lion's den.

From *The Most High God* by **Renald Showers** p.91

LION
BABYLON

BEAR
MEDIA-PERSIA

LEOPARD
GREECE

FIERCE BEAST
ROME

TEN HORNS
DIVIDED KINGDOM

7

God's View of Man's Kingdoms

The first 6 chapters of Daniel are almost only history. The last 6 are only prophecy. Heretofore Daniel interprets other's visions and dreams but hereafter Daniel receives dreams and visions that are interpreted by an angel. Heretofore the third person is used but hereafter the first person is used showing Daniel's intimate relation with his experiences. In this chapter Daniel has a vision and the quiet confidence he showed earlier left him. He trembled and turned pale and needed angelic help (7:15-16).

Daniel received the dream in the first year of Belshazzar's co-regency; about 553 BC (Swindoll, *Daniel*, vol. 2, p. 3). His dream is basically the same as Nebuchadnezzar's dream in chapter 2. This one gives more details to the chapter 2 dream and the prophetic vision from God's point of view. God views mankind's "exalted grandeur of great strength and wonderful exalted accomplishments," represented in the great majestic glittering statue of chapter 2 as no more than the wild ferocious beasts of chapter 7. Jesus said, "That which is highly esteemed among men is detestable in the sight of God" (Luke 16:15). Animals have no consciousness toward God. God elevates man as he communes with his creator. When he is independent of God he, like Nebuchadnezzar descends to the beast's level and becomes beastlike. Isaiah 40:15-17 declares that the nations are as a drop in a bucket and dust on scales. Isaiah 2:17 declares;

The pride of man will be humbled and the loftiness of man will be abased; and the LORD alone will be exalted in that day.

In this dream there are 4 winds of heaven stirring up the sea where 4 beasts come out. In symbolic prophecy the seas usually represent humanity at large (Isaiah 17:12-13, Revelation 17:1, 15).

In chapters 7 and 8 animals are used to convey truth. Today we use animals to describe characteristics of people. He is so fearful; he's chicken. He's as stubborn as a mule. He has a backbone of a jellyfish. He's as wise as an owl. He is as sly as a fox. He's as gentle as a lamb. He smells like a skunk. He's as strong as an ox. He has eagle eyes. Don't allow your daughter to see him because he's a wolf. He is as slow as a snail. (Have you heard of snail mail?) He's bull-headed. I smell a rat. He's a snake in the grass. Don't invest in stocks now because it's a bear market. Please don't bug me. He clams up.

Our savior is called a lamb and a lion (Isa. 53:7, John 1:29, 36, Rev. 5:5). Jesus declared that Herod is a fox (Lk. 13:32). We are all called sheep (Ps. 100:3, Isa 53:6). "The righteous are as bold as a lion." (Pr. 28:1). Since we generously use animals to show human behavior we should not be surprised to see that they are generously used in Scripture.

The winged lion = Babylon

The first beast, the winged lion, is the national symbol of Babylon. The 2 Ishtar gates of Babylon have 2 carved winged lions guarding the city (D. Jeremiah, *The Handwriting on the Wall*, p. 134). Jeremiah 4:7 declares that the lion, the destroyer of nations has come out to make Judah a waste land. Jeremiah 4:13 declares that Babylon's horses are swifter than eagles. "Our pursuers are swifter than the eagles." (Lam. 4:19). The flying swift fierce lion is an excellent symbol for Babylon because its empire was conquered faster than any other up to that time. His wings are plucked and he's given a man's heart. "The successors of Nebuchadnezzar were comparably weak and indolent princes as if the wings had been plucked." (Barnes, 48-49). The plucking of the wings began with King Nebuchadnezzar's arrogance and 7-year adventure with the animals and culminated with the feeble reign of Belshazzar. When Nebuchadnezzar regained his sanity he received a man's heart.

The bear = Persia

The second beast represents the Medo-Persian Empire. The bear is an excellent representative of this kingdom because of its extreme fierce and severe treatment of its enemies. Like the bear, the Medes and Persians were tactless, greedy, stupid, strong, rapacious, and cruel. The bear is the most ferocious animal when robbed of its cubs (2 Sam. 17:8, 2 Kings 2:24, Pr. 17:12, Hos. 13:8). It obeyed the command to "devour much flesh" (v. 5) and the Persian Empire became much larger than the Babylonian one. The ponderous bulk of the bear vividly represents the Persian armies. Xerxes led 5,000,000 troops in his attempt to conquer Greece (Barnes p. 210). The 3 ribs are the 3 nations it conquered: Babylon, Egypt, and Lydia. One side was higher than the other representing Persia's dominance over the Medes.

The leopard = Greece

The third beast is a leopard with 4 wings and 4 heads. This is Alexander's Macedonian-Greek empire. The leopard is a very swift, agile, cruel, and cunning predator with a tremendous appetite for blood (Hab. 1:8, Jer. 5:6, Hosea 13:7). It's known for silently stalking its prey and then suddenly springing on it. The 4 wings symbolize the incredible speed of Alexander's army in conquering the empire. Alexander's army of 35,000-40,000 defeated the 300,000 man Persian army in several decisive battles in about 3 years and 11,000 miles of territory between Greece and India in another 8 years.

Alexander could conquer everyone but himself. He was very irresponsible and permissive in his moral lifestyle and died in a drunken stupor when he was almost 33. He complained that there were no more worlds to conquer. The 4 heads coming out of the leopard's head represent the 4 generals who divided the kingdom after Alexander's untimely death.

The indescribable horrible hideous 4th beast = Rome

The fourth beast was so hideous and horrible that no animal could adequately represent it. It had large iron teeth and devoured everything in its way. "There is a kind of man whose teeth are like swords and their jaw teeth like knives to devour the afflicted from off the earth" (Pr. 30:14). Rome's teeth were iron spears and arrows (Ps. 57:4). Rome far surpassed the cruelty and corruption of the previous kingdoms as it freely crushed and devoured everything in its way just for the sadistic pleasure of doing it. Super sadistic Rome freely tortured many to death through crucifixion including Peter, Andrew, and our Lord Jesus Christ. Paul was severely beaten by the Roman lector before he was beheaded. Many Christians were burned alive or fed to the wild animals.

The 10 horns like the 10 toes of chapter 2 represent the division of Rome that will be in effect when the rock, supernaturally cut out without hands, crushes the image at the second coming of Christ (2:44-45).

The little horn

Another horn arises from within the ten horns with the eyes of man and "speaks great things." In Scripture eyes are symbolic of intelligence (Ezekiel 1:18, Gen. 3:5). This 11th horn, though little at first plucks up 3 of the 10 horns (kings) by their roots and dominates all the others. The little horn (24-25) boldly speaks against the most high, seeks to change times and laws and persecutes the saints for a time (1 year), times (2 years), and half a time (1/2 year). This totals 3 1/2 years or 1260 days. This is Antichrist; the beast of Revelation 13:1-10.

Who Is Antichrist?

Apostle John is the only Scripture writer to use the term, *Antichrist* (I John 2:18, 22; 4:3, II John 1:7). *Anti* usually means to be against something. Indeed Antichrist is against God and Christ as he blasphemes God (Daniel 7:25, 2 Thess. 2:3-8, Rev. 13:5-6). It also means, "in place of" or "instead of." Antichrist wants to take Christ's place and be loved, adored, honored, and worshiped as the true savior of mankind. He mimics Christ and charms the world with his smooth speech (Ps. 5:9; 55:21, Pr. 26:24-28, Jer. 9:8). The world at large will follow him (Rev. 13:4) but he will be destroyed with the brightness of Christ's coming (2 Thess. 2:8).

According to David Jeremiah (*The Coming Economic Armageddon*, p. 115) over 100 passages describe Antichrist. He will be dynamic (Dan.7:25, Rev. 13:2), defiant (2Thess.2:2-4, Dan. 11:36-37), deceitful (2Thess. 2:10-12, Rev.13:4), diabolical (Dan. 7:21-25. Zech. 14:1-3), and dramatic (Rev. 13:3). The Antichrist will be Satan's CEO (Chief Executive Officer) and filled with evil. He perfectly represents Satan in the flesh (Rev. 13:1-2) just as Jesus Christ perfectly represents Yahweh, our heavenly Father as God in the flesh (John 14:9-11).

John Phillips gives the following graphic description of Antichrist (D. Jeremiah, *The Coming Economic Armageddon* p. 105).

> The Antichrist will be an attractive and charismatic figure, a genius, a demon-controlled, devil-taught charmer of men. He will have answers to the horrendous problems of mankind, He will be all things to all men; a political statesman, a social lion, a financial wizard, an intellectual giant, a religious deceiver, a successful orator a gifted organizer, He will be Satan's masterpiece of deception, the world's false messiah With boundless enthusiasm the masses will follow him and readily enthrone him in their hearts as this world's savior and god.

Antichrist will be cheerfully welcomed as he arrives. Belgium's Prime Minister Paul-Henri Spaak during the 1930s and 40s reportedly said;

The truth is that the method of international committees has failed. What we need is a person, someone of the highest order or great experience, of great authority, of wide influence, of great energy. Let him come and let him come quickly. Either a civilian or a military man, no matter what his nationality, who will cut all the red tape, shove out... all the committees, wake up all the people, and galvanize all governments into action., (D. Jeremiah, *Agents of the Apocalypse* p. 141).

The pope is Antichrist according to many students of prophecy. His Latin title, *Vicarious Filii Dei* (the substitute for the Son of God) equals

666, the number of the beast (Rev. 13:18). The title itself is blasphemous as the pope claims to be the substitute for Christ here on earth. Before the Protestant Reformation many Catholics called the pope Antichrist. St. Bernard in the 12th century called Anacletus the Antichrist and Frederick II, ruler of the Holy Roman Empire declared Gregory IX to be Antichrist. Martin Luther, John Calvin, Philip Melanchthon, Huldreich Zwingli, William Tyndale and many heroes of the reformation, declared that the pope is Antichrist (p. 147, D. Jeremiah, *The Handwriting on the Wall*).

Papal Rome was free to develop its power in 538 after fully expelling the Heruli, Ostrogoths, and Vandals from Rome; fulfilling the little horn's plucking up 3 kingdoms. According to JFB, Papal Rome plucked up the Ravenna, the Lombard, and the state of Rome. This became the pope's first dominion.

Antichrist's reign was 1260 years according to this system of interpretation. The time, times and dividing of a time (3 1/2 years or 1260 days) should be interpreted symbolically as 1260 years because "a day equals a year in prophecy," (Numbers 14:33-34 and Ezekiel 4:4-6).

In 1798 French General Berthier took the pope prisoner: 1260 years after the papacy was supposedly established in 538. Thus the years between 538 and 1798 constitute Antichrist's reign. The interval between the Council of Nice in 325 and the death of Pope Gregory XIII in 1585 is 1260 years. The interval between the Edith of Justinian and the French Revolution is also 1260 years (533-1783). Emperor Phocas conferred the title of Pope to Boniface in 606 and 1260 years later (1866-1870) the temporal power was overthrown (Anderson, CP p. 268).

In chapter 9 we will see how God generously uses cycles of 7 in world events. The year of 529 and 754 are also possible dates for the commencement of the papacy's antichrist rule (JFB, p. 423). The temporal power of the Roman Church was broken and fully removed in 1870 as the papal states became a part of Italy but in 1929 it's temporal power was restored (Was this the deadly wound healed as prophesied in Revelation 13:3?)

The Roman Church's persecution of Christian believers during the dark ages was indeed very severe. Millions of believers were tortured and killed during its reign of terror but it's only a pale preview of the final three and a half year persecution of Antichrist. (*Fox's Book of Martyrs* documents the persecution, torture, and death of many believers by Pagan and Papal Rome) The Roman Church definitely has the spirit of Antichrist (I Jn. 2:18, 22) as it "wore out the saints of the most high" (v. 25; Rev. 13:7), tried to change times and laws, and blasphemed as it accepted titles that belong only to God. It's therefore understandable why many declare the pope to be Antichrist. However this interpretation is not possible because Revelation 13 makes it clear that Antichrist is one individual; not a system or group of men.

Revelation 17 accurately describes the Roman Catholic Church as, "drunk with the blood of saints" (v. 6), a great city that rules over the kings of the earth (v. 18), and a city on 7 hills (v. 9). The woman rides the beast but in verse 16 the beast destroys this harlot. It would therefore be impossible for the Roman Catholic pope to be the beast and the Revelation 17 harlot because the pope destroys the Roman Church. Quite absurd!

Robespierre, the leader of the French Revolution would also be a good antichrist. He ruled over France in a severe reign of terror as he executed many by the newly invented guillotine. Eventually Robespierre was also beheaded by the guillotine. They tried to change times and laws as their month contained 3 10-day weeks; replacing God's ordained 7-day week.

Wicked rulers and officials like Haman, Hitler, Himmler, Mussolini, Nero, Domitian, Diocletian, Antiochus Epiphanes, Togo, Stalin, and Mao are excellent types of Antichrist. If A=100, B=101, and 1 is added to each succeeding letter in the alphabet Hitler's name equals 666.

Some suggest that Judas Iscariot is Antichrist because like Antichrist he is also called the "son of destruction" (John 17:12, 2 Thess. 2:3) and the only one the Scriptures state that Satan entered into (John 13:27).

Frank Abagnale (born 1948) is one of the greatest scam artists of all time. This incredibly brilliant teenager successfully presented himself as a US Bureau of Prisons agent, Harvard lawyer, medical doctor, Pan American airline co-pilot, and college professor. He taught sociology at Brigham Young University with a bogus degree from Columbia University. He successfully forged checks worth $2,800,000. Abagnale's very successful deception is nothing compared to Antichrist's successful deception of the world at large.

President Nixon's Jewish secretary of State, Henry Kissinger was also suspected of being Antichrist because of his negotiating skills in helping to bring peace between Israel and Egypt. The middle of his name is *sin* and so he must be the "Man of sin" of 2 Thessalonians 2:3. (Don't laugh too hard!) If the value of 6 is given to A, 12 to B, and 6 is added to each succeeding letter of the English alphabet, his name equals 666.

President Ronald Wilson Reagan was also suspected of being Antichrist because he established diplomatic relations with the Vatican and all three of his names have 6 letters.

Some thought that John Kennedy, our first Roman Catholic president was Antichrist. He went through "death" and "resurrection" as a PT boat commander in the South Pacific during World War II. He received 666 votes in the Democratic convention as he ran for president in 1956. After his assassination his brother Bobby became the deadly wound that was healed (Rev. 13:3). That theory died after Bobby's assassination.

Ellen Gould White, the 19th century charismatic Seventh Day Adventist prophet's name also equals 666.

We don't know *who* the Antichrist is but we can know *what* he is! He is everything that Christ is not. Zechariah 11:16-17 gives an excellent description of Antichrist. Bank tellers spend virtually no time studying counterfeit money but spend lots of time handling genuine notes. As they repeatedly handle the genuine bank notes they become intimately familiar with them and when a counterfeit appears it is immediately recognized and rejected.

We should always concentrate our attention on the true Christ and spend lots of time "handling Him" in prayer and reading the Bible and then all that is not of God will be repulsive like same charges on the magnet. Let's ask Him to protect us from all that is not of God and fervently sing out from our hearts the following song;

Turn Your Eyes Upon Jesus.
By Helen H. Lemmel

O soul are you weary and troubled? No light in the darkness you see?
There's light for a look at the savior and light more abundant and free!
Thro' death into life everlasting, He passed and we follow Him there;
Over us sin no more has dominion- For more than conquerors we are!
His Word shall not fail you He promised; Believe Him, and all will be well:
Then go to a world that is dying, His perfect salvation to tell.
Turn Your Eyes upon Jesus Look full in His wonderful face;

And the things of earth will grow strangely dim
In the light of his glory and grace

The deterioration of mankind

The statue starts with gold and ends with mud. Daniel's dream begins with the noble lion and ends with an indescribable super ugly hideous creature. Evolutionists and modern illusive positive idealistic dreamers put the statue upside down. They think mankind is improving and advancing in civilization but history, prophecy, and reality teach otherwise. The world is continually deteriorating as evil men get worse and worse (2 Timothy 3:13). ISIS boldly demonstrates this truth as they regularly chop off heads, crucify, and burn alive infidels (Non-Muslims).

We glory in the advances and achievements of civilization, but God clearly sees human history as a chronicle of immorality and brutality, and depravity. Governments and political leaders may mask their true character for a time but they are unmasked before God. Just as we have moved from the head of gold to the feet of mud, from the royal lion to the nondescript beast, as history unfolds it does not get better, it gets worse (D. Jeremiah, *The Handwriting on the Wall* p. 137).

Christ made it clear that mankind would indeed get worse and worse as wars will continue until His second coming (Mt. 24:6). This truth was stressed in a prophetic conference held in California in February, 1914. Modern "enlightened expert theologians" laughed and scoffed at the conference and declared that the world was actually getting better as man was indeed learning how to reject war and solve his problems peacefully. They rejected this clear truth of Scripture and sneeringly scoffed at the prophetic conference and called it a *pathetic* conference.

Things looked fairly good in early 1914. Many peace treaties had been signed. In August, 1914 the modern enlightened liberal theologians were no longer laughing as the *Great War* commenced claiming over 9,000,000 lives. After the war the Versailles Peace Treaty was signed by the belligerents and all rejoiced because; "This was the war to end all wars."

Many more treaties were signed and the League of Nations was formed to "ensure that disputes would be settled peacefully." The treaties were not worth the paper they were written on as they were honored only when it was convenient to do so. Who can forget British Prime Minister Neville Chamberlain's exuberant excitement as he proudly proclaimed, "We have peace in our time" after signing the Munich peace agreements with Adolf Hitler. This super first-class coward and chicken very generously, naively, callously, and shamefully caved in to the demands of one of the most wicked men of all time. Chamberlain's appeasement postponed the war for a little over 11 months. He strengthened Hitler and helped foment a far worse war than the Great War of 1914-1918. Chamberlain died in late 1940 while his "trusted peace partner" Hitler was severely and savagely bombing England.

After World War II ended US President Harry Truman signed the United Nations Charter and naively declared,

> (This charter) is a declaration of great faith by the nations of the earth- faith that war is not inevitable, faith that peace can be maintained. If we had had this charter a few years ago and above all the will to use it- millions now dead would be alive. If we should falter in the future in our will to use it, millions now living will surely die (Swindoll, Daniel, vol. 2, p. 67).

President Truman, like many others naively felt that mankind can end war with his own will, wisdom and strength (Pr. 28:26). He did not realize that wars happen not because of the lack of will, wisdom, or strength but because of man's severe corrupt moral character (Js. 4:1-2, Jer. 17:9, Mt. 15:19) which can only be rectified by the shed blood of the Son of God, our Lord Jesus Christ (Col. 1:20, Eph. 1:7; 2:13).

The situation in the earth will continue to deteriorate (2Tim. 3:13) until Jesus Christ, the Prince of Peace comes to rule (Rev. 11:15; 19:6, 11-16). Without the Prince of Peace, there is no peace (Isa. 48:22).

The Ancient of Days

"The LORD has established His throne in the heavens, And His sovereignty rules over all." (Psalm 103:19). The little horn and every earthly ruler will understand this truth as well as the message of Proverbs 21:1, Psalm 47:2-9, and Revelation 1:5. The little horn (Antichrist) prevails against the saints until the Ancient of Days, the high and exalted one of Isaiah 57:15 comes and gives judgment in favor to the saints of the most high to possess the kingdom (Mt. 5:5).

This is the only place in Scripture that the phrase, "Ancient of Days" is used. God is Spirit (John 4:24) but Daniel sees Him in human form as one who has existed forever. He is overwhelmed with awe and wonder as he views Yahweh's majesty, eternity, holiness, splendor, and glory. "Before the mountains were born or you gave birth to the earth... from everlasting to everlasting you are God" (Ps. 90:2). In 7:9 God's throne and wheels are described as a burning fire. A similar description is found in Ezekiel 1:4-28. "Fire goes before him and burns up His adversaries roundabout" (Ps. 97:3).

> Smoke rose from His nostrils and consuming fire came from His mouth... The LORD thundered from heaven; the voice of the Most High resounded; He shot his arrows and scattered the enemies; great bolts of lightning and routed them. (Ps. 18:8, 13-14, NIV).

> Billions of angels bow down and worship before the throne of the Ancient of Days, depicting His deity and His Godhead, for He alone is worthy to be worshiped. (D. Jeremiah, *The Handwriting on the Wall* p.141).

The Son of Man

In 7:13 the son of man is coming in the clouds of heaven appearing before the Ancient of Days. Revelation 4-5 gives details of this awesome majestic scene. The clouds are the chariot of God (Isa. 19:1, Ps. 104:3). This is Jesus Christ, the Son of Man and the Son of God (Mt. 26:64).

There are many titles that describe Christ. *Son of God* expresses His deity. *Son of David* expresses His royalty. *Son of Man* expresses His humanity. Many titles of God the Father are given to Him (Isaiah 9:6-7) but Christ almost always referred to Himself as the *Son of Man*: 69 times in the synoptic gospels and 12 times in John. He claimed the fulfillment of this verse as He identified himself as the Son of Man who would come in the clouds of Heaven (Mt. 24:30; 25:31; 26:64). Why did He not use a more exalting title? Christ wanted to humbly and fully identify with man in His humanity. In Hebrew there are few adjectives so when a person is wealthy he is called a son of wealth. A woman who shows care, kindness, and concern for others is referred to as a daughter of kindness. In freely identifying himself as the Son of Man, Christ is basically saying,

> "Though I am fully God, I am happy to identify with you by becoming fully human like you. I have become a son of man like you so you can become a son of God like me (I Jn. 3:1-3, Rom. 8:29) and as you are like me, you are fully and unconditionally accepted by my Father."

During His ministry Christ used only two adjectives to describe Himself. These are found In Matthew 11:28-29 as he issues His great invitation to mankind;

> "Come to me all who are weary and heavy laden and I will give you rest. Take my yoke upon you for I am *gentle, (meek, mild, friendly, pleasant,) and humble in heart, (bowed down, small)* and you will find rest for your souls. For my yoke is easy and my burden is light."

Christ is the perfect man with the perfect example of humility, gentleness, kindness, and meekness. Christ is equal to the Father, the Ancient of Days (John 10:30-38). Christ is *Everlasting Father* in Isaiah 9:6 and everything His Father is (Jn. 14:9-11), but He does not flaunt, arrogantly display, nor show off His greatness but with humility and meekness comes to earth to compassionately and gently minister to His fallen creation. In Philippians 2:5-7 Paul tells us to;

> Have this attitude in yourselves which was also in Christ Jesus who although He existed in the form of God, did not regard equality with God a thing to be grasped, but emptied Himself, taking the form of a bond servant and being made in the likeness of men.

When Christ emptied Himself He did not cease being God but voluntarily yielded His right as God to use His attributes for His personal use. He never performed a miracle for His own benefit (Mt. 4:3-4) but freely performed miracles for the benefit of others. "There is one God and one mediator also between God and man, the *man* Christ Jesus" (I Timothy 2:5). Christ is Almighty God (Isaiah 9:6): Big enough to rule the universe and small enough to live in our hearts. Christ is the only member of the trinity to become man and so the title, *Son of Man* differentiates God the Son from God the Father and God the Holy Spirit (John 3:13).

In verse 14 Yahweh, the Ancient of Days gives complete sovereign rule and dominion over all the earth to the Son of Man (Ps. 110:1-2; 72, Rev. 11:15 19:11-21).

> "Ask of me and I will surely give the nations as Your inheritance and the very ends of the earth as your possession. You will break them with a rod of iron. You shall shatter them like earthenware." (Ps. 2:8-9).

Paul proclaims that Christ will reign until He puts all his enemies under His feet (I Cor. 15:25). Gabriel declares in Luke 1:32-33 that Jesus Christ will be,

> "great and will be called the Son of the Most High and the Lord God will give Him the throne of His father David and He will reign over the house of Jacob forever and His kingdom will have no end."

After receiving the kingdom Christ will rule over the world forever and ever (Rev. 11:15; 19:6-16). The Lamb of God Who takes away the sins of the world (John 1:29, 36. Isa. 53:7) is also the fierce warrior and conquering Lion of Judah who "treads the wine press of the fierce wrath of God the Almighty" as He rules the world with a rod of iron (Dan.2:44-45, Rev. 5:5; 19:11-15).

Daniel is greatly disturbed (v.28) as the angel reveals the difficult times ahead for his people but the angel comforts and assures Daniel and all who read the prophesy that Almighty God, the *Ancient of Days* will not allow the persecution to go on forever but will step in and inaugurate His perfect eternal kingdom of love, peace, and grace that the saints will inherit and enjoy as they rule with Christ forever. In I Corinthians 2:9 Paul quotes Isaiah 64:4 as he declares that, (author's paraphrase)

> "Our eyes haven't seen nor have our ears heard nor have we imagined in our hearts the glorious wonderful things God has prepared for us who love Him."

R.G. Lee (1886-1978), former pastor of the Bellevue Baptist Church, Memphis, Tn. USA, and 3-time president of the Southern Baptist Convention received a vision of Heaven while on his deathbed. He was so surprised, filled with awe, and overflowing joy that he said, "I've preached on Heaven many times but I never gave it justice." God graciously permitted Pastor Lee to experience the awesome truth of Psalm 31:19, Isaiah 64:4 and I Corinthians 2:9.

We have seen beautiful sights, heard beautiful sounds, and imagined great fantastic things but they are nothing compared to the sights, sounds, and things Christ has in store for all of us who love Him. Paul tells us to comfort each other with this encouraging glorious truth of the second coming of Christ (I Thess. 4:13-18). This hope should motivate us to live pure and holy lives (I Jn. 2:2-3).

David Jeremiah tells of a 5-year old girl waiting for her father to honor his promise to play with her. He assured her he would after finishing the preparation of his sermon. She told him that she would give him a hug when he's finished. While leaving she made a U-turn and returned and gave him a bone-crushing hug and and said, "That's a sample of what you will get when you are finished."

No doubt the pastor's daughter gave him encouragement to finish the preparation and fulfill his promise. The embrace of Christ is more precious than the pastor's daughter. The promises of God and the Holy Spirit (Jn. 12-16) are the samples of God's glory which are realized at the 2nd coming of Christ.

Let us never forget the solemn and awesome warning of Hebrews 12:14:

"Without holiness no man will see the Lord"

While being severely stressed in his spirit and mind with this vision Daniel probably prayed as David did in Psalm 4:1 as the LORD delivered him from his stress and gave him supernatural strength to recover so he could receive more revelations (Isa. 40:29-31, 2 Chron. 16:9).

8

More Trouble for Israel

In the 3rd year of Belshazzar's reign, about 2 years after the chapter 7 vision, Daniel receives a more detailed vision concerning the 2nd and 3rd kingdoms. In this new vision the emphasis shifts from the Gentile nations to Israel. Daniel is written in Hebrew (1:1-2:3; 8-12) and Aramaic (2:4-7:28). Since the message of 2:4-7:28 is directed mainly to Gentile nations, Aramaic, the dominant language of that time is used but starting at chapter 8 through the end God's message is directed to Israel and so understandably the Holy Spirit directs Daniel to use Hebrew, the language of Israel.

In this vision Daniel is transported to Susa, an insignificant and nondescript suburb of Babylon that was virtually unnoticed by everyone in the Babylonian world. About 25 years later Persia conquered Babylon and made Susa the nerve center of the new empire (Neh.1:1, Esther 1:2).

The bear and silver kingdom of the Medo-Persian Empire is represented by the ram with 2 horns. One horn came up last and grew longer and more powerful than the other. This shows that Persia though at first was the lesser of the 2 kingdoms became greater than Media (The first shall be last and the last shall be first. Mark 10:31). This corresponds to one side of the bear being higher than the other in 7:5. The ram is an accurate representation of the Persian Empire because its guardian spirit was a ram with sharp pointed horns. The Persian king wore a ram's head as he stood in front of his army (Keil, p. 290 from Showers, p. 97).

The leopard and bronze kingdom of Greece is represented by the goat; an accurate representation of Greece. In 814 BC Caranus, the first Macedonian ruler was led into Edessa by goats. He made it the seat of his government and renamed the city *Egae* (Greek, goat). It's next to the Aegean Sea (Goat Sea). Bronze figures of a goat with one horn have been found as a symbol of Macedon (Barnes p. 104). They have also found one horned goats on Greek coins (Barnes p. 105).

Macedonia, the oldest European nation with connected and regular history, is represented by the goat with the horn. About 500 BC King Amyntas I was threatened with invasion from Persia and became tributary to Persia. This event is illustrated on a rectangular carving on a wall in Persepolis showing a Persian holding the long horn of a goat. This signifies the subjection of Macedon to Persia (Barnes, 104).

The goat has a horn between its eyes (v. 5). Eyes are used symbolically in Scripture to denote human intelligence (Ezek. 1:18, Genesis 3:5). Goats usually have 2 horns above their eyes but this goat has 1 horn between its eyes representing a very intelligent as well as a very powerful ruler.

Alexander the Great was born in the late summer of 356 BC and died June 13, 323 BC; living almost 33 years (Collier's Encyclopedia, p. 519-522). His father Philip taught him how to fight and told him, "Alexander, my son, seek out a kingdom worthy of yourself. Macedonia is too small for you." (D. Jeremiah, *The Handwriting on the Wall*, p.161). At 20 he became the Macedonian king after his father's murder. Alexander wrote the following letter to Darius:

> Your ancestors entered into Macedonia and other parts of Greece and did us damage, when they had received no affront from us as the cause of it; and now I, created general of the Grecians, provoked by you and desirous of avenging the injury done by the Persians have passed over into Asia (Barnes p. 210).

Even though Persia never conquered Greece in its attempted invasions at Salamas, Thermopylae, Leuctra, and Marathon, much wrong and damage was inflicted on Greece; especially by Xerxes and his 5,000,000 soldiers. Alexander understandably had no problem inspiring and motivating his army to fight. They remembered the repeated unprovoked Persian attacks on Greece and therefore very furiously and joyfully attacked the Persian Empire with raving revenge in their hearts (Barnes, p. 107).

The goat never touching the ground of verse 5 is a perfect description of Alexander's military genius and his incredible speed of conquest.

Even though he had far less resources than the enemy and was vastly outnumbered about 300,000 to 35,000 he furiously attacked the ram and shattered the 2 horns as he made the Persian Empire helpless (8:7). He slaughtered the Persians at Issus and killed the king's bodyguard, causing King Darius to flee and completely destroyed the Persian Empire at Gaugamela (8:7). After fleeing again, King Darius was killed by his own men (Collier's Enc. p. 522).

Alexander through his intelligence was able to conquer the Persian Empire in just 3 years (334-331 BC) and the known world in just another 8 years; never losing a battle (Ps. 33:16). No other conquests were made so rapidly as Alexander's. He was the progenitor of *blitzkrieg*, lightning warfare. Even Julius Caesar envied Alexander.

The goat greatly magnified himself (v. 8). "To receive recognition as the supreme ruler, he (Alexander) required the provinces to worship him as a god." (WBE, 1985 edition. p.327). The sudden breaking of the goat's horn represents Alexander's unexpected sudden death in the full strength of the empire. His mother, Olympias told him he was a descendant of Achilles and Hercules (WBE) and taught him how to sin. He fought well and sinned well in his very irresponsible promiscuous sex lifestyle and therefore in the zenith of his power he died in a drunken orgy when he was almost 33. The 4 horns replacing Alexander's broken horn represent the 4 generals who divided the empire among themselves after his death. This corresponds to the four-headed leopard of 7:6. Two of the 4 horns represent the king of the North (Syria) and the king of the South (Egypt). Chapter 11 details the prominence these 2 kingdoms have in relation to Israel.

Unlike the vicious, ravenous, fierce beasts of chapter 7, Persia and Greece here are represented by relatively harmless barnyard animals. Why? Compared to the severe harsh treatment that Persia and Greece gave to the other conquered nations these 2 nations were relatively harmless and even kind to Israel. The Persians encouraged the Jews to return to Israel in order to rebuild Jerusalem and its temple at government expense (Ezra 1:3-5; Nehemiah 2:1-8).

Alexander was also kind to the Jews. The high priest Jaddas was warned by God in a dream to welcome him into Jerusalem and so he opened the gates for Alexander and showed him Daniel's prophecy predicting that a Greek would conquer Persia. Alexander was so greatly encouraged by the prophecy that he offered sacrifices in the temple and promised protection for the Jews in his empire (Henry, p. 1450). Alexander guaranteed the Jews freedom to practice their religion.

Unlike the 2nd and 3rd kingdoms, the 1st kingdom (Babylon) and the 4th kingdom (Rome) were not represented by "relatively harmless barnyard animals" for obvious reasons: They were very harsh, severe, and cruel in their treatment of Israel (2 Chronicles 36:17-21. Lk. 19:43-44; 21:20-24). Josephus gives details of Rome's devastation of Jerusalem as over 1,100,000 Jews perished when Vespasian and Titus crushed the rebellion. (More details in chapter 9).

The second little horn

Yes, the Persians and Greeks under Alexander and his immediate successors treated Israel well but the little horn in verse 9 did not!

It's important to understand that the little horn in chapter 8 is NOT the little horn of chapter 7. The chapter 7 little horn appears in the 4th kingdom as the 11th horn in the midst of 10 other horns. It uproots and supplants 3 horns (kingdoms) and persecutes God's people for 42 months. The chapter 8 little horn appears in the 3rd kingdom and uproots no one but grows out of one of the original 4 horns that replaced Alexander after his death. It was insignificant at first but waxes great as it exalts itself as God among the hosts of heaven and casts down the stars (v. 10). The priests and leaders and the Jewish people, the chosen people of God were considered to be stars and the host of heaven (12:3, Gen. 15:5; 22:17, Isaiah 24:21).

This chapter 8 little horn is Antiochus IV Epiphanes, the "illustrious one": The 8th king of the Seleucid dynasty (king of the North). He is the perfect Old Testament type of Antichrist and one of the fiercest and bitterest enemies of Israel. This very cruel, wicked maniac caused severe suffering for the Jews. He appears during the latter time of the Greek Empire as the sins of Israel run their course (vs. 12, 19, and 23). The blasphemous inscription, *THEOS EPIPHANES* "God Made Manifest" is placed on the coins that bore his image (Boice, p.91).

Moses declared that Israel had been rebellious since he first knew them (Nu. 27:14, Dt. 1:26, 43; 9:7, 24). The Hebrew prophets constantly exposed and denounced Israel's rebellion (2 Chron. 36:16, Ez. 2:3-5; 20:8, 13, Hosea 13:16, Neh. 9:17; Isa. 30:1, 9; 65:2, Jer. 5:6, 23-29) but Israel continued to ignore the prophets' warnings and rebel. Judah's bent to idolatry was so great that God was determined to bring disaster on her and therefore declared that it was useless to pray for her (Jer. 7:16-18; 11:11-14). Yahweh therefore delivered Judah to Nebuchadnezzar (Jer. 44:17-30; 17:21-27; 13:8-11, 2 Chronicles 36:15-21).

The Babylonian captivity delivered the Jews from idolatry but Malachi 1:7-10 and 2:1-2, 8 inform us that the Jews profaned the holy things of God; thus continuing their typical rebellion against God. Apostate Jews introduced heathen customs into Jerusalem (I Macc.1:11-16) resulting in God's wrath through Antiochus. They, "made themselves uncircumcised and forsook the holy covenant, and joined themselves to the heathen..." (v.15). They erected theatres and sacrificed to Hercules as well as Yahweh.

Through deceit Antiochus seduced those who disdained the holy covenant (Dan. 11:32, I Macc. 1:20-53). Antiochus forbade the observance of the Sabbath and circumcision, and introduced the Feast of Bacchanalia, the worship of Bacchus, the god of pleasure and wine into the temple. He also required the Jews including priests to participate in Greek games outside the temple. In Greek games participants were stripped naked (D.Jeremiah, *The Handwriting on the Wall*, p. 164).

Like Satan (Isa. 14:13), Antiochus exalted himself above God. Pagan writers describe him as "base, rude, boisterous, sordid, silly and mad" (Henry, p. 1458). He was also called *Epimanes,* the maniac. He stomped down hard with harsh indignation and contempt on the stars (leaders) and the host (people) as he freely slaughtered many Jews.

He tortured Eleazar, a faithful 90-year old scribe to death after he boldly spit out swine's flesh forced into his mouth. Eleazar preferred to "die gloriously" rather than compromise the faith. Antiochus cruelly murdered brave mothers who circumcised their sons. He tortured to death another mother and her 7 sons because of their refusal to deny the faith. Tongues and limbs were chopped off before frying them in a heated pan. The third son while dying said, "You take us out of this present life but the king of the world shall raise us up who have died for his laws unto everlasting life."

(I Macc 1:24-64, 2 Macc. 5:11-14; 23-26; 6; 7, Daniel 11:33-34, Heb. 11:32-40). Those who defied Antiochus and continued to worship God were, "mutilated, strangled, or crucified, with their children hung from their necks." (Maier, p. 210).

He crushed truth to the ground (Isa. 59:14) and prospered in everything he did (24). The little horn waxed exceedingly great to the south, east, and Israel (8:9). In 171 BC Antiochus plundered Egypt and Jerusalem and gained great riches (I Macc. 1:16-19, Dan. 11:22-32). He slaughtered 80,000 Jews and sold 40,000 into slavery on his way back to Syria (2 Macc. 5:5-14).

Egypt formed a defense treaty with Rome but Antiochus miscalculated that Rome was too busy fighting in Macedonia to honor the treaty and frustrate his adventures and so he invaded Egypt again (Swindoll, *Daniel* vol. 2, p. 29).

On this invasion (170-169 BC) ships from Khittim (islands and the coastland of the Mediterranean, the emerging Roman Empire), came against him (11:30). Popilius Laenas, the Roman ambassador presented him a decree from the Roman senate gaving him an ultimatum to either leave Egypt alone or face the wrath of Rome. After Antiochus requested time to consider his response, Laenas drew a circle around him with his sword and told him that he must have a reply for the Senate before he could leave the circle (JFB, p. 448).

Antiochus was greatly grieved, humiliated, and infuriated as he was forced to back down. After replenishing his treasury n Persia he went to the *pleasant land* (Israel) where he expressed his frustration, bitterness, and anger on the Jews with his severe reign of terror.

In December, 168 BC, Antiochus seized Jerusalem by treachery, stripped the temple of anything of value, and made Jerusalem and the temple a wilderness. General Apollonius with 20,000 troops erected an idol in the temple area and poured swine fat on the altar; a supreme insult to the Jews. The Jews understood the idol as the "abomination of desolation" of Daniel 11:31. The regular sacrifice is canceled and Antiochus' abomination of desolation is set up. This is a preview and type of the future supreme abomination of Antichrist in the last days (9:27; 12:11, Mt. 24:15).

In Exodus 29:38-42 God instructs Israel to offer sacrifices every evening and morning. Since God instituted the sacrifices God alone had the right to end them. When Antiochus terminated the sacrifices he did what only God had the right to do; thus making himself "equal with the commander of the host" (v. 11).

The 2300 evenings and mornings

In verse 13 Daniel hears one saint (angel) ask another saint, (author's paraphrase), "How long will the temple and the saints be trampled down as the daily sacrifices are suspended due to the desolation and pollution brought to the temple by the little horn?" The other angel answers in verse 14, "For 2,300 evenings and mornings; then the holy place will be properly restored."

2 Maccabees 10:5 declares that the sacrilege happened exactly 3 years before it was cleansed by Judas (Kislev 25, 168 BC- Kislev 25, 165 BC). This obviously doesn't equal 2300 days and so the passage possibly refers to the whole series events starting in September, 171 BC (2300 days earlier) when Antiochus practically suspended the sacrifices as he began to attack the Jews (Barnes, p. 115).

Antiochus and the Jews had a good, cordial, and peaceful relationship with each other until 171 BC. A series of events that year led to the disaster of Jerusalem and the temple. In 172 BC Menelaus supplanted his brother Jason of the high priesthood by offering more money for it. Later he paid the required tribute to Antiochus by taking treasures out of the temple and selling them in Tyre. Onias III, the lawful high priest strongly rebuked Menelaus for this sacrilege. Menelaus seduced Onias to come to Daphne where he was murdered by a high official of Antiochus. The Jews were angry at the sacrilege and murder of the lawful high priest and therefore rose in rebellion against the Syrians who protected the murderer, Lysimachus, "The assault on the officer of Antiochus, and rebellion against him was the commencement of the hostilities which resulted in the ruin of the city and the closing of the worship of God" (Barnes, p. 116). From this time Antiochus attacked the Jews, the temple, the priests, and made life miserable for them until his death. Barnes correctly concludes that the sacrifices and the worship of God were "practically suspended and interrupted during that time." (Barnes, p.115).

The following is the more probable interpretation.

God instructs Israel to have 2 regular daily sacrifices in the temple: One every morning and one every evening (Dan. 9:21, Ex. 29:38-42, Nu. 28:3-31). In Daniel 8:11, 12, 13; 11:31, and 12:11 the word *sacrifice* is not in the original Hebrew. Only the Hebrew word, *tamid,* meaning *regular* or *continual* is used. This adjective obviously refers to the regular sacrifice that is offered every evening and morning in the temple (2 Chron. 2:4; 13:11; 31:3). The word *sacrifice* is therefore justifiably inserted by translators. In verse 14 there is no *and* in Hebrew and the singular, *arev-boker* (evening-morning) is used. Like the regular of 8:11, 12, 13; 11:31, and 12:11, *evening-morning* is used as an adjective referring to the regular sacrifice offered every evening and morning in the temple. In I Chronicles 16:40 we read that Zadok the priest was entrusted with the responsibility;

> To offer burnt offerings to the LORD on the altar of burnt offering <u>continually morning and evening</u> according to all that is written in the law of the Lord, which He commanded Israel.

This supports the teaching that both *evening-morning* and *continual* refer to the regular daily temple sacrifices offered every evening and morning.

Today we say; "The poor need help", "the wealthy are generous", "the wicked face judgment" the locals are angry," and the healthy are exercising." Even though the word *people* is not used, we understood that these adjectives refer to people. We are talking about poor *people*, wealthy *people*, wicked *people*, local *people*, and healthy *people*. The same reasoning should be applied to *regular* and *evening-morning*. An amplified translation of Daniel 8:14 would be;

> "The temple will be rectified and properly restored to its original purpose after being suspended for 2300 consecutive evening and morning sacrifices that would be offered in 1150 days."

The context of verses 11-13 strongly supports this interpretation.

Judas Maccabeus restored the temple on Kislev 25, 165 BC: Exactly 3 years after the Greek idols were set up by Antiochus on Kislev 25, 168 BC. Yahweh's altar was removed about 2 months earlier which accounts for the difference between 1,095 days in exactly 3 years and the 1150 days of 2300 sacrifices that are specified here (NIV note on Daniel 8:14).

Gabriel seeks to comfort Daniel after his frightened appearance. The vision pertains to the "time of the end" (v. 17), "the appointed time of the end" (19) or "many days in the future" (v. 26). Gabriel is referring to the end time events of this chapter 8 prophecy; about 300-450 years later.

Yes, indeed Daniel's people will suffer more in the future for yet more sinful and rebellious behavior but it's comforting to know that it will not continue indefinitely as the little horn will be supernaturally broken (v. 25). In 8:15-25 Gabriel interprets the vision for Daniel and in verse 26 Gabriel assures Daniel that the vision of the "the evening-morning (2300 sacrifices of 8:14) is true. The exciting story of Judas Maccabeus, his bothers, and the men of Judah cleansing the temple is given in chapter 11.

Daniel was told to shut up the vision and keep it secret for the time being. The Persians would soon conquer the Babylon Empire and if Babylonian officials read this prophecy predicting their fall they might consider Daniel a traitor and therefore give him lots of trouble.

Daniel was happy to know that very soon the 70-year Babylonian captivity would end and the Jews could return to Israel and reestablish their lives with the rebuilt temple but was discouraged as this prophecy revealed that the temple would be cast down by this little horn. He understandably became exhausted as he fainted and got sick. He would need more strength and encouragement as he will learn in the chapter 9 vision that the temple would be destroyed again and his people would suffer under Antichrist, the cruel little horn of chapter 7, (9:26-27).

Daniel, though blessed abundantly by God like David after being anointed king (I Sam. 16:13) did not get proud by thinking that he no longer needed to work. After recovering he went back to his usual job of doing the king's business (v. 27).

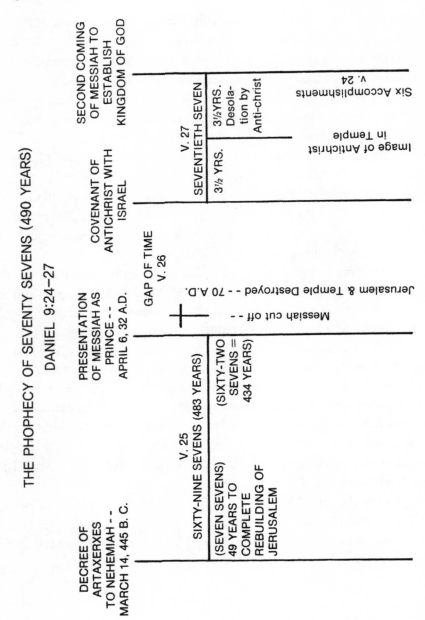

From *The Most High God* by **Renald Showers** p. 138

9

Daniel's Intercession for Israel and God's Response. When Will Messiah Come?

Daniel became very sick after receiving the chapter 8 vision but he sufficiently recovered as God strengthened and enabled him to receive the backbone of the skeleton of prophecy in 9:24-27. Daniel, like Apostle Paul in Romans 9:1-3, had great grief, love, and concern for his people Israel. Though he was a prophet, Daniel knew the importance of reading and diligently studying the Scriptures and praying. (Let's follow his example!) He knew the prophecy of Jeremiah 25:11 predicting Judah's 70-year captivity and calculated that the time was almost fulfilled. He was therefore motivated to pray that God would be gracious to the Jews, deliver them from captivity, and restore Jerusalem and Israel.

Daniel never read James 5:16 but obviously knew its truth. "The effective prayer of a righteous man can accomplish much." In Daniel's effective and model prayer, he addresses God as "Lord God" and "Yahweh God." He shows a nice balance between the great and dreadful God (v. 4, Isaiah 6:1) and the God of mercies and forgiveness (v. 9, Ex. 20:6). He prayed for God's mercy and forgiveness for Israel not because Israel deserved them but because God is gracious and merciful. The Wycliffe Bible Commentary (p. 793) gives 8 reasons why Daniel's prayer was so effective and a great model prayer for us.

(1) Daniel's prayer was persistent as he rejected discouragement (Dan 6:1-10; 9:1-3). He waited 68 years without losing hope, **(2)** He had determination

(v. 3). **(3)** He was importunate (9:3, Lk. 18:1-8; Matthew 9:27-30; 15:22-28; 17:15; 20:30-34). **(4)** He showed humility by identifying with his people's sins (Lk. 18:10-14). **(5)** He made confession (Daniel 9:4-5, Psalm 32:5, James 5:16). **(6)** He displayed submission (9:14) and engaged in **(7)** petition and **(8)** intercession.

Daniel is a perfect model for Godly living. Like Joseph (Gen. 37-50), Jonathan, Elisha, and John the Baptist Scripture records nothing negative about his life. He perfectly and diligently did his work and earned the trust of pagan monarchs.

Daniel however knew the truth of Psalm 14:2-3 and 53:2-3 (quoted in Romans 3:10-18) and therefore knew he was a sinner and so he freely confessed his sins along with the sins of his people. "We have sinned against you" (v. 8, 11). "We have rebelled against you" (v. 9), "We have refused to listen to the prophets" (v. 6). "We have not obeyed Him" (v.14). Even though he was innocent of idolatry, rebellion, and refusing to listen to the prophets, he freely identified with his people as he fervently prayed for forgiveness and restoration. Daniel knew that God would deliver Israel as she cries out for God's help and searches for God with "all your heart." (Jer. 29:10-14).

Unlike the situation in 10:1, Daniel gets an immediate response direct from the throne of God. Gabriel gives Daniel the marvelous prophecy of the 70 weeks; (70 seven-year periods or 490 years), the backbone of the skeleton of prophecy (Isaiah 30:19; 65:24, Psalm 32:5). Gabriel reveals the exact day Messiah will be revealed in Israel.

The 70 weeks (70 seven–year periods or 490 years) of Daniel 9:24–27 (The backbone of prophecy)

After studying this passage, Leopold Kahn, a European Jewish rabbi concluded that Messiah had already come. After asking another rabbi where he is he was told that he might be in New York City. Kahn sold everything he had and went there to look for Messiah. After attending a gospel meeting Messiah found Leopold Kahn. He learned and understood that Yeshua Hamoshiakh (Jesus Christ) is the promised messiah of Israel and he therefore repented of his sins and gave his life to Him. He founded the American Board of Missions to the Jews and now called *Chosen People Ministries* (D. Jeremiah, *The Handwriting on the Wall*, p.185).

When a Christian asked a rabbi in Israel if he had read Daniel he answered, "No.... When I was studying to be a rabbi I was told not to read Daniel." (D. Jeremiah, *The Handwriting on the Wall*, p.192). Rockmael Frydland, a Polish Jew accepted Jesus Christ as Messiah after reading Daniel 9:24-27. He severely suffered under the cruel Nazi holocaust but survived it. This backbone of prophecy has helped many Jews understand that Yeshua of Nazareth (Jesus Christ) is the promised Messiah of Israel.

God's Word is full of 7s. The first verse of the Hebrew Bible (Gen. 1:1) has 7 words and 28 letters. The 4th and 5th words have 7 letters and the 6th and 7th words have 7 letters. The shortest word is the middle word with 2 letters. When combined with the word to its right there are 7 letters and when combined with the word to the left there are 7 letters.

There are 7 days in the week, 7 good years, and 7 bad years in Egypt (Gen.41:26-27). 14 lambs were sacrificed daily during the 7-day Passover feast. At Sukkot (Tabernacles) 14 lambs were sacrificed daily and 70 bullocks. 7 weeks after Passover 7 lambs were offered at Pentecost. Joshua led the children of Israel for 7 days around Jericho and 7 times on the 7th day as 7 priests blasted 7 trumpets before the walls fell (Josh.6). Naaman dipped 7 times in the Jordan in order to receive healing (2 Kings 5:1-14). Nebuchadnezzar spent 7 years with the animals before his sanity returned (Dan.4:23). There are 14 generations between Abraham and David; 14 generations between David and the Babylonian captivity; and 14 generations between the Babylonian captivity and Jesus Christ (Mt. 1:17).

Revelation has 7 letters to 7 churches, 7 candlesticks (1:12, 20), 7 angels (1:20), A lamb with 7 horns and 7 eyes (5:6), 7 Spirits (1:4), 7 stars (1:16), 7 lamps (4:5), 7 seals, 7 trumpets, 7 bowls of wrath, 7 thunders, (10:3), 7 crowns (12:1), a leopard-like beast with 7 heads (13:1), a scarlet-colored beast with 7 heads (17:3), 7 mountains and 7 kings (17:9-10), 7 dooms, 7 personages, and 7 new things.

7 beatitudes are proclaimed in Revelation. Blessings are promised for those who read it (1:3), who die in the Lord (14:13), watch for His coming (16:15), invited to the Lamb's marriage supper (19:9), partakes of the 1st resurrection (20:6), keep the words of the book (22:7), and wash their robes (22:14).

Multiples of seven are interwoven in Israel's history. In 1586-1585 BC Joshua led Israel into Canaan and 490 years later (1096-1095 BC) the kingdom was established under Saul. In 605 BC, 490 years later the servitude under Nebuchadnezzar commenced. Solomon's temple was dedicated in his 11th year (1006-5 BC) and 490 years later (515 BC) the second temple was dedicated. 497 years later in 18 BC Herod started to enlarge the temple (p. 227-228, CP).

God's works are also full of 7s. The rainbow has 7 colors and the musical scale has 7 major notes. The human body is constantly changing and in 7 years it is completely different from what it was 7 years earlier. The potato bug hatches in 7 days after being laid. The canary hatches in 14 days; chickens in 21; ducks and geese in 28; mallards in 35; and parrots and ostriches in 42. The normal gestation period for rats is 21 days; 35 days for rabbits; 56 for cats; 63 for dogs and wolves; 98 for lions; 147 for sheep; 280 for humans and cattle; 336 for horses; 364 for donkeys, and 623 for elephants. Since God generously uses 7s in His Word and works it should be no wonder that He also generously uses 7s in this all important backbone of prophecy.

The purpose of the 70 seven-year periods (490 Years)

In Daniel's prayer he referred to the 70 years of captivity (v. 2) and the angel responded by stating that (9:24) "Seventy 7-year periods have been decreed (Hebrew, *Khatak*), for your people (Israel) and your holy city (Jerusalem). This is the only place in Scripture where *khatak* is used. It can also be translated as *cut off, determined,* or *set aside.* Gabriel makes it clear that the 70 seven-year periods of years are set aside for Daniel's people, Israel, the Jews and for the holy city, Jerusalem. God says that even though He took 70 years away from Israel He will give them 7 times that amount back. The purposes for the 490 years are to:

(1) **Finish the transgression.** The root meaning of the Hebrew word translated transgression is *to rebel* (Leupold, p. 414 from Showers, p. 118). Israel has continually rebelled against the rule of God from its beginning.

Moses said, "You have been rebellious against the LORD from the day I knew you" (Dt. 9:7, 24, 27). The prophets continually cried out against Israel's rebellion (Neh. 9:17, Hosea 13:16, Isa. 30:1-9; 65:2, Jer. 5:6-31). In Acts 7 Stephen documents Israel's history of constant rebellion and he is stoned to death. The strongest example of Israel's continual determined obstinate stubborn rebellious behavior is recorded in John 19:14-15 where Israel demands that its messiah and king be crucified. The Jews cried out, "We have no king but Caesar." Israel demanded Caesar as her king and the request was granted. Israel has continually rebelled against Yahweh and His anointed king, Yeshua, but at the end of the 490 years the root of rebellion will be destroyed.

(2) Make an end of sin. Sin is plural in Hebrew. This refers to the habitual daily sins that naturally happen but will end as the root of rebellion is destroyed (Wood, p. 249 from Showers, 118). Sin is fully restrained as the Word is sealed as in Job 9:7 and 37:7.

(3) Make atonement for iniquity. The atonement for Israel's sins was made at Calvary but the application will take place as the 490 years are completed at the second coming of Christ. Calvary's reconciliation will then become effective for Daniel's people, Israel (Jer. 50:4-5; 17-20, Isa. 59:20, Rom. 11:25-27, Rev. 1:7).

> "I will pour out on the house of David and on the inhabitants of Jerusalem the spirit of grace and supplication, so that they will look on Me whom they have pierced and they will mourn for Him as one mourns for his only son, and they will weep bitterly over Him like the bitter weeping over a firstborn" (Zech. 12:10).

John 19:37 records a partial fulfillment of this prophecy but the complete fulfillment happens at the second coming of Christ.

A speaker at the Narkis St. Baptist Church in Jerusalem told a story of seeing a deeply religious Jew at the western wall earnestly pleading for God to, "Send the messiah. We desperately need Him! We promise to welcome him; even if he's Jesus!"

(4) Bring in everlasting righteousness. Jesus Christ, the Messiah of Israel is everlasting righteousness in person. He will dwell in the hearts of the Israelis who will never rebel against God again (Jer. 31:31-34; 33:14-18; 23:5-6, Ez. 36:22-32; Isa. 11:1-5).

(5) Seal up the vision and the prophecy. The Hebrew word translated *to seal up* is the same word used earlier and is translated, *to put an end to sin*. As the people stop sinning, the warnings, visions, and discipline of the prophets are no longer needed.

(6) Anoint the most holy *place*. This speaks of a rebuilt temple during the millennium (Ezekiel 40-48, Isaiah 4:2-6).

Does a day represent a year in prophecy?

Many sincere students of the Bible prophecy have concluded that Numbers 14:34 and Ezekiel 4:4-6 teach that a day in prophecy represents a year. The 70 weeks equal 490 days which should be interpreted as 490 years. A careful study of Numbers 14:34 and Ezekiel 4:4-6 will clear up this misunderstanding.

In Numbers 14, the Israelis, exhibiting their typical stubborn rebellious character, rebel against the LORD. In judgment Yahweh determined that no Israeli 20 years old or older would enter Canaan except Caleb and Joshua. God decreed that Israel would spend 40 years in the desert as the spies spent 40 days in the land of Canaan. Each year spent in the wilderness represents each day the spies spent in Canaan. The prophecy here is not in days but in years and it's based on something that happened earlier in days.

Ezekiel is instructed in 4:4-6 to lie on his left side for 390 days representing Israel's 390 years of rebellion and on his right side for 40 days representing Judah's 40 years of rebellion. There is no prophecy given here. No indication here nor in Numbers 14 that in all prophetic time prophecies one day equals a year. Those who support the day for a year theory for all time prophecies have problems. Christ gave a time prophecy concerning His death and resurrection but He did not spend 3 years in the grave. Jeremiah 25:11 teaches that the desolation of Judah would be

70 years. 70 years = 25,200 days. Thus, the day for a year theory would have to teach 25,200-year captivity. No one teaches that the 1,000 year reign of Christ will really last 365,000 years. If the literal, plain meaning of Scripture makes good sense, seek no other sense. Days mean days and years mean years.

The Hebrew for the 7-day week is *shavuot*. The Hebrew word used in this passage is *shavu'im*. It's translated "weeks" but literally means groups of 7. A better translation would be "70 groups of 7 are cut off and set aside for Israel." Daniel is already thinking in terms of years (9:1-2) and so it's obvious that Gabriel's message is to be interpreted as 70 7-year periods or 490 years that are set aside for Israel. If someone said, "I was born 40 years ago, graduated from college 20 years ago and married 18 years ago and in another 10, I will retire," we would understand that the 10 obviously refers to years. Therefore logic tells us that Gabriel is referring to 490 years; not days. In 10:2-3 it reads literally in Hebrew, "three 7s *of days*" making it clear that it means 3 literal 7-day weeks.

Dr. Jeremiah's *Handwriting on the Wall* (p.193) gives a humorous story of a man who received a prescription. After it was filled he successfully used it every day as a railway pass for 2 years. It got him into Radio City Music Hall and once into the symphony. The cashier gave him a raise when he showed it as a note from his boss. His daughter found it and played it and won a scholarship to the conservatory of music.

The numbers in this prophecy can be as confusing but remember that Gabriel did not give this prophecy to confuse us but to reveal the day when Messiah would be revealed to Israel. We will understand it as we diligently study and seek the Holy Spirit's guidance (Pr. 3:5-7).

Countdown to Messiah

There are many prophecies in the Hebrew Scriptures predicting Messiah's coming and ministry. The first prophecy of Messiah is in Genesis 3:15 where God promises that the seed of the woman will bruise the serpent's head. Moses predicted another prophet like himself will come (Dt. 18:15-19). Isaiah 7:14 predicts Messiah's virgin conception and birth. Micah 5:2 predicts Messiah's birth place. David (Ps. 22) and Isaiah (52:13-53:12) predict Messiah's suffering. These prophecies like all other messianic prophecies refer to Jesus Christ but none use the term, *Moshiakh* (Hebrew, Messiah, anointed one). Daniel 9:24-27 is the only prophecy where the word *Moshiakh* is used. Here Gabriel reveals the exact day of Messiah's appearing to Israel.

> "So you are to know and discern that from the issuing of the decree to restore and rebuild Jerusalem until Messiah the Prince *there will be* seven weeks (seven 7-year periods) and sixty-two weeks (62 7-year periods); it will be built again, with plaza and moat, even in times of distress" (v. 25).

62+7=69. 69 seven-year periods equal 483 years. Messiah, the Prince is revealed to Israel after the completion of the 69 periods of 7 years or 483 years later.

Gabriel's message is completely clear! The *terminus a quo* (the starting point or beginning date) for the countdown to the time of Messiah is the day when authorization is given to restore and rebuild the city of Jerusalem! It's NOT an authorization to rebuild or adorn the temple or the house of God in Jerusalem. It's so vitally important that we understand this. The following brief study in Ezra and Nehemiah will help clear it up.

A brief study of Ezra

The book of Ezra like Daniel is written in Aramaic (4:8-6:18) as well as Hebrew. It gives the story of the Jews returning to Jerusalem and rebuilding of the temple that Nebuchadnezzar tore down. In Ezra Persian kings issue 3 decrees authorizing the rebuilding and adorning of the temple of God in Jerusalem. Over and over the phrase, "house of God" or "temple" is used in Ezra (1:2, 3, 4, 5; 3:8, 10, 11; 4:1, 3, 24; 5:2, 8, 11, 14, 15, 16, 17; 6:3. 5, 7, 8, 11. 12. 16. 17, 22; 7:16, 17, 19, 20, 23, 27; 8:25, 30, 33, 36; 9:9; 10:1, 6, 9). **In Ezra there is absolutely no authorization to rebuild the city!**

Cyrus conquered Babylon in October, 539 BC and began to rule over Babylon in March, 538 BC (NIV note, Ezra 1:1). King Cyrus issued the first decree authorizing the rebuilding of the temple of Jerusalem in 538 BC (Ezra 1:1-3). Cyrus restored all the articles of the temple that

Nebuchadnezzar had taken to Babylon and authorized the Jews to fully restore their temple worship services with all its sacrifices. Yahweh's altar was restored. The people shouted for joy and sang praises of thanksgiving as the foundation was laid (3:11-13).

In 734 BC, Isaiah (7:8) prophesied that within 65 years the northern 10 tribes that were taken into captivity by Assyria would cease to be a distinct people. The prophecy was fulfilled by 669 BC when the Assyrian king, Esarhaddon (680-668 BC) transported foreigners into Samaria who intermarried with the Israelis (2 Kings 17:24-41).

In chapter 4 these Samaritans, the enemies of Judah and Benjamin tried to sabotage the rebuilding of the temple. They deceitfully declared to Zerubbabel (v. 2), "Let us build with you, for we, like you seek your God: and have been sacrificing to Him since the days of Esarhaddon, king of Assyria, who brought us up here." Zerubbabel knew that these Samaritans had mixed idolatry with the worship of Yahweh and therefore saw their deceit (2Cor. 6:14-18; 11:14-15). He knew it was impossible for these pagans to help build Yahweh's temple on an equal basis with the Jews and so he wisely rejected their request. To honor their request would seriously compromise the faith and again invite God's wrath upon his people. The Samaritans revealed their true character when after further rejections they built their own temple on Mt. Gerizim.

When these early Samaritans failed to sabotage the building of the temple internally they bribed high ranking Persian officials (4:4-5) to give the king false reports of what was happening. They told the king in 4:12-16 (author's paraphrase);

> "You might think these Jews are only rebuilding the temple but you need to realize they are also rebuilding the city of Jerusalem and fortifying its walls so they will no longer be required to pay you any taxes. Check the historical documents and you will easily ascertain and understand that they have always been a very rebellious people and are currently rebelling against you. Instead of being thankful for your very generous provision to rebuild and restore the temple these miserable rebellious Jews are secretly rebuilding the city itself. You gave them an inch and they are taking a mile. You need to stop this Jewish venture immediately before they complete the walls or else you will not

be able to collect any taxes from them. You are about loose your possession in the province beyond the river."

Understandably the king got alarmed and upset. He immediately stopped the rebuilding project until an investigation was made (vs. 21-24). The king knew that there was a vast difference between rebuilding the temple and rebuilding the city. The temple merely gave the Jews religious freedom but the rebuilding of the walls and fortifications around Jerusalem would give the Jews political autonomy. The king willingly gave religious freedom as he authorized, encouraged, and even financed the rebuilding of the temple but he absolutely refused to give political autonomy. He wanted to continue to collect taxes as he ruled over Israel. He clearly said, "This city will not be rebuilt until I authorize it" (4:21 author's paraphrase). The work on the Jerusalem temple was stopped until the second year of Darius (Ezra 4:24). The king no doubt thought,

> These sorry, ungrateful Jews! Instead of appreciating my very generous authorization to return to their homeland and rebuild their temple at my expense they have decided to rebuild the city too. I am therefore forced to stop the Jews from building anything.

An investigation was made and after learning that the accusations were false and making sure that the Jews were building only the temple, King Darius reinstated Cyrus' decree of 538 BC as he issued his own decree in 520 BC to finish building the temple as quickly as possible at government expense (4:24-6:15). Three weeks after Prophet Haggai began preaching the people again laid the foundation and resumed rebuilding the temple (Haggai 1:14-15). The events of Zechariah 7 occurred during that time. The temple was completed in 515 BC, the 6th year of King Darius and all Israel greatly rejoiced as they celebrated the first Passover in the rebuilt temple (6:16-22).

In the 7th year of Artaxerxes (Ezra 7:8, 458 BC) another decree is issued concerning the temple. (His reign is reckoned from July, 465 BC when his father Xerxes was murdered). The king gave permission to every Jew to return to Jerusalem and bring gold and silver in order to beautify and adorn "the house of the LORD which is in Jerusalem" (7:8-27). It makes no reference to building anything. The temple had been completed 57 years earlier and Jerusalem's walls remain torn down for another 13 years. Like Cyrus' and Darius' decrees it has *absolutely nothing* in it authorizing the rebuilding of the city of Jerusalem.

This decree would be hardly noticed except that many intelligent sincere students of Bible prophecy teach that it's the *terminus a quo*, the starting point for the countdown to Messiah. <u>Gabriel made it absolutely clear that the starting point for the countdown to Messiah is the authorization to rebuild Jerusalem! Not the authorization to beautify the temple with gold and silver</u> (Daniel 9:25). Therefore the 7th year decree of Artaxerxes (458 BC) must be firmly and completely rejected as the *terminus a quo*, the starting point for the countdown to Messiah!

According to Sir Robert Anderson (*The Coming Prince,* page 61), Dr. Pusey wrote a great book, *Daniel* but like many others he erroneously decided that Artaxerxes' 7th year decree should be the starting point for the countdown to Messiah. Dr. Pusey writes:

> "The little colony that Ezra took with him (...some 8,400 souls) was itself a considerable addition to those who had before returned *and involved a rebuilding of Jerusalem.* This rebuilding of the city and reorganization of the polity, begun by Ezra, and carried on and perfected by Nehemiah, corresponds with the words of Daniel, 'from the going forth of a commandment to restore and build Jerusalem'" (p. 172).

Anderson replied,

> This argument is the feeblest (weakest) imaginable and indeed this reference to the decree of the seventh year of Artaxerxes is a great blot on Dr. Pusey's book. If an immigration of 8,400 souls involved a rebuilding of the city, and therefore marked the beginning of the seventy weeks, what shall be said of the immigration of 49,697 souls seventy-eight years before? (Ezra 2:64-65). Did this not involve rebuilding? But Dr. Pusey goes on to say, "The term also corresponds to the 483 years to the time of Christ." Here is the real ground (reason) for fixing the date ...BC 458, as given by Prideaux who unfortunately Dr. Pusey has followed at this point. With more *naiveté* the author

of the *Connection* pleads that the years will not tally if any
other date be assigned and therefore the decree of the seventh
of Artaxerxes must be right!'...Such a system of interpretation
has done much to discredit the study of prophecy altogether.

If 483 years (69 X 7) is added to 458 BC we come up with 25 AD. We
add 1 year because time is reckoned as one year between 1 BC and 1 AD
(There is no zero year) and another year could be possibly added because
some say the decree was 457 BC. We therefore come to 27 AD which was
about the time Christ started His ministry. (He was born about 3 BC and
Luke 3:23 states He was about 30 years old when He started the ministry).
The 70th week (final 7-year period) begins when Christ makes a 7-year
covenant with many (Israel). 3 1/2 years later in the middle of the 7-year
period Christ is crucified and therefore the temple sacrifices are stopped.
Three and half years later the Jews stone Stephen; thus confirming their
rejection of their messiah. This completes the 70 weeks of years (490 years)
that are set aside for Israel.

Israel is therefore rejected by God. Therefore all the positive prophecies
concerning Israel's future are transferred to the church, the new spiritual
Israel but all the negative ones still apply to Israel. This is called replacement
or covenant theology. A careful study will prove that this interpretation is
erroneous and therefore needs to be rejected!

2 Peter 1:20-21 makes it clear that no prophecy is to be subjected to
private interpretation because it's not the result of human origin but was
the result of holy men who were moved by the Holy Spirit. It's so vitally
important not to put one's preconceived ideas into Scripture but let the
Scriptures speak for themselves!

The story is told of a man who visited a farmer who had many targets
painted on the side of the barn with an arrow shot right in the middle
of the bull's eye on every target. The man is so amazed and generously
complemented the farmer on his accuracy but the farmer replied, "It's very
easy to hit the bull's eye every time. All you have to do is shoot the arrow
first and then paint the target around the arrow where it lands and you
become a perfect marksman."

Yes, the years tally out well in this interpretation as prophetic arrows are shot and targets are drawn around them but that still does not make it correct! The years will tally out perfectly with the correct interpretation.

I strongly reiterate again. **In Ezra there is absolutely no authorization to rebuild the city of Jerusalem! Authorization is given ONLY for the rebuilding and beautifying of the temple, the house of God in Jerusalem!** Therefore all the dates in Ezra including 458 BC are to be firmly and completely rejected as starting points for the countdown to Messiah. No authorization in Ezra but very clear authorization in Nehemiah.

The *Terminus* a Quo (the starting point)

Nehemiah served as the cupbearer to Artaxerxes, the son of Ahasuerus (Xerxes) who took Esther as his queen. Nehemiah (1:3) is greatly disturbed because Jerusalem is defenseless with its walls torn down. Like Daniel (9:3-19) Nehemiah fasted and prayed fervently for Israel (Neh. 1:4-11) and came before the king.

The ancient cupbearer had a dangerous job. He was required to taste all the wine and food that the king would consume and hopefully make sure it was free of poison. Many monarchs were killed from poisoned food and drink. Nehemiah is looking and feeling very sad which understandably bothers the king. The king wonders if his cupbearer is being moderately poisoned as he tastes the king's wine and food. He wants his cupbearer to look and feel well and healthy and so he asks Nehemiah, (2:2, author's paraphrase), "You look sad. You're not sick are you?" Nehemiah answers, "I cannot help being sad because Jerusalem, the city of my ancestors is defenseless because all the walls and gates are torn down." The king then asked him, "How can I help you?" Nehemiah answered, "Please give me authorization to rebuild Jerusalem."

The king freely granted Nehemiah's request and also made provision for all the material needed to accomplish the project (2:3-8). This authorization was granted on Nisan 1, 445 BC, the 20th year of Artaxerxes (2:1). Thus, here is the *terminus a quo,* the starting point for the countdown to Messiah.

The preceding should make it absolutely clear that the 20th year of Artaxerxes (445 BC) is the proper starting time for the countdown to

Messiah. It's the only time that authorization is given to rebuild the city of Jerusalem.

For argument's sake let's consider that Dr. Pusey is correct and therefore 458 or 457 BC is the proper *terminus a quo*. If Dr. Pusey is correct and authorization was indeed given in Artaxerxes' 7th year to rebuild Jerusalem why would Nehemiah need to ask the king for the authorization since he already had it for 13 years? The king would have gotten very exasperated and angry as he answers,

> "Look, Nehemiah! Are you blind and ignorant? Can't you see that I gave Ezra and your people permission to rebuild Jerusalem 13 years ago! If it's still left in ruins it's your fault! What's your problem? It's obvious that you and your people are very lazy and irresponsible since you have ignored the authorization I gave you 13 years ago. You have dragged your feet while you could have easily rebuilt Jerusalem. Since you did not respond to my generous provision 13 years ago but completely ignored it why should I think that you would respond to any provision that I would give you now? Quit bothering me and wasting my time with your needless moaning and groaning! Get to work and take advantage of my decree I gave you 13 years ago!"

Obviously this very silly, stupid, ridiculous conversation between Nehemiah and the king did NOT take place nor could it! <u>Both King Artaxerxes and Nehemiah knew that no authorization whatever had ever been given to rebuild the city!</u> Authorization was definitely needed and generously granted by Artaxerxes to rebuild Jerusalem in his 20th year (445 BC). Nehemiah 2-6 gives the story of the successful rebuilding of the wall in very troubled times.

Circumstances in the lives of individuals and nations can suddenly and drastically change; sometimes overnight. Adam and Eve had a perfect, joyful life together until the events of Genesis 3. Abraham (100) and Sarah (90) were obviously too old to be parents but God decided otherwise (Gen. 15:1-4, 17:16-17, Heb.11:11-12). Joseph was languishing in prison in the morning but later that day became the ruler of Egypt (Gen. 41:40-41). Pharaoh's army with 600 chariots was ready to slaughter the Israelis but in Exodus 14:26-28 we see the results of Pharaoh's adventure.

Goliath terrorized Israel but the situation drastically changed. (ISam.17:48-51). Haman's plans to destroy every Jew in Persia would soon be realized (Esther 3:8-11) but things drastically changed in chapter 7. Christ was dead and forever securely sealed in a Roman tomb but we know what happened to Him 3 days later. Mass murderer Saul, the most vehement feared arch-enemy of the Christian church became probably the greatest missionary and hero for Christ (Acts 9:1-16).

In early 1864 very few Americans believed that President Lincoln would be renominated by his party to run for president again since he obviously had no chance of being re-elected. (Smile!).

On June 25, 1950, the "illustrious Lord of heaven," Kim Ilsung and North Korea invaded South Korea and conquered all of it except a small perimeter around Busan. The situation drastically changed when US General Douglas MacArthur successfully invaded Incheon and soon liberated all of Korea from communist rule. In November China entered the war and ensured that Korea would remain divided.

In early 1989 East German leader Honecker declared that the Berlin Wall will stay up another 50 years and no one argued with him. In November of that year the wall was torn down and soon East and West Germany were reunited. To almost everyone's surprise the Soviet Union disintegrated in 1991 (Don't forget Daniel 3 and 6).

President Obama presided over 8 years of unparalleled hostility to Israel. He regularly praised Islam and bowed to Saudi monarchs. He boldly insulted Christianity and Israeli Prime Minister Netanyahu. He used US taxpayer money to support a modern-day Neville Chamberlain in the Israeli election. All the polls predicted Netanyahu's defeat but he won anyway. Obama's popularity in Israel was about 4%.

In the US presidential election of 2016 virtually all the polls declared that Mrs. Clinton would be elected president but God had other plans. Franklin Graham led prayer meetings in all 50 state capitals for God's mercy, grace, guidance, and help in the election. God graciously granted his request.

After Trump's victory but before his inauguration for the first time in history the US ambassador refused to veto a Security Council resolution of strong condemnation for Israel. Mrs. Clinton showed her very strong hostility and contempt for Israel by choosing Virginia US Senator Tim Kaine, a strong, vehement anti-Israel candidate for her running mate.

Situations can drastically change quickly. We wonder what happened to change the Persian king's mind from being vehemently opposed to giving any autonomy to the Jews (Ezra 4:21) to freely granting it to Nehemiah, Milman in his *History of the Jews* (p. 342-343) sheds some light on this:

> ..Jerusalem was open and defenseless; the jealous policy of the Persian kings would not permit the Jews to fortify a military post of such importance as their capital. On a sudden, however, in the twentieth year of Artaxerxes, Nehemiah, a man of Jewish descent, cup-bearer to the king, received a commission to rebuild the city with all possible expedition. The cause of this change in Persian policies is to be sought, not so much in the personal influence of the Jewish cupbearer, as in the foreign history of the times. The power of Persia had received a fatal blow in the victory obtained at Cnidos by Conan, the Athenian admiral. The great king was obliged to submit to a humiliating peace, among the articles of which were the abandonment of the maritime towns, and a stipulation that the Persian army should not approach within 3 days journey of the sea. Jerusalem being about this distance from the coast, and standing so near the line of communication with Egypt, became a post of utmost value. The Persian court saw the wisdom of entrusting the command of a city and the government of a people always obstinately national, to an officer of their own race, yet one whose fidelity they might have full reliance.

Secular history confirms the edict. Herodotus, the father of history visited Artaxerxes' court and Thucydides, the prince of historians were contemporary of Artaxerxes. Xerxes (Ahasuerus), the son of Darius and father of Artaxerxes came to the throne in 485 BC and was murdered in July, 465 BC. Artabanus usurped the throne in July 465 BC for 7 months. Artaxerxes came to the throne in February, 464 BC but his reign was reckoned from July, 465 BC, the king's *de jure* ascension. We know this because Nehemiah states that Chisleu (November) and Nisan (March) of the 20th year are both in the same year of the king's reign (Nehemiah 1:1;

2:1). The 20th year started in July, 446 BC and ended July, 445 BC. The edict was given on Nisan, 445 BC (p. 64-66, CP).

The dates tally out well if we use the 458 BC date but they don't if we use the 445 BC date. 483 years added to 445 BC brings us to 39 AD which is 7 years past the time of Christ's death. (Remember there's 1 year between 1 BC and 1 AD).What can we do? We simply study deeper into the Scriptures and find answer.

A solar year is based on the time it takes the earth to orbit the sun. We measure the year by determining the interval between 2 successive passages of the sun through the vernal equinox which is 365.242199 days or 365 days, 5 hours, 48 minutes, and 46 seconds. That's 11 minutes and 14 seconds shorter than the 365.25 days calculated by the Julian calendar.

The winter solstice (shortest day in the northern hemisphere) fell on December 25 at the time of Christ but by 1580 it fell on December 11. With the astronomers' advice, Pope Gregory XIII declared in 1582 that the day after Thursday, October 4 would be Friday, October 15 in order to make the winter solstice on December 21. To synchronize the year with the earth's revolving around the sun, an extra day is added every 4 years for a leap year but since the year isn't quite 365.25 days long there would be no leap year during the turn of the century except every fourth turn of the century The moon completes its full cycle of phrases in 29.53059 days (*World Book Encyclopedia*, (WBE) 1985, "Calendar" vol. 3, p. 28-30). The Hebrew calendar is based on the lunar year, lasting 354 days. There are 13 months every 3rd year and seven 13-month years every 19 years.

The prophetic year

Gabriel's message to Daniel and Israel is not given in lunar or solar years but in prophetic years. A prophetic year contains exactly 12 thirty-day months which equal a 360-day year. The prophecy was given in Babylon whose calendar contained twelve 30-day months (*The Coming Prince* by Anderson, p. 75). Sir Isaac Newton, a Jewish believer in Yeshua (Jesus Christ) and one of history's greatest scientists states that:

> All nations before the just length of the solar year was known, reckoned months by the course of the moon, and years by the return of winter and summer, spring, and autumn; and in making calendars for the festivals, they reckoned thirty days to a lunar month and twelve lunar months to a year. (CP, p.68).

The ancient nations of India, Persia, Egypt, Greece, Italy, Central America, and China had 360-day years containing twelve 30-day months (Velikovsky, 330-34, Showers, p. 123). Noah's flood started on the 17th day of the 2nd month (Gen. 7:11). The water prevailed upon the earth for 150 days (v. 24) and the ark rested on the mountains of Ararat on the 17th day of the 7th month (8:4). Here we see that there is in interval of 150 days: Five 30-day months between the 17th day of the 2nd month and the 17th of the 7th month. In the Encyclopedia Britannica under the title *Chronology* tradition teaches that Abraham preserved his family with a 360-day year (p. 68, CP).

In Daniel 12:7 the angel tells Daniel that Antichrist will rule for a time (1 year), times (2 years), and half a time (1/2 year), or 3 1/2 years. In Revelation 12:6 Satan, the great dragon persecutes the woman for 1260 days. In verse 14 she is nourished "for a time (1 year) and times (2 years) and a half a time (1/2 year): Antichrist speaks arrogant words of blasphemy against God and has authority for 42 months (13:5). The city is trampled on for 42 months and two witnesses are given power for 1260 days (Rev. 11:2-3). This should make it clear that 1260 days = 42 months =3 1/2 years as these periods of time are used interchangeably throughout Revelation. If Julian years were meant the 42 months would equal 1278 days.

In Ezekiel 24:1-2 we learn that Nebuchadnezzar laid siege to Jerusalem on the 10th day of the 10th month of the 9th year of Judah's King Zedekiah. Jeremiah (25:11) prophesied that Jerusalem would be desolate for 70 years. The cornerstone for the rebuilding of the temple was laid on the 24th day of the 9th month, in the 2nd year of Darius (520 BC, Haggai 2:10-19). Anderson (CP, p. 70) calculates that the interval is exactly 25,202 days. Seventy years of 360 days equals 25,200 days and so we conclude that the desolation of Jerusalem began 1 day after Jerusalem's siege and ends 1 day before the temple foundation is laid.

The division of the 70 seven-year periods

In Daniel 9:25 we see that the time prophecy is divided into 3 parts. In the first part we have 7 seven-year periods (49 years). It took only 52 days to complete the wall (Neh. 6:15) but it took about 49 years to complete the fortification and defense of Jerusalem (Showers p. 123). Gabriel said the city would be built in times of distress (9:25). Nehemiah 4 and 6:1-7:4 give details of the stress the Jews faced while rebuilding the walls. Malachi completed his prophecy 49 years after the edict to rebuild Jerusalem; thus completing the Hebrew Scriptures. There are no more messages from God until Gabriel gives his message to Zacharias in Luke 1:11-20. The second part is 62 seven-year periods. When they are added to the first group of 7 seven-year periods we have a total of 69 seven-year periods equaling 483 years. The 3rd part is the final 7-year period that is explained later.

Anderson's calculations

Most of the information on this section is gleaned from *The Coming Prince* (CP) by Sir Robert Anderson (1841-1918). He was raised in a devout Christian home but as a teenager had doubts about his conversion. He accepted Christ as his personal savior about 1859 and became an active lay preacher. Anderson became the Scotland Yard Assistant Commissioner of Metropolitan Police and Chief of the Criminal Investigation Department until he retired in 1901. Through his diligent work crime decreased during his time there. During his life many doubted the dependability and truthfulness of Scripture but through his very careful and diligent research the validity and dependability of Scriptures were vindicated. Anderson proves again that the Bible is the anvil that wears out many hammers (Psalms 119:89, 105, 140, 142 144, 160, Mt. 5:18, Lk. 21:33, Jn. 17:17).

The day of the edict is not given and so we must follow the Jewish custom of understanding that if the day is not given it's understood to be the first day of the month. Therefore Nisan 1, (March 14), 445 BC is the *terminus a quo,* the starting date for the countdown to Messiah (p. 122 CP). Astronomer Royal of England's Royal Observatory calculates that the new moon appeared over Jerusalem on March 13, 445 BC at 7:09

AM. The following day, March 14 is the first full day of the new moon (p. 123-124, CP). Gabriel made it clear that 69 seven-year periods (483 years) later Messiah is revealed to Israel (9:26).

The 483 years are prophetic years containing 360 days each. If we multiply 483 by 360, we have 173,880 days. When these 173,880 days are added to Nisan 1 (March 14), 445 BC we come to the 10th Nisan, (April 6), AD 32 (Anderson, *The Coming Prince)*. It was on this Palm Sunday that Jesus freely and boldly presented Himself as the promised King and Messiah of Israel and gladly received the praise of the People (Luke 19:20).

This is absolutely amazing! Marvelous! Phenomenal! Awesome! Gabriel carried from the throne of God the prophecy concerning the time when Israel's messiah would come and it's accurate even to the exact day! Anderson substantiates these calculations (p. 128) and no one has ever disputed them.

The 1st Nisan in the twentieth year of Artaxerxes (the edict to rebuild Jerusalem) was 14th March, BC 445. Palm Sunday, 10th Nisan, 6th April, AD 32, was the day of Christ's triumphal entry into Jerusalem. The intervening period was 476 years and 24 days (the days reckoned inclusively as required by the language of the prophecy, and in accordance with the Jewish practice).

But 476 X 365 = - - - - - - - - - - - - - - 173,740 days
Add (14 March to 6th April, both inclusive) - - - - -24 days
Add for leap years - - - - - - - - - - - - - - 116 days

Total - - - - - - - - - - - - - - - - - - 173,880 days

Secular history substantiates Anderson's calculations. Collier's Encyclopaedia states that Tiberius became the Roman emperor on August 19, 14 AD. The Word of God came to John the Baptist in the 15th year of Tiberius (between August 19, 28 AD and August 18, 29 AD). He baptized many people including Christ Who began His ministry at that time (Luke 3:1). It is virtually universally accepted that Christ had a 3 1/2 year ministry and celebrated 4 passovers. John specifically mentions 3 (2:13; 6:4; 13:1), and if John 5:1 is another Passover we have all 4 Passovers of Christ's ministry in the gospel of John. Bishop Epiphanius of Cyprus, who lived in the 4th century, declared that Christ was baptized in November, 28 AD and died in the spring of 32 AD (Finegan, p. 253 from Showers, p. 126).

Christ cleansed the temple during His first Passover (Jn. 2:14-17). Herod began building the temple in 18 BC and it was completed in 64. The Jews stated that it took 46 years to build it (Jn. 2:20). This means that the temple was in its 46th year of building when Christ cleansed it. When 46 is added to 18 BC we have 29 AD (There is one year between 1 BC and 1 AD). Thus the first Passover of Christ's ministry is the spring of 29 AD (Showers, p. 126-127).

These calculations from Anderson and Showers prove that Yeshua (Jesus Christ) began His ministry in the fall of AD 28 and was killed in the spring of 32 AD. Those who use 458 BC as the starting date for the countdown to Messiah also teach that Christ began His ministry in 27 AD but that date is impossible in light of this previous information.

Christ's about face

Throughout His ministry, Christ shunned the limelight of publicity as He continually forbade those He healed to tell any one about the miracle. After healing the afflicted He instructed them to "tell no one" (Mt. 9:30; 16:20, Mk. 7:36; 8:30). Christ firmly shunned and rejected the vain glory of being an exalted superstar and therefore refused to flaunt His greatness with great pomp and fanfare before men. He sought only to gently and humbly demonstrate His Father's rich tender love and compassion by ministering to mankind's needs.

After cleansing the leper He instructed the man to; "See that you tell no one but go show yourself to the priest and present the offering that Moses commanded as a testimony to them" (Mt.8:4). The religious leaders of Christ's day rejected Him from the beginning (Lk. 4:24-30) and therefore were very prejudiced against Christ. It's therefore very unlikely that the priest would have pronounced the man clean if he knew that Christ healed him.

On Palm Sunday, 10th Nisan, (April 6, 32 AD), Christ rode a donkey into Jerusalem and fulfilled Zechariah 9:9 (Luke 19:28-38). On His triumphal entry He did a full 180-degree about face from His previous instructions of shunning public recognition and freely welcomed the high exalted praises and adulation of the people. They joyfully praised Him with a loud voice, shouting;

"BLESSED IS THE KING WHO COMES IN THE NAME OF THE LORD: Peace in Heaven and glory in the highest!" (Lk. 19:37-38, Ps. 118:26).

The praise was so great that the Pharisees told Him to rebuke the people in their "uncontrolled enormous fanatical wild praise and adulation" (author's paraphrase). Instead of rebuking the people, Christ firmly rebuked the Pharisees and boldly proclaimed that the stones would cry out if the people remained silent (v. 39-40).

Why did Christ make this 180-degree about face? Because on His triumphal entry into Jerusalem on Palm Sunday, April 6, 32 AD, Daniel's prophecy of 9:25 was fulfilled. It's therefore no wonder that Christ wept so bitterly over Jerusalem (Luke 19:41). The Jewish people and the leaders had access to Daniel's prophecy but ignored it and refused to believe it. In deep anguish with a broken heart Christ bitterly wept over Jerusalem because, "If you had known in *this day* even you, the things that make for peace! But now they are hidden from your eyes."

The *this day* that Christ referred to was the *terminus ad quem,* of Daniel 9:25; the fulfillment of the 69 periods of 7 years (483 years) between the authorization to rebuild Jerusalem (March 14, 445 BC) and the revelation of Israel's messiah (April 6, 32 AD): This is the last day of the 173,880 days of Daniel's prophecy. He knew that He was the Prince of Peace (Isa 9:6) and Israel's only hope for peace.

He so earnestly wanted to bring peace to Israel, the nation He dearly loved but also knew that the Jewish leaders had rejected Him and were determined to murder Him (John 8:40). He grieved deeply because the rebellious nation refused to allow Him to bring peace and therefore would face the horrible disaster in 70 AD (Luke 13:34). Disaster comes to Israel because, "you did not recognize the time of your visitation" (Lk. 19:43-44).

Messiah cut off? Killed?

In John 12:32 Christ tells the people that He will be lifted up; thus revealing how He would die. The people answered;

> "We have heard out of the law that the Christ is to remain forever: and how can You say, 'the Son of Man must be lifted up?' Who is this Son of Man?" (v.34).

The people knew the message of Psalm 2:6-9; 10:16; 24:7-10, and Isaiah 9:6-7 which teach that Messiah and His kingdom would bring everlasting peace to Israel and the world. Like King David, Messiah would be a fearless victorious warrior king who defeats all the enemies of Israel and proclaims and enforces peace with his rod of iron (Ps. 2:5-11). Messiah proclaims the day of vengeance, takes charge of Israel's government (Isa. 9:6), and comforts all who mourn (Isa. 34:8; 35:5; 61:2). Zechariah 14:3-9 promises that Yahweh through Messiah will rule over all the earth.

The people were therefore confused. Daniel (7:13-14) knew that the Son of Man (Messiah) would rule over the earth but like the Jews of John 12:32 he felt confused as he learned that Messiah is cut off after being revealed to Israel (9:26).

"Cut off" refers to the death penalty (Isa. 53:8, Obadiah 9, Nahum 3:15). Yes, Messiah would be violently tortured to death as prophesied in Psalm 22 and Isaiah 52:13-53:12. How can Messiah rule Israel and the world if He's put to death? We who are blessed to be living today on this side of the cross have the obvious answer with the story of the death and resurrection of Jesus Christ but Daniel and the Hebrew prophets did not fully understand the message of Psalm 16:10-11 predicting Messiah's resurrection (I Peter 1:10-11). They did not understand that Messiah is first a Lamb (Isa. 53:7, Jn. 1:29) and then a Lion.

After His resurrection Christ anonymously joined 2 very dejected, disillusioned, and discouraged men traveling on the Emmaus road. They were discussing (literally in the Greek, *antiballo* throwing back and forth) how and why their expectations of Jesus Christ had come to such a tragic and bitter end. Their dearest friend was dead! When Christ asked them what things they were talking about. Cleopas answered with strong surprise and disbelief,(author's paraphrase);

"Are you a hermit living in a cave? Where have you been? Are you the only one who does not know about the horrible, tragic death of this great prophet who spoke like no one else and performed many miracles? We were hoping and expecting Him to redeem Israel from this cruel harsh Roman bondage but obviously He hasn't. He's dead! Some women have shared rumors of his resurrection but we know He's really dead and therefore gone for good!"

Christ must have smiled as He listened to their despair. He obviously knew first hand and therefore far more than anyone else about the previous events they were talking about. He gave a gentle rebuke in Luke. 24:25-27:

"O foolish men and slow of heart to believe in *all* that the prophets have spoken. Was it not necessary for the Christ to suffer these things and to enter His glory?" Then beginning with Moses and with all the prophets, He explained to them the things concerning Himself in all the Scriptures.

Christ rebukes the men because they were slow to believe <u>all</u> the writings of the prophets about Himself. They, like Israel understood Messiah only as the fierce warrior lion king like David who would redeem Israel from all her external enemies and establish perfect justice for all. They did not understand that Christ would first redeem Israel from a far more horrible bondage and a far worse enemy than Rome; the severe inner corruption and depravity of the heart. Neither Israel nor mankind understands that the worst enemy is not external but internal. Martin Luther understood this as he prayed, "Deliver me from the pope in me."

Christ through His sacrifice on the cross provided redemption for Israel and the whole world from mankind's worst enemy; the severe internal corruption of the sinful human heart (Jer. 17:9, Mt. 13:15; 15:19, Ecc. 9:3, Mk. 7:20-23). All who willingly receive His redemption will be free (Jn. 8:32-36) and never perish (Jn. 3:16, 36; 10:10, Rom. 5:8).

I chuckle as I think about this because today the world and Christianity in many cases understand Messiah *only* to be Jesus Christ, the sweet, loving, compassionate, tender Lamb of God who takes away the sin of the world (Isa. 53:7, John 1:29, 36) but not the fierce warrior, Lion of God who stomps down hard on the winepress of God's wrath as He rules the world with a rod of iron (Ps. 2:6-9, Rev. 5:5; 6:16-17; 19:11-16).

I have seen many beautiful stain glass paintings on church windows of Christ knocking on a door (Rev. 3:20), tenderly holding children or a lamb, walking on water, being baptized by John the Baptist, feeding the 5,000, healing lepers, blind, and all diseases, but I have never seen a stain glass painting of Christ in His anger as He cleansed the temple (Mt. 21:12-13, Jn. 2:14-16) or riding a white horse with a sword coming out of His mouth with eyes like a flame of fire and slaying the wicked (Rev. 19:11). Messiah is both Lamb and Lion and to teach only one aspect and neglect the other is unbalanced and improper (Jos. 1:7, Dt. 5:32, 28:14, Pr. 4:27).

Messiah is cut off after 69 7-year periods (483 years): Not after 69 and half 7-year periods (486 1/2 years). Those who teach this erroneous teaching are the same ones who teach that the 7th year of Artaxerxes is the edict to rebuild Jerusalem. One error leads to another and we will see that it leads to even more serious errors.

Messiah is cut off and has nothing. The Hebrew, *ain* always conveys the idea of emptiness or non-existence. Yahweh's appointed Prince and Ruler of Israel lost the authority to rule over Israel as He's cut off and another prince, an impostor, *the coming prince,* usurps the crown that rightly belongs to Messiah the true Prince: the King of Israel.

Scriptures never exaggerate but always objectively and accurately convey reality. The Scriptures tell it like it is. Gabriel declares that Messiah would have nothing: Absolutely nothing! Paul declares in 2Corinthians 8:9 that, "He (Christ) became poor so that you through His poverty might become rich." This began when the Creator of the universe became a helpless embryo and fetus in the womb of Mary and a babe in Bethlehem. It culminated when He was crucified. He was stripped naked, sarcastically mocked, and His flesh was torn to a bloody pulp.

Not only physically but spiritually He had nothing. In Mark 2:10 Jesus proclaims that He had power to forgive sins while He's on the earth but after being lifted above the earth He apparently no longer had that authority since He asked His Father to forgive the men who were crucifying Him (Lk. 23:34).

Christ with joy freely accepted crucifixion, the most cruel, sadistic, torturous death invented by man, for our benefit (Heb.12:2). However, the most horrible torture Christ received was not the severe physical suffering of the crucifixion but His awful severe spiritual torture of separation from His beloved Father. His most cherished relationship with His heavenly Father which He enjoyed from eternity past was broken as He was completely abandoned by His heavenly Father (Mark 15:34, Ps. 22:1). Christ cried out 2 times, "My God, My God" indicating that God the Father and God the Holy Spirit forsook Him. "But the LORD was pleased to crush him, putting him to grief... The good pleasure of the LORD will prosper in His hand" (Isa. 53:10). Christ was made sin for our benefit (2Cor. 5:21). Sin was so repulsive and abhorrent to our heavenly Father that He could not look on His Son as He was made sin. He had to turn His face away and completely abandon Him. Even as God the Father abandoned His Son Apostle Paul declares that God was in Christ reconciling the world (2 Cor. 5:19).

Jesus Christ was put to death and had absolutely nothing but His sacrifice was fully and freely accepted by our heavenly Father (Isaiah 53:11-12). We who have trusted Him as Savior receive what He deserved because He so willingly received what we deserved (2Cor. 5:21). Halleluyah! What a Savior!

Yes, after the 69 seven-year periods (483 years) Messiah is revealed and cut off, dead, and gone for good. This is obviously not true for those of us who know Jesus Christ as personal Savior but tragically it is true for Israel and the world at large.

Rome and the Jews

As stated earlier the Jewish people have always been in constant rebellion against God (Isa. 48:8). Despite God's strong prohibition against making treaties with the nations (Ex. 23:32; 12:12-15, Dt. 7:2; 23:6, Jud. 2:2-3, Ezra 9:12, Isa. 30:1-5, Jer. 5:30-31; 23:16-21) Simon, the last survivor of the Maccabees, high priest, and leader of Judea rejected these warnings and made a defense treaty with Rome.

> He directed his whole attention to the consolidation and the internal security of the Jewish kingdom. He sent an ambassage which was honourably received at Rome... To secure the alliance

of the Romans, the great safeguard of the new state, he sent a golden shield weighing 1,000 pounds to Rome. The Romans in return sent a proclamation to many of the kings of the East, to all the cities in the empire in which the Jews were settled, announcing their recognition of Simon as the prince of Judea; and while on the one hand the Jews at their command were to acknowledge Simon, On the other they haughtily intimated to the kings and cities under their dominion that the Jews were under their protection and alliance with Rome. (Milman, p.378).

In Judges 2:2 God pronounces judgment on Israel because of their failure to obey His command. The nations Israel made agreements with would be thorns in their eyes. The Romans will be far worse than thorns in Israel's eyes. Simon's bold rejection of God's clear warning in these Scriptures will be a disaster for Israel. A famous poem demonstrates the consequences of his actions.

> There was a young lady of Niger
> Who smiled as she rode on the tiger
> They came back from the ride
> With the lady inside
> And the smile on the face of the tiger

For 76 years the Jewish lady smiled as she rode the tiger and then the Roman tiger smiled after swallowing the lady.

The Jews regularly fought each other in civil wars. In 67 BC civil war erupted again. Simon's grandsons, 2 brothers, Aristobulus and Hyrcanus fought each other for the privilege to rule over the Jews. Both sought Rome's aid to defeat the other and Hyrcanus' faction invited Pompey and the Roman army into Jerusalem in 63 BC (Maier, p. 227). Pompey basically told the warring brothers, "I come not to take sides but to take over." The Jewish lady is thus "safe" inside the Roman tiger.

Roman governors were generally insensitive to Jewish feelings, beliefs, and customs but the first governors made some reasonable attempts to accommodate them. Roman policy was to respect the local people's religion and culture.

Rome made an extremely irresponsible choice when it sent Pontius Pilate, a very rabid, vehement anti-Semite to govern Judea. He strongly disdained the Jews and their "ridiculous silly customs" and enjoyed insulting them. The Jews complained to Rome because of his insensitivity and ill-treatment and Pilate was therefore under investigation by the Roman Senate. This is why Pilate, so very much out of character, so easily caved into the mob's desire to have Jesus Christ crucified though himself fully knowing that Christ was innocent (Jn. 18:38; 19:4). His personal well-being and high position in government was far more important to him than executing Roman justice and so this "brave, courageous Roman governor" became a first class chicken as he cowardly and callously yielded to the sadistic blood thirsty mob's demand for Christ's crucifixion. Later Emperor Caligula banished him to Gaul where tradition says he committed suicide.

The Romans strongly disdained the Jews and their "ridiculous, silly festivals like Passover" One soldier was beheaded after publicly blaspheming and tearing in half the Law of Moses. Another soldier during Passover made a very obscene demonstration revealing his utter contempt and disdain for the Jews. He lifted his tunic, showed his genitals and turned his backside to the Jews and broke wind. The enraged Jews reacted by hurling stones at the soldiers. When reinforcements were sent 20,000 were trampled to death as they tried to escape (Maier, p. 273).

Judea and Rome were in constant conflict and finally in 66 AD open rebellion erupted against Rome. The Jews had early success but after Emperor Nero dispatched his best general Vespasian to Judea, the Jews were slowly being pushed back. Vespasian conquered all of Galilee and laid siege to Jerusalem. Josephus, one of the Jews' finest generals clearly saw that it would be futile to fight Rome and so he surrendered and encouraged his fellow countrymen to do likewise. After surrendering to Vespasian he wrote his eye witness account of the horrible devastation of the Jews and Jerusalem.

Jerusalem and the temple destroyed again

After Messiah the Prince is cut off we read about the next event in the prophecy. "The people of the prince who is to come will destroy the city and the sanctuary" (v. 26). The people of the coming prince is his army (Joshua 8:1, Judges 7:1; 9:49, I Sam 11:11). Gabriel thus prophesied that the Roman army would destroy the temple and Jerusalem.

Jesus bitterly wept over the city (Lk. 19:41-44) because as stated earlier, "You did know the time of your visitation" Israel very stubbornly and obstinately refused to accept and understand Daniel's prophecy which revealed the specific day for the revealing of Israel's messiah. Because of Israel's willful obstinate refusal to receive God's visitation in Christ Jesus, she would suffer horrible, severe consequences.

Christ gave a strong warning to His people in Luke 21:20-21.

"But when you see Jerusalem surrounded by armies, then recognize that her desolation is near. Then those who are in Judea must flee to the mountains and those who are in the midst of the city must leave, and those who are in the country must not enter the city; because these are days of vengeance.....Woe to those who are pregnant and to those who are nursing babies in those days; for there will be great distress upon the land and wrath to this people, and they will fall by the edge of the sword, and will be led captive into all nations; and Jerusalem will be trampled under foot by the Gentiles until the times of the Gentiles are fulfilled."

Vespasian surrounded and laid siege to Jerusalem but after hearing of Nero's suicide he lifted the siege and went to Rome to become the new emperor. Many robbers and murderers entered Jerusalem and along with the Zealots brought a horrible reign of terror for everyone there. Those who heeded Christ's warning and fled after Vespasian's siege was lifted escaped the devastation and lived. Tragically many ignored or rejected Christ's clear warning and trusted the false prophets or their own strength and wisdom (Pr. 3:5-7; 14:12; 12:15; 28:26, Jer. 17:5-9; 23:16-21) and reaped severe consequences. They perished or were sold into slavery (Maier, p. 361).

The Zealots were the first century's Al Qaida, Taliban, ISIS terrorists. John Gischala and Eleazar were 2 rival Zealot leaders who fiercely fought each other inside the city. Simon, son of Giora led a 3rd faction. All 3 factions fought each other, burned each other's food and supplies, and killed anyone who tried to escape their self imposed famine and reign of terror. Many of the Jews who escaped begged Vespasian to rescue the people from the horrible situation inside Jerusalem (Maier, p. 329-330).

Titus, Vespasian's son resumed the siege. The severe suffering of the people was extremely horrible and indescribable. Titus' troops captured any who ventured out to look for food. If they resisted they were tortured and crucified before the walls as a terrible warning to the people within. Titus pitied the 500 who were captured daily. "Out of rage and hatred, the soldiers nailed the prisoners in different postures, and so great was their number that space could not be found for the crosses." (Maier, p.347).

Deserters swallowed gold coins and retrieved them from their excrement. When Arab and Syrian soldiers saw this they ripped open the bowels of about 2,000 deserters looking for gold and valuable coins. Titus forbade it but was unable to enforce his command (Maier, p. 350). The people searched for herbs to eat but when they could no longer find them they ate cow dung (p. 351).

The famine in the city was so severe that relatives fought over the smallest morsel of food. They gnawed on belts, shoes, leather from shields, and even ate wisps of hay. One woman baked and ate half her infant and hid the other half. Robbers smelled it and demanded a portion but were paralyzed and totally repulsed when she told them what she did.

The whole city and even Titus and the Romans were horrified. Titus swore to bury this infant cannibalism in the ruins of the city (Maier, p. 358-359).

Titus tried very hard to save the temple from destruction. After the temple was set afire he ordered the troops to put it out and also ordered a centurion to club those who disobeyed his orders. The soldiers were so filled with fury, bitterness, hatred for the Jews, and desire for revenge and plunder that they disobeyed their general's command (p. 360-361). They also disobeyed Titus' command to kill only those who are armed and offered resistance. The soldiers, weary of battle killed the old and feeble and everyone in their way. The shouts of the legions, howls of the Jews, and shrieks of the people were deafening. There were so many corpses that the soldiers had to climb over large piles in order to pursue the fugitives (Maier, p. 361). 1,100,000 died in the siege and 97,000 were taken as prisoners (Maier, p. 367).

Four years of bitter defeats at the hands of the Jews had made mockery of the vaunted invincibility of the Roman legions, and only killing could now soothe their bruised vanity. The temple was put to the torch, infants thrown into the flames, women raped, priests massacred, Zealots thrown from the wall. Survivors of the carnage were earmarked for the triumphal procession to be held in Rome, sold as slaves, held for the wild beasts in the arenas, or saved to be thrown off the Tarpeian Rock in Rome for amusement. At no time did the Romans more justly earn the grim words of their own historian, Tacitus, who said, "They make a desolation and call it peace." (Dimont, *Jews, God, and History,* p.105-106)

Milman in *History of the Jews,* (vol. 2, p.77) sums up the situation well.

The blood runs cold, and the heart sickens, at these unexampled horrors; and we take refuge in a kind of desperate hope that they have been exaggerated by the historian: those... (who face stark reality) admit of no such reservation; they must be believed in their naked and unmitigated barbarity.

Moses predicted this horrible disaster in Deuteronomy 28:53-57. Verse 49 predicts the Roman destruction of the Jews and verse 68 predicts their return to Egypt as slaves. Over and over in the exodus the Hebrews demand to return to Egypt (Ex. 14:11, Nu.11:18-20; 14:1-4). Their request is granted in 70 AD.

Christ saw this disaster coming to Jerusalem and its temple (Lk. 19:44). It's therefore no wonder that in His deep anguish of spirit He wept so bitterly over Jerusalem; the city He so dearly loved and so earnestly wanted to protect and save from destruction (Lk 13:34-35).

"O Jerusalem, Jerusalem, the city that kills the prophets and stones those sent to her! How often I wanted to gather your children together just as a hen gathers her brood under her wings, and you would not have it. Behold your house is left to you desolate: and I say to you, you will not see Me until the time comes when you say, 'BLESSED IS HE WHO COMES IN THE NAME OF THE LORD!'"

In Vietnam on September 4, 1965, South Korean soldier, Captain Kang Jae-Ku (born 1937) was teaching soldiers how to use grenades and one soldier accidentallly dropped a live one. Kang fell on top of it as he gave his life for the soldiers (John 15:13-14).

On Friday, March 2, 2012, Stephanie Decker of Henryville, Indiana was in her house with her 2 children; Dominac 8 and Reese 5. As a killer tornado tore down their house she covered them with her body and lost both legs near the knee. Stephanie willingly laid down her life in order to protect her children. They are safe and sound because of their mother's love and sacrifice.

On March 31, 2008, Navy Seal Mike Monsoor, 25 was awarded the Congressional Medal of Honor by US President George W. Bush. He freely sacrificed his life, to save 45 of his comrades as he fell on the grenade in Ramadi, Iraq on September 29, 2006. A fellow warrior said, "He never took his eye off the grenade; his movement was only down toward it." Kristen Scharmberg of the Chicago Tribune reported, "The men who were there that day say they see the option flicker across Michael Monsoor's face: save himself or the men he had long considered brothers. He chose them."

On Friday, December 14, 2012, at Sandy Hook Elementary School in Newtown, Connecticut, USA, Adam Lunza, murdered his mother and cruelly massacred 20 children and 6 adults before taking his own life. Anne Marie Murphy, 52, was found dead as she covered children. Dawn Hochsprung, 47, school principal lunged at the murderer and was killed. School psychologist, Mary Shulach, 56, shielded students and was killed. First grade teacher, Victoria Soto, 27, hid students in the bathroom and died as she shielded them from the bullets. "You have a teacher who cares more about her students than herself." said John Harkin, mayor of Stratford, Soto's hometown. "That speaks volumes to her character, commitment, and dedication."

On Monday, September 30, 2013 Dwayne Johnson (46) was hiking with his wife, his children, and their cousins along a scenic route at Buena Vista, Colorado. An unexpected rockslide killed everyone in the group except Dwayne's daughter Gracie (13) because Dwayne shielded her with his body.

On December, 2014, Zaevion William Dobson, a 15-year old Fulton High School football player in Knoxville, Tn. died shielding 3 friends from gunfire. President Obama declared, "Zevion Dobson died saving 3 friends from being shot. He was a hero at 15. What's your excuse for not acting?" (Knoxville, Tn. News Sentinel, Feb.12, 2016).

After wildfires devastate a forest or a farm, officials look at the damage and sometimes find a chard dead bird. After kicking it over they are surprised to see little chicks running out. The bird gathered and protected her chicks under her wings while she faced the torturous pain of death by fire.

These are tremendous, rich illustrations of our Lord Jesus Christ's love and sacrifice for Jerusalem, for Israel, and for all mankind! He freely took the bullets, the grenade blast, the crushing rock, and the fire of judgment on Himself with His sacrifice on the cross. Tragically the Jewish people refused to come under His wings and therefore are tortured and consumed by the fire of God's holy indignation and judgment.

All who reject Christ's offer of protection from this fire will perish in the Lake of Fire (Rev. 20:15). We who know Jesus Christ as Savior are safe as we are under His wings (Psalms 91:4; 17:8; 36:7; 57:1; 61:4; 63:7, Ruth 2:12, Isaiah 31:5). William Cushing must have had these verses in mind when he wrote the following hymn:

Under His Wings.

Under His wings I am safely abiding,
Though the night deepens and tempests are wild.
Still I can trust Him. I know He will keep me.
He has redeemed me and I am His child.

Under His wings, under His wings.
Who from His love can sever?
Under His wings my soul shall abide.
Safely abide forever.

Under His wings what a refuge in sorrow
How the heart yearningly turns to His rest
Often when earth has no balm for my healing
There I find comfort and there I am blest.

Under His wings, O what precious enjoyment.
There I will hide till life's trials are over.
Sheltered, protected, no evil can harm me.
Resting in Jesus I'm safe evermore

In her excellent commentary on Psalm 91 Peggy Joyce Ruth gives the following insight on Psalm 91:4 (p.26). On her farm she noticed a hawk threatening newly hatched chicks. The mother hen did not run to her chicks and jump on top of them and force them under her wings but squatted down, spread her wings and began to cluck. After running to their mother the hen tightly tucked the chicks under her wings thus making it impossible for the hawk to get to the chicks. It had to get the mother hen first.

This rich analogy is obvious. Christ does not force His love and protection on anyone but freely unconditionally receives all who come under His wings of protection and invite Him to rule over them (Mk. 10:42-43, John 3:16-17, 6:37, 2Pe. 3:9, Rev. 3:20, 22:17). The Gerasene businessmen asked Christ to leave their area since He was bad for business. He politely complied (Mk. 5:17).

Israel rejected Yeshua (Jesus Christ) as king as they cried out, "We have no king but Caesar" (Jn. 19:15). Christ will rule over Israel only after the stubborn nation repents of her very obstinate, arrogant, rebellious behavior, and invites Him in and cries out, "Blessed is He who comes in the name of the LORD. We have blessed you from the House of the LORD" (Ps. 118:26).

The 70th week: The final 7–year period set aside for Israel

Lenin said that treaties, like pie crusts are made to be broken. Many peace treaties were signed before World War II "guaranteeing peace" but they weren't worth the paper they were written on.

French President Daladier guaranteed assistance to Czechoslovakia if she were threatened or attacked by Germany but Daladier and British Prime Minister Chamberlain boldly revealed their severe corruption as these super first class chickens very naively, shamefully, callously, and cruelly sacrificed Czechoslovakia on the altar of the very heinous, wicked, ravenous, satanic beast, Adolf Hitler at Munich. Later French President Mitterrand solemnly assured French protection for Israel if she would withdraw to the 48 ceasefire border between Israel and the Arabs. Israeli Prime Minister Begin scornfully laughed and boldly rejected the offer stating, "No thank you Mr. President. We know the worth of your French guarantees."

Stalin and Hitler signed at least 10 treaties between August 24, 1939 and May, 1941 and even sent Christmas greetings to each other in 1939 and 1940. Daniel 11:27 states that 2 kings whose hearts are bent on evil will sit at the same table and lie to each other: A perfect description of Hitler and Stalin and the many "peace" treaties that were signed before and after both world wars.

A hunter was pointing his gun at a bear. The bear asked, "What do you want?" The hunter answered, "A fur coat." The bear said, "I need a full stomach. Put your gun down and let's negotiate." They reached an agreement. Both received what they wanted. The bear got his full stomach and the hunter got his fur coat.

God clearly commanded Israel not to make covenants with other nations (Ex. 23:32; 34:12-15, Dt. 7:2-5; 23:6, Jud. 2:2, Isa. 30:1-5, Ezra 9:12, Jer. 5:30-31; 23:16-21) and to reject false prophets who bring false hope with their covenants with death because they will not stand (Isaiah 28:15-18; 57:8-13). Tragically Israel in her typical rebellious behavior continues to reject God's true prophets and freely embraces the false hope that false prophets give resulting in death (I Kings 20:34, Jer. 23 and 28).

As in the days of the Hebrew prophets, modern Israel continues to honor false prophets and make covenants with death. Shortly before the 3rd and final Jewish rebellion against Rome (132-135) Rabbi Akiva proclaimed Simon Bar Kochba (Son of the Star) as messiah and seduced many Jews to follow this charismatic charlatan. Like the first 2 rebellions Rome crushed this one too and many Jews perished as they followed this false prophet and false messiah. Bar Kochba died in battle and the greatly revered rabbi was tortured to death by the Romans. Even though it's very obvious that Rabbi Akiva and Bar Kochba were corrupt, evil, false leaders (Mt. 24:23-26, Jn.

5:43) Israel continues to honor these charlatans by naming streets and public places after them.

In 1993 Israeli Prime Minister Rabin freely lied to his people while negotiating with and signing a "peace treaty" with arch-murderer and granddaddy of terrorists Yasser Arafat and the Palestine Liberation Organization (PLO). The PLO was founded in 1964; 3 years before Israel was forced in a defensive war to conquer the so-called "occupied territories of the West Bank." Even though the PLO has made it clear in its charter its determination to liberate *all* of Palestine from the "racist Zionist invaders," Israel and Prime Minister Rabin very naively signed this covenant with death. (Rabin was assassinated on November 4, 1995).

Stephen, the first Christian martyr boldly asks the Jewish leaders in Acts 7:52;

> "Which one of the prophets did your fathers not persecute? They killed those who previously announced the coming of the righteous one, whose betrayers and murderers you have now become; you who received the law as ordained by angels, and yet did not keep it."

The Jewish leaders obviously had no answer and so in their deep, irrational overflowing, uncontrolled, hateful, emotional rage that caused them to murder Jesus Christ, the Prince of Life, they also killed Stephen (vs. 54-58). Christ tells the Jews in John 5:43;

> "I have come in my Father's name and you will not receive me. If another comes in his own name you will receive him."

Pompey, the Roman conqueror was welcomed into Jerusalem and later the Jews demanded Caesar for their king and their request was granted (John 19:15). Israel rejected all the Hebrew prophets and the greatest prophet of all, Yeshua Hamoshiakh (Jesus Christ) but freely welcomes false prophets (Jude 1:11, Jer. 23:9-39, Nu. 16:1-3, 31-35).

Egypt's Anwar Sadat, the architect of the devastating 1973 Yom Kippur War that nearly destroyed Israel, was warmly welcomed into Jerusalem as a hero of peace. Like Pompey and Sadat, the future Roman prince, who comes in his own name, will be freely and warmly welcomed into Jerusalem as he easily seduces Israel to sign his 7-year covenant with death. Antichrist, the little horn of Daniel 7:7-8, 24-25, the coming prince of 9:26-27, the man of sin and son of destruction (2 Thess. 2:3-12) and beast of Revelation 13 gives Israel his "most solemn assurance of peace" (Ps. 5:9; 55:21, Pr. 26:24-28, Isa. 48:22, Jer. 9:8). Like severely naïve and seduced British Prime Minister Chamberlain, Israel now naively thinks she can rest in peace and security as she signs a 7-year peace treaty with someone more evil and demonic than Adolf Hitler (Jer. 6:14; 8:11, Ezek. 13:10, I Thess. 5:3).

The Abomination of Desolation

In Revelation 13:11-13 we see another beast who exercises the authority of the first beast (Antichrist). He performs miracles and calls fire to come down from heaven.

Elijah is the only prophet to call fire down from heaven (1Kings. 18:38, 2Kings 1:10-12). Malachi 4:5 declares that Prophet Elijah will come before the "great and terrible day of the LORD." Satan deceives many Jews and the world through this counterfeit "Elijah" who encourages the people to worship the beast.

Antichrist proclaims "peace" under his iron rule and requires everyone to worship his image and receive his mark of 666 (Rev. 13:15-18). He earns the trust of the Jews and guarantees their protection and authorizes sacrifices to be practiced in the rebuilt temple but 3 1/2 years later in the middle of his 7-year contract of peace he double crosses the Jews and puts a,

> Stop to sacrifice and grain offering and on the wing of abominations will come one who makes desolate even until a complete destruction, one that is decreed, is poured out on the one who makes desolate (Dan. 9:27).

The sacrifices are a form of worship of Yahweh and so it's no wonder that Antichrist stops the sacrifices because he wants to replace Yahweh and be worshiped himself as God. The wing is the pinnacle or extreme point of the temple. This is where Satan tempted Christ to be an exotic show-off superstar hero who floats down to the ground but Christ successfully resisted the temptation (Mt. 4:5-7). Antichrist is a great show off superstar to Israel and the world as he makes himself the center of attention and demands to be worshiped as God (Rev. 13:13-14).

The abomination of desolation Antiochus Epiphanes caused in 168 BC (Dan. 11:31) was a preview of the future supreme abomination of Daniel 9:27 and 12:11 that Christ referred to in Matthew 24:15. Apostle Paul sheds light on Antichrist's abomination (2 Thess. 2:3-4. Antichrist is;

> ...the man of lawlessness .., the son of destruction, who opposes and exalts himself above every so-called god or object of worship, so that he takes his seat in the temple of God: displaying himself as being God.

In the middle of the 70th 7-year period Antichrist enters the Jerusalem temple and demands to be worshiped as God. He will do the same things Antiochus did but on a much grander scale. Pious Jews will be outraged and then Antichrist will persecute Israel for the last 3 1/2 years of the 490 years allotted to her (Rev. 12:13-14). This is the time of Jacob's trouble (Jer. 30:7): The great tribulation of Daniel 12:1.

Matthew 24:15-18, 21-22a confirms this as Christ gives instructions to Israel concerning the abomination spoken of in Daniel 9:27 and 12:1;

> "Therefore when you see the abomination of desolation which was spoken of through Daniel the prophet standing in the holy place (let the reader understand), then those who are in Judea must flee to the mountain. Whoever is on the housetop must not go down to get the things out that are in his house. Whoever is in the field must not turn back to get his cloak... (v.21) For then there shall be a great tribulation such as has not occurred since the beginning of the world until now, nor ever will. Unless those days had been cut short, no life would have been saved."

Christ then assures the disciples that it will culminate in the glorious return of Christ to rule over the whole world in truth and righteousness for 1,000 years (Mt. 24:29-31; Lk. 21:27-28; Rev. 11:15; 19:6; 20:6).

"And its end will come with a flood; even to the end there will be war; desolations are determined." The Hebrew word, *shetef,* means a gushing overflow of water (Job 38:25, Pr. 27:4, Ps. 32:6). In Nahum 1:8 it is used to describe the outpouring of God's wrath and also vividly describes the 70 AD devastation of Jerusalem. God's wrath abides on Jerusalem as she continues to reject her God ordained prince of peace. God's wrath will be poured out on the coming prince; the Antichrist. Daniel 7:25-27 predicts that Antichrist (the little horn) makes war against God and His people right up till the second coming of Christ: The end of the 490 years (Showers, 128). Jesus confirms this in Matthew 24:6-7. God ordains the desolations in order to bring stubborn rebellious Israel to repentance through her Messiah, Yeshua Hamoshiakh (Jesus Christ).

The Jews have faced much tribulation from the beginning. They were callously and cruelly enslaved by ancient Egypt and ruled over by many nations in the book of Judges. The northern kingdom was conquered and uprooted by Assyria, the 8th century BC Nazis. Judah was conquered and uprooted by Babylon. Haman came close to destroying the Jews (Esther 3-9). Antiochus severely persecuted them and Rome devastated the Jews in 70 AD. They were scattered all over the world and mistreated by virtually all the nations they were driven to. (Eduard Flannery documents the difficulties of the Jews in his book, *The Misery of the Jew*). They were driven from one country to another and made second class citizens of the *Christian lands* of Europe. Hitler and Nazi Germany slaughtered 6,000,000 Jews: 2/3 of Europe's Jews and 1/3 of the world's Jewish population. The many tribulations of the Jews have been great but they will be pale compared to the future one of Daniel 12:1 and prophesied by Christ in Matthew 24:21.

The tribulation Jesus warns about corresponds with the 3 1/2- year tribulation in Revelation 11:2; 12:6; 12:14; 13:5, and Daniel 12:1-7. He said that the time would be shortened because otherwise no flesh will be saved (24:22).

> "Immediately after the tribulation of those days the sun will be darkened and the moon will not give its light, and the stars will fall from the sky, and the powers of the heavens will be shaken. And then the sign of the Son of Man will appear in the sky, and then all the tribes of the earth will mourn and they will see the SON OF MAN COMING ON THE CLOUDS OF THE SKY with power and great glory" (Mt. 24:29-30).

This is Revelation 11:15, 19:11, Daniel 7:13-14, 27 and the stone's crushing the earth's kingdoms to powder in Daniel 2:35.

Divine covenants

The covenants of God and Christ are everlasting (Ps. 105:10, Ez. 16:60; 37:26, Jer. 32:40; Isa 61:8). Nowhere in Scripture do we find God making terminal ones like the 7-year covenant in 9:27. Those who insist that the 458 or 457 BC edict is the edict to rebuild Jerusalem also teach that the coming prince is also Messiah the prince who makes the 7-year covenant with Israel. Messiah stops the sacrifices 3 1/2 years later in the middle of the 7-year period as He offers Himself as the supreme sacrifice. (The temple sacrifices were not stopped after Christ's death but continued until the destruction of the temple in 70 AD). The 490 years were completed 3 1/2 years later when Stephen was stoned.

This erroneous interpretation has to be firmly and completely rejected because it makes Christ the initiator of the abomination of desolation which He specifically warns us to be aware of (Mt. 24:15-21). This is utterly absurd! Stupid! Ridiculous!

There is no record of Christ ever making any kind of agreement with the Jewish leaders! They hated and rejected Him and plotted His death from the beginning and throughout His ministry (Mt. 12:14, Mk.3:6, Lk. 4:29, Jn. 5:18; 7:1; 8:40-59; 10:31). He boldly exposed their hypocrisy and wickedness (Mt. 23) and declared they were snakes (Mt. 23:33) and children of the devil (Jn. 8:42-44). If Christ wanted a covenant with Israel He certainly would have been far more conciliatory with the Jewish leaders and never make such a public scene at the beginning of His ministry (John 2:13-22).

Christ had absolutely no desire to flatter these very miserable, corrupt, wicked leaders of apostate Israel. Therefore it's impossible for the coming prince to be Christ! The coming prince is Antichrist! Unlike Christ Antichrist will freely flatter Israel as he makes the covenant with Israel and causes the abomination of desolation that Christ warns the disciples to be aware of (Mt.24:15).

Messiah the Prince and the coming prince are 180-degree opposites! Messiah the prince is the Hebrew prince of Life who gives His life as a sacrifice for Israel and all mankind (Isa. 53:8, Jn. 10:10-18; 11:49-52, Romans 5:6-8). The coming prince is the Roman prince of death who seeks to exploit and destroy Israel and mankind for his own selfish benefit (Daniel 7:25, Zech. 11:16, Jn. 10:10, Rev. 13).

Woodrow Kroll, former Bible teacher on the Back to the Bible broadcast of Lincoln, Nebraska told of a time he was leading a tour on a bus in Israel. He emphasized the Scriptural truth that the shepherd gently and tenderly leads the sheep and never drives them.

While shocked and embarrassed he saw a "shepherd" mercilessly driving the sheep by beating their rearends with his staff. He got off the bus and told the shepherd, "I tell the people that the shepherd gently leads the sheep and never drives them like you are doing. What kind of shepherd are you? Why do you do beat and drive the sheep?"

The "shepherd" answered. "You are right. The shepherd gently and tenderly leads the sheep and never drives them as I am doing. I am not the shepherd. I'm the butcher."

"The thief (Satan, the butcher) comes only to steal, kill, and destroy but I (Jesus) come to bring abundant life" (Jn. 10:10)

A 2,000–year gap in prophecy?

There is obviously a gap of about 2,000 or more years between the 69th and the 70th 7-year period of Daniel. That seems strange since the 2nd 7-year period immediately follows the 1st and the 3rd immediately follows the 2nd etc. but the 70th 7-year period does NOT immediately follow the 69th. Why do we have this gap in this prophecy since all the other time prophecies have no gaps? Why do we interpret this prophecy this strange way?

There are no gaps in other time prophecies but there are many gaps in prophecies. Isaiah 9:6 states that a child will be born (1st coming) and that the government will upon His shoulders (2nd coming). Zechariah 9:9-10 states that Israel's king comes in humility riding a donkey (1st coming) and his dominion will be all over the earth (2nd coming). In Psalm 2:6-8 Messiah the King is installed on Mt. Zion (2nd coming), formally begotten by God (1ˢᵗ coming), and rules them with a rod of iron (2ⁿᵈ coming). Isaiah 35:4-6 says, "Take courage, fear not. Behold your God will come with vengeance" (2ⁿᵈ coming)... "Then the eyes of the blind will be opened and the ears of deaf be unstopped. Then the lame will leap like a deer. And the tongue of the mute will shout for joy" (1ˢᵗ coming). Isaiah 11:1-3 tells us that an offspring of Jesse would have the Spirit of wisdom, understanding, counsel, and strength and knowledge of the fear of the LORD. He would judge fairly (1ˢᵗ coming) and in verse 4 He will strike the earth with the rod of His mouth and with His breath slay the wicked" (second coming). Verses 6-10 prophesy of the animal kingdom being at peace after the second coming of Christ.

The best illustration of a gap in prophecy is Isaiah 61:1-2. One Sabbath in the synagogue Jesus quotes these verses in Luke 4:18 but stops in the middle of the 2ⁿᵈ verse after reading, "to proclaim the favorable year of the LORD." He handed the scroll back the attendant and told the crowd that, "Today this Scripture is fulfilled in your hearing." As you read Isaiah 61:1-2 you will see that Christ did not quote, "and the day of vengeance of our God: To comfort all who mourn" for obvious reasons. He came the first time neither to proclaim the day of vengeance nor to comfort <u>all</u> who mourn (Jn. 3:17). Christ proclaims the day of vengeance at His second coming. He takes vengeance on all who don't obey the gospel (2 Thess. 1:8, Isa. 34:8; 35:4, Micah 5:15, Nahum 1:2).

While living in Glennallen, Alaska in 1970 I saw 2 high mountains east of Glennallen "next to each other": Mt. Drum, 12,010 feet high (3661 meters) and Mt. Wrangell, 14,163 feet high (4317 meters). From Glennallen Mt. Drum appeared higher than Mt. Wrangell as it is 25 miles from my place while Mt. Wrangell is about 40 miles away. Though appearing to be next to each other, they were not. I was unable to see the 15 mile gap between them. The Hebrew prophets saw and understood the 2 mountains of Messiah's comings to be together. They did not see the 2,000+ year gap between them (Eph. 3:1-12, 1 Peter 1:10-12). Just as all the prophecies concerning the first coming have been literally fulfilled; we can rest assured that all the prophecies concerning the 2ⁿᵈ advent will also be literally fulfilled. Dale Crowley in his book, *The Soon Coming of Our Lord*, says it so well:

The 2 comings of Christ: A contrast

When Christ comes the second time, it shall not be as it was on His first advent.

He came the first time to die in the sinner's place. He is coming the second time to execute judgment on the sinner.

He came the first time to seek and to save that which was lost. He is coming the second time "in flaming fire to execute judgment on all them that know not God."

He came the first time to be man's representative before a God of love and grace. He is coming the second time as God's representative against a rebellious world.

He came the first time in great humility. He is coming the second time in great power and glory.

He came the first time to be the lowly Nazarene; He is coming the second time as the King of kings and Lord of lords.

He came the first time to be "despised and rejected of men." He is coming the second time to be acknowledged by all, both high and low, rich and poor, bond and free.

He came the first time to ride the lowly ass into Jerusalem. He is coming the second time to ride the great white horse, leading the armies of heaven.

He came the first time to submit to the unjust judgment of earthly potentates. He is coming the second time to compel all earthly rulers to yield their scepters to Him.

He came the first time to shed His blood on a cross. He is coming again as the mighty Conqueror whose "'vesture is dipped in blood."

He came the first time to save men from a devil's hell. He comes the second time to say to all the workers of iniquity, "Depart ye into everlasting fire prepared for the devil and his angels."

Showers' concluding remarks on Chapter 9

Dr. Renald Showers wrote an excellent commentary on the book of Daniel, *The Most High God*. His concluding comments on Daniel 9 are well worth reading.

> The new revelation delivered by Gabriel offered Daniel the twofold prospect of despair and hope. Jerusalem would be rebuilt with its defenses after the Babylonian captivity, but that would not be the end of Israel's troubles. In spite of the fact that this prophecy informed Israel of the exact time when Messiah would be present to present Himself as Prince to the nation, the Jews would have Him put to death. As a result of their rejection of the Messiah in the His first coming, Israel would miss the opportunity of lasting peace at that time and would bring upon itself many more desolations including the destruction of Jerusalem and the Temple by Antichrist, the last Roman ruler. Once all the chastening which God had decreed for Israel and Jerusalem would run its course, then Israel would return to God forever and experience blessing. Ultimately there would be blessing, but Israel would have to experience a long time (including 490 decreed years) of chastening to reach that blessing.

In light of the revelation in Daniel 9, it can be concluded that Israel's present independence and possession of Jerusalem is only a temporary lull in what is to be the norm for that nation and city until the end of the 490 years. In essence, it is calm before the worst storm that Israel will ever experience. Jesus said that Jerusalem will be trampled under foot by the Gentiles until the times of the Gentiles will be fulfilled (Lk. 21:24). Daniel 2 and 7 indicated that those times will not be fulfilled until the second coming of Christ. (Showers, p. 137).

Dear reader, are you ready for Christ's second coming? Dr. Jeremiah states that there are 1845 prophecies in the Bible on Christ's 2nd coming; outnumbering the prophecies on His 1st coming 8-1 (devotional: March 22, 2012). Accept Christ's sacrifice freely offered for you, me, and all mankind at His first coming and you will be ready to share in the glory of His second coming (2Tim. 2:12). A special reward is given to all who eagerly await Christ's coming (2 Tim. 4:8).

9B

The Fullness of Time

In Galatians 4:4 Apostle Paul declares, "But when the fullness of time came, God sent forth is Son..." The "fullness of time" is rich with meaning. Alexander made Greek the common spoken language of the ancient world which made it easy to communicate the gospel all over the empire. The Romans built a great network of paved roads, bridges, aqueducts, and tunnels throughout the empire thus making it easy for travel throughout the empire. Many of these are still being used today. With their very severe penalty for crime Rome also made travel safe.

The following information is gleamed from Barry Settlefield, an Australian astronomer (http.//settlefield.org)

The message of chapter 9 was given to Daniel while he was in Babylon and preserved in Persia. It reveals when the *fullness of time* would come.

Daniel was held in high esteem in the Persian Court. The Parthian Dynasty of the Persian Empire east of Judea was ruled by 2 houses called the Megistanes. They are equivalent to the US Senate and the US House of Representatives of the US Congress. The lower house members were called *Sophoi* or "Wise ones": The upper house members were called *Magoi*, "Great Ones." The *Magoi* (translated "Magi" in Matthew 2:1) understood Daniel 9:24-27 and calculated that Israel's king messiah would be revealed about 32 AD in the midst of His years (about 35). They backtracked 35 years from 32 AD and calculated that He would be born about 3-2 BC and so at that time they follow the star that leads them to Jerusalem.

King Herod freely murdered his wives, children, and anyone for the slightest suspicion of treason. Roman Emperor Augustus declared that it was far safer to be Herod's pig rather than his son because Herod was too religious to eat pigs.

Matthew 2:3 records that Herod and all Jerusalem were greatly troubled when the Magi arrived. Why were fierce cruel Herod and the whole city troubled when 3 old men came into Jerusalem riding camels? The answer is simple. These *magoi* (magi) were NOT 3 old men riding camels. They were crack cavalry units of the Persian army of the Parthian Dynasty from the east. Judea was a buffer between them and the Roman Empire. These fierce horsemen could pen down the Romans indefinitely and usually won when they clashed with the Romans. They successfully defied the Romans as they penetrated 750 km into the empire to worship the king of the Jews. It's therefore no wonder that Herod and all Jerusalem were upset. His army was away fighting the Homonadensian War, thus leaving Jerusalem undefended and very vulnerable. Augustus declared Herod to be king of the Jews and so understandably he was very disturbed when he learned that the magi were looking for another king of the Jews. The Magi understood that the king of the Jews would be born in Jerusalem, the capital of Judea and so they arrive at Herod's palace.

Josephus declared that Herod died before Passover and shortly after a lunar eclipse that could be seen in Jericho. The Jews celebrated his death on Shebat 2, 1 BC which came 15 days after the eclipse. Since the eclipse happened on January 9, 1 BC we calculate Herod's death on January 24, 1 BC.

Shepherds watched the sheep in the open fields in the spring and autumn when they give birth to lambs. In other times of the year they were kept in the sheep-folds in order to protect them from wild animals and harsh weather. The flocks bred in Bethlehem were used in the temple sacrifices. Significantly Christ, the Lamb of God (Jn. 1:29, 36) was probably born in late September, 3 BC when the shepherds were in the fields watching over the birth of lambs (Luke 2:8). The bread of life (Jn. 6:35) was born in the *house of bread* (Hebrew: Bethlehem).

The magi visited Christ probably 15 months after His birth (near December 25) and brought the precious gifts of gold, frankincense, and myrrh. The Persians controlled the silk route to China and India and therefore brought the most valuable items available. These king makers from the east proclaimed Christ as king as valuable metals like gold were given from one monarch to another. Frankincense was used in temple worship services and so Christ is also proclaimed priest. Myrrh is used to anoint dead bodies. This signifies that Christ would offer Himself as the sacrifice for our sins (Heb. 9:14). These gifts no doubt supported the family after they fled into Egypt.

Wow! We believers in Yeshua Hamoshiakh (Jesus Christ) shout again, "Halleluyah! What a Savior!" Christ rules as king in our lives by stooping down to minister to our needs (Jn. 13:12-17, Mt. 11:28-30). As our high priest He offers Himself as a sacrifice for our sins (Heb. 9:11-15).

Obviously our savior was not born on December 25 but He possibly started His life in the womb of Virgin Mary about that time (Lk. 1:26-38). Therefore let's celebrate Christ's incarnation, birth, sinless life, sacrificial death, resurrection, and return (Ps. 2:9, Rev. 19:11-16) not on Christmas Day and Easter only but every day of the year! We cheerfully obey Christ's instructions in Matthew 10:8. "Freely you have received, freely give."

10

Interlude between Asking and Receiving

Daniel received this final revelation in 536 BC; 2 years after the Babylonian captivity ended. This chapter introduces us to the detailed prophecies for Israel in chapter 11 and 12 on up to the second coming of Christ.

Daniel fasted and prayed for 3 weeks. His prayer was immediately heard in Heaven but the answer was delayed because of spiritual warfare (v.12). The demonic prince of Persia tried to stop the angel from carrying the answer to Daniel but with Archangel Michael's help, the answer got through (v. 13).

Like Daniel, we who are in Christ are greatly beloved (Eph. 1:6). Our prayers are registered in Heaven the moment we pray but answers are many times delayed because of the severe spiritual warfare going on in the heavens. That is why Christ tells us in Matthew 7:7-8 to continue to ask, seek, and knock and then the request will be granted. Paul tells us not to be discouraged in doing what is right because in due season we will reap if we faint not (Gal. 6:9). "Those who wait hopefully for me will not be put to shame" (Isa.49:23, Ps.25:2-3, 27:14. 37:34, 40:1-2, 62:5-6, 147:11, Isa.30:18, 40:31, 64:4).

Isaac was married when he was 40 but waited 20 years before the Lord answered his request for a child (Genesis 25:20-26). Yahweh tells Habakkuk (2:3), "For the vision is for the appointed time; it hastens toward the goal and it will not fail. Though it tarries, wait for it. For it will certainly come and it will not delay." Moses' earnest desire to enter

Canaan was temporarily denied (Nu. 20:8-12, Dt. 3:23-27; 32:48-52) but ultimately granted (Mt. 17:3). God's delays are not God's denials.

Another example of God acting immediately but with delayed results is Joshua 3 when Israel crosses the Jordan River. The priests carried the Ark of the Covenant and led Israel across the Jordan River on dry ground. The ark was used to dry up the river just as Moses' staff was used to lead Israel through the Red Sea (Ex. 14:15-18). The priests were instructed to "stand still" as soon as they entered the edge of the Jordan River (Jos. 3:8). When the priests entered the Jordan the flowing waters stopped and stood at a heap or mound near Zarethen and Adam; about 30 miles upstream (v.6). The water was immediately cut off 30 miles upstream but it still flowed where the priest entered the Jordan. Its flow became less and less until the water was gone and so all Israel crossed over the river (v. 17). The priests did not see where the water was cut off but they exercised faith as they stood at the edge of the river and watched it dry up as they led Israel over the Jordan on dry ground.

In John 11:1-6, Christ got word that His dear friend, Lazarus was sick. Instead of immediately rushing to his aid He stayed where He was for 2 days. Martha was somewhat disillusioned and irritated because He "dragged His feet." She knew that no one could die in the presence of the Prince of Life and so she could not understand why Christ did not immediately come and heal him and prevent his death. Christ wanted the people to see the glory of God as He demonstrated His power over death by raising Lazarus from the grave. This gave Christ the opportunity to proclaim the rich truth in 11:25-26;

> "I am the resurrection and the life; he who believes in Me will live even if he dies, and everyone who lives and believes in Me will never die."

Mary and Martha, like Daniel learned that God's delays are not God's denials.

Henry Holloman lists 7 requirements for a successful prayer life. It is necessary to have a pure heart and faith (Ps. 66:18, Js. 1:5-8), be obedient (I Jn. 3:22), abide in Christ (Jn. 15:7), glorify God (I Cor. 10:31), have a desire to mature in Christ (2 Peter 3:18), and pray in the Holy Spirit (Eph. 6:18). Let's make sure that we fulfill these requirements in our prayer life so that delays come only because of spiritual warfare (Swindoll, *Daniel, God's Plan for the Future*, Vol. 2, p. 62).

After praying and fasting for 3 weeks an awesome supernatural being appeared and Daniel trembled with fear (10:5-9). The majestic description of this man is basically identical to the description of Jesus Christ in Revelation 1:13-16. Some commentaries declare that this man is Jesus Christ but there is a problem. The Persian prince prevented this being from bringing the answer to Daniel for 3 weeks. He could bring the answer only after receiving help from Archangel Michael. Since Jesus Christ is Sovereign how could an evil prince delay His mission to Daniel and why would He need Michael's help? A possible answer is that God sometimes sovereignly chooses to limit His sovereignty for His sovereign purposes. God could have destroyed Satan right after his rebellion but chose not to. Christ freely chose to live in the womb of Mary for 9 months and be born a helpless babe in Bethlehem, He permitted Satan to tempt Him during His 40-day fast and allowed sinful men to torture and crucify Him on wood coming from a tree He created. He accepted angelic help after the temptation (Mt. 4:11) and in Gethsemane (Lk. 22:43). He will receive angelic help at His 2nd coming (Mt. 13:41-43; 49-50; 24:30-31, Rev. 19:14).

Like Apostle Paul's friends who became as dead men when confronted by the glorified Christ (Acts 9:7), Daniel's friends became so frightened that they ran away and hid (v. 7). Daniel's strength left him as his natural appearance turned to "deathly pallor" and fainted with his face to the ground (v. 8-9). Like John in Revelation 1:17, Daniel received reassurance as this supernatural being told him not to fear (v. 10-12). In verse 19 we see this supernatural being encouraging Daniel with, "O man of high esteem, do not be afraid! Peace be with you; take courage and be courageous." Daniel immediately received his strength.

11

Detailed History in Advance

Introduction

In his excellent commentary of the book of Daniel (The *Handwriting on the Wall*, p.215) Dr. Jeremiah tells the following very shocking story.

> A professor at a liberal theological seminary was teaching from the book of Daniel…At the beginning of his lecture he said, "Now I want you to understand that Daniel was written during the Maccabean period in the second century B.C., not by the historic Daniel who lived in the sixth century B.C. The facts were written as all history is, after the events took place."
>
> One young man raised his hand and asked, "How can that be, sir, when Christ said in Matthew 24:15 that it was written by Daniel?"
>
> The professor paused a moment, looked the student in the eyes and said, "Young man, I know more about Daniel than Jesus did."

Wow! How "blessed" we are to have modern enlightened liberal professors who, "know more about Daniel than Jesus did." Even if a pseudo-Daniel wrote the book about 150 BC, liberals still have problems because it still predicts the exact day when Messiah is revealed to Israel (April 6, 32 AD) and the Roman destruction of Jerusalem and its temple. How would our "enlightened professor" explain that?

Another modern "enlightened" liberal preacher decided to "expose the myths of Scripture" as he told the congregation "what really happened to Jonah". He said that the message of Jonah is a good allegory about the importance of following God but that the events described there could not have happened because, "it's impossible to live for 3 days and 3 nights in a fish." A distraught listener confronted the preacher and said, "The Bible says that Jonah was swallowed by a great fish and we should believe it." The preacher asked, "Can you explain how a man can live for 72 hours in a fish?" She answered, "No, but when I get to Heaven I'll ask Jonah how he did it." The preacher asked, "What if he's not there?" She answered, "Then you can ask him."

Christ obviously believed in the authenticity of Jonah (Mt.12:39-40, Lk. 11:29) as well as Daniel and we should believe it too.

Another "enlightened" liberal theologian declared that Moses led Israel through the Red Sea when the water was only 3 inches deep. Someone shouted, "Halleluyah! Pharaoh's army drowned in 3 inches of water!"

Back to the Bible is an excellent radio broadcast originating in Lincoln, Nebraska. USA. Dr. Woodrow Kroll, the former host, gave a very interesting lesson on February 21, 2006 from Jericho. He told the story of the fall of Jericho under Joshua and he quotes Joshua's strong warning in 6:26:

> "Cursed before the LORD is the man who rises up and builds this city Jericho; with the loss of his firstborn he shall lay its foundation, and with the loss of his youngest son he shall set up its gates."

Over 500 years later Hiel tried to rebuild Jericho but he paid the price that Joshua declared would be paid (I Kings 16:34).

Dr. Kroll interviewed Avid, his Arab friend and guide. Avid's father was the first mayor of Jericho and his mother was a midwife who delivered over 35,000 babies. Avid is the second oldest in his family. The oldest son was healthy but mysteriously and unexpectedly died as a baby. His parents could not understand why. 70 other normal healthy babies died mysteriously and unexpectedly and no one understood why. After Avid read the story of Joshua's curse on Jericho he realized that his father built an apartment inside the ancient *cursed* city of Jericho. Other people also built apartments inside the ancient city and 70 healthy first-born babies mysteriously died. These residents found out the hard way that even in the 20th and 21st century this ancient curse of Joshua is still in effect. Always remember that we can always trust God's Word!

According to Donald Campbell, over 134 detailed prophecies in Daniel 11:1-35 have been literally fulfilled and are now history (Swindoll, *Daniel*, Vol. 2, p. 69). God is omniscient (Ps. 139:1-4; 94:11; 147:5, Pr. 24:12, Isa. 46:10) and is quite capable of revealing the detailed history of Daniel 11 in advance. The prophecies are so detailed that modern "enlightened" liberal theologians have decided that Daniel did not really write the book. Instead a deceitful historian wrote this "fraud" after the events happened and decided to ascribe it to Daniel. I do not need to defend the authenticity of Daniel or even the Bible no more than I need to defend a lion. Daniel, like a lion is fully capable of defending itself. Since Jesus Christ obviously believed it to be genuine (Mt. 24:15) we need to accept it too. Messianic Rabbi Robert Solomon of Beth Hallel Synagogue of Roswell, Ga. declared, "If you have a reservation on Scripture; the devil has a reservation for you." It's very dangerous to reject what Yeshua (Jesus Christ) accepts!

Two men were watching a cowboy movie. One said to the other, "I bet you $10 that this man will fall off the horse". The second man said, "Ok I accept the bet." Sure enough the man fell off the horse. The second man felt distraught as he pulled out his wallet to give the other the $10 he had just won but the first man's conscience bothered him and said, "I can't take the money. It's not fair because I saw the movie earlier and therefore knew he would fall off the horse." The second man replied, "Oh, its ok. I also saw the movie but I thought this time he had learned his lesson and be more careful and not fall off the horse again."

All history from Adam to the end of the millennium is on God's video and He's perfectly able to reveal it. John Calvin takes 40 pages explaining the first section (11:1-19) which covers the events up to Antiochus Epiphanes. Barnes uses 50 pages explaining the details of chapter 11. In addition to Calvin and Barnes, there are other good commentaries covering the details of these events. I will give only a brief superficial overview of these events.

Never Ending War

While teaching English in Korea I learned that China and Japan were in constant warfare. Each ran over Korea as they conquered each other. Japan cruelly occupied and exploited Korea from 1910-1945. The US and USSR callously divided Korea after the war and continues to remain divided. Korea has received a difficult history but today sends out more foreign Christian missionaries than any other nation except the US. Percentage wise Korea sends more than the US.

Israeli history is similar to Korean history. The king of the north (Syria) and the king of the south (Egypt) constantly fight each other and run over Israel in the process.

The 3 Persian kings of verse 2 are Cambyses, Smerdis, and Darius Hystaspis. In 480 BC after 4 years of preparation, Xerxes, the 4th Persian king invaded Greece with his abundant riches and 5,000,000 troops. (Barnes 208-209). The mighty king of verse 3 is Alexander who took revenge on Persia 150 years after Xerxes' failed attempts to conquer Greece. Virtually all of Alexander's relatives were murdered (Boice, 112) and so there was no descendant available to take the throne after his death (v. 4). His kingdom was therefore divided by his 4 generals. Starting with verse 5 special attention is given to 2 of the 4 divisions that directly affect Israel: The king of the North (Syria) and the king of the South (Egypt). The land of Israel was continually ravaged and devastated in the long bloody wars between these 2 powers as each side trampled down Israel as they invaded each other.

In order to have peace with Syria the Egyptian king gives his daughter, Berenice, in marriage to Antiochus, the king of the North (v. 6). He is required to first divorce his wife, Laodice. After the death of Ptolemy Philidelphus, the king of the South, Antiochus divorced Berenice and remarries Laodice, his first wife who killed her husband for his fickleness. Berenice and her children were also put to death and her brother, Ptolemy Energetes, (Benefactor) avenged her death by attacking Syria and looting the temples as described in verse 8 (Barnes, 213).

In verse 11 Ptolemy invaded Syria with 70,000 foot soldiers, 5,000 cavalry, and 73 elephants. He defeated Antiochus who had 62,000 foot soldiers, 6,000 cavalry, and 102 elephants. Ptolemy was not strengthened by the victory because it caused the victor's heart to be lifted up in arrogant pride as tens of thousands were slain (v. 13). He failed to exploit the victory because of his love of pleasure, luxury, and his irresponsible lifestyle. This caused the people to rebel against him.

In 203 BC, Antiochus, the Syrian king invaded Egypt and the wars continue (Barnes 217-218). Many join the invasion including Philip of Macedon, Egyptian rebels, and "The robbers of the people" (rebellious Jews). The Jews support Antiochus, hoping to get an independent kingdom but fail (JFB, 445). Antiochus does what he wants to do as he brings Israel completely under his control and desolates the land of Israel (v. 16). In 17 Antiochus gives his daughter, Cleopatra I to Ptolemy in marriage in order to secure Egypt's neutrality in his war with Rome and if possible even to conquer Egypt. The plan backfired as Cleopatra became loyal to her husband instead of her father (v. 17). Antiochus conquered many Greek isles but Roman General Lucius Scipio Asiaticus defeated him in 190 BC at Magnesia. He was slain trying to loot the temple of Jupiter (JFB p. 446).

His son, Seleucus Philopator gathered taxes and claimed the throne. He dispatched Heliodorus to loot Yahweh's temple. Heliodorus poisoned Seleucus 12 years later as Heliodorus tried to secure the throne for Demetrius; Seleucus' only son and heir. God used Heliodorus to slay Seleucus; the same instrument Seleucus used to desecrate the temple (v. 20, Zech. 9:8)

In 175 BC, Antiochus Epiphanes deceitfully used flattery to usurp the throne from Demetrius, the rightful heir. He feigned peaceful intentions with the Egyptian king and possessed Memphis and all the other rich places of Egypt. Only Alexandria successfully resisted. The conquest was easy because Ptolemy Philometor was betrayed by his ministers and guardians (v. 26). The 2 leaders lie to each other (v. 27) as Antiochus accomplished what his fathers could not do (v. 24). On his return to Syria, he took revenge on the Jews as they were celebrating his death.

Antiochus' 2nd invasion of Egypt was not successful. The ships of Khittem (Greek Isles, referring to Rome) frustrate his adventures there as explained in chapter 8. This culminates into the abomination of desolation of verse 31.

Judas Maccabeus

In 11:32 we read that Antiochus seduced many Jews to abandon their faith with his smooth words (Ps. 5:9; 55:21, Pro. 26:24-28, Jer. 9:8) but, "the people who know their God will display strength and take action." The exciting story of the bravery of Judas Maccabeus, his brothers, and the Jews in their successful guerrilla warfare against Antiochus with a "little help" (11:34) is the fulfillment of this prophecy. Judas took as the motto of his standard the initial letters of the Hebrew sentence from Exodus 15:11, *Mi Kamokha Baelim, Yahweh* "Who is like unto thee Yahweh, among the gods?" (JFB p.449). The story is in I Maccabees 2.

Mattathias, a Jewish priest from the village of Modin, had five sons: John, Simon, Judas Maccabeus, Eleazar, and Jonathan. Antiochus' men came to Modin to compel the Jews to sacrifice to the Greek gods as the king had ordered. They wanted Mattathias to set a good example and be the first to sacrifice, knowing his fellow citizens would follow. Mattathias and his family were offered the king's friendship and lots of gold and silver if he obeyed. Verses 19-22a gives Mattathias' heroic reaction.

> Then Mattathias answered and spoke with a loud voice, "Thou of all the nations that under the king's dominion obey him and fall away from the religion of their fathers, and give consent to his commandments: Yet I and my sons and brothers walk in the covenant of our fathers. God forbid that we should forsake the law and the ordinances. We will not hearken to the king's words."

When another Jew came forward and sacrificed as Antiochus commanded, Mattathias and his sons killed the man, the king's officer, and his soldiers. They overturned the pagan altar and Mattathias cried out, "Whoever is zealous for the laws of our country and worship of God, let him follow me" (v. 27).

Mattathias and his sons fled to the mountains and commenced guerilla warfare. Many others followed with their wives and children and lived there in caves. The Jews did not resist the Syrians when they burned them inside their caves on the Sabbath day. They even refused to block the mouths of the caves, and about 1,000 suffered. Mattathias directed them to fight on the Sabbath in order to survive.

Mattathias and his men destroyed the pagan altars, killed those who had sacrificed on them, and circumcised all their boys. He got ill and urged his sons to continue the struggle he had begun. He appointed Judas as their leader because of his courage and strength and Simon as adviser. He told them in verse 62, "Fear not then the words of sinful men: for his glory shall be dung and worms." He died and was buried in Modin, where he was greatly mourned by the people (v. 70).

Judas Maccabeus, his brothers, and followers, "fought with cheerfulness the battle of Israel" (3:2) and drove the enemy from the country. Though greatly outnumbered, Judas defeated and killed Apollonius, the governor of Samaria and Seron, the governor of Coele-Syria,

Judas proclaims in verse 19, "For the victory of battle stands not in the multitude of the host; but strength comes from heaven." In verses 38-39 Ptolemee led the Syrians against Judas with 40,000 infantry and 7,000 cavalry. Judas urged his army to be bold and put their trust in God even though he had only 3,000 poorly armed men left (4:8). Even though Ptolemee was helped by Jewish traitors as guides, Judas humiliated him with his skillful maneuvers and strategy. They got scared and fled when they saw their camp destroyed (4:14).

In 4:28 Antiochus' general, Lysias, invaded Judah with an army of 60,000 infantry and 5,000 cavalry. Judas met him with 10,000 and prayed (v. 30), "Blessed art thou savior of Israel, who did quell the violence of the mighty men by your servant David." He asked for God's help and killed about 5,000 (v. 34). "Now when Lysias saw his army put to flight and the manliness of Judas' soldiers and how they were ready to either to live or die valiantly, he went to Antiochin..." (v.35). He prepared to invade again with an even larger army.

Judas gave glory and thanks to God for these victories and went to Jerusalem to purify the desecrated temple and offer sacrifices. He rebuilt the altar and restored the sacred implements. Incense was rekindled on the lamp-stand exactly three years after Antiochus desecrated the temple (Kislev 25. 168 BC- Kislev 25, 165 BC). Judas and his men celebrated this great festival of lights, or dedication (Hanukkah) for 8 days. They "offered burnt offerings with gladness, and sacrificed the deliverance of praise"

(4:56). There was only enough oil to light the Hanukkah lamp for 1 day but miraculously the oil lasted 8 days. Jesus was at the temple during the Feast of Dedication indicating that He also observed it (Jn. 10:22). Today Jews continue to observe it.

Judas again defeated the enemy and rebuilt the walls of Jerusalem. His brother Simon defeated the invaders of Galilee while Judas and his brother Jonathan attacked Gilead and their enemies in Idumea, Hebron, and Ashdod.

Matthew Henry in his commentary gives a very vivid detailed description of Antiochus' death (p. 1450). Antiochus would not be assassinated or killed by any human means but supernaturally. He,

> Shall fall into the hand of the living God and die by an immediate stroke of his vengeance. He hearing that the Jews had cast the image of Jupiter Olympus out of the temple, where he had placed it was so enraged at the Jews that he vowed he would make Jerusalem a common burial- place, and determined to march thither immediately; but no sooner had he spoken these proud words than he was struck with an incurable plague in his vowels; worms bred so fast in his body that whole flakes of flesh sometimes dropped from him; His torments were violent, and the stench of disease such that none could endure to come near him. He continued in his misery very long. At first he persisted in his ... (evil desires) against the Jews' but ...despairing of his recovery, he called his friends together, and acknowledged all those miseries to have fallen on him for the injuries he had done to the Jews and his profaning the temple in Jerusalem.... When he could no longer endure his own smell he said, 'It is meet to submit to God and for man who is mortal not to set himself in competition with God' and so died miserably in a strange land on the mountains of Pacata, near Babylon.

After the death of Antiochus IV his son, Antiochus V became king. Judas had to continue to fight the Syrians. He and his 2,000 men slaughtered 9,000 attacking Syrians. When another 20,000 attacked him all but 800 of his army fled because of fear. When encouraged to do the same thing Judas replied,

> May the sun never see me turn my back on the enemy: I would
> rather die in this battle than tarnish my honor.

He broke the ranks of the right wing but many from the left wing chased and surrounded him. He fought bravely killing many but died of exhaustion. He was buried in Modin in much public mourning by his brothers, Jonathan and Simon (Maier, p. 214).

Many Jewish and Christian theologians believe that there is a gap of time between verses 35 and 36. The prophecies through 35 have been fulfilled but the remaining ones have not. The king in verse 36 seems to refer to the end time Antichrist, the man of sin and lawlessness (2 Thes, 2:3-4, Dan. 7:25, Rev. 13:5-6). He shows no regard for all other gods or for the desire of women. This possibly means that he does not have the normal masculine physical desire for women, or he freely massacres women and children like other conquerors, but it probably has another meaning. The desire of virtually every woman living before Christ was to be the mother of Messiah (Gen, 3:15). Since the angel is talking about objects of worship, it seems likely that he is talking about Messiah, the desire of women. Antichrist has no regard for Messiah as he is only interested in glory for himself. Like Lucifer he magnifies himself above everyone including Yahweh and His Son (Isa. 14:12-15).

Antichrist is ultimate man achieving deity through his own efforts. Man was created on the 6th day of the week and so a trinity of man is made from his day of his creation (666); a fitting symbol of Antichrist (Rev. 13:18). Like the doom of Antiochus Epiphanes, the doom of Antichrist is certain (v. 45; Rev. 19:20).

12

The Triumph of Jesus Christ and Righteousness

In Dr. Jeremiah's book, *Agents of the Apocalypse*, (p. 127-128) he gives the following illustration that vividly demonstrates the triumph of Jesus Christ over Satan and evil.

> As a kid I loved missions Sundays, when missionaries on furlough brought special reports in place of a sermon...
>
> One day they told us, an enormous snake—much larger than a man slithered its way...into the kitchen of their simple home. Terrified, they ran outside and searched frantically for a local who might know what to do. A machete-wielding neighbor came to the rescue, calmly marching into the house and decapitating the snake with one clean chop.
>
> The neighbor reemerged triumphant and assured the missionaries that the reptile had been defeated. But there was a catch, he warned. It was going to take a while for the snake to realize it was dead.
>
> The snake's neurology and blood flow are such that it can take considerable time for it to stop moving even after decapitation. For the next several hours the missionaries were forced to wait outside while the snake thrashed about smashing furniture and flailing against walls and windows, wreaking havoc until its body finally understood that it no longer had a head...

On March 15, 1986 in Raburn County Georgia Sheriff Deputy Dan Page arrested a man who shot and wounded Page. After Deputy Page shot the man in the heart the man gave 6 shots from his gun.

Ripley's *Believe or Not* cartoon (World Jewish Review, May 13, 2015) told about a Chinese chef while preparing soup died in August, 2014 after being bitten by a cobra whose head was chopped off 20 minutes earlier.

These stories demonstrate Satan's situation today. At the cross and resurrection he was decapitated (Eph.1:22) but he can still cause terrific damage to mankind. Even though he's been shot in the heart he can shoot at you and me.

1Peter 5:8-9 informs us that Satan is a roaring lion seeking anyone to devour. I've seen many National Geographic documentaries with lions attacking their prey but I never saw a lion roar before attacking its prey. They quietly stalk the prey and suddenly attack it. Older male lions roar up wind from their prey in order to frighten them to run into the trap where the females kill them.

All things (including Satan) have been placed under Christ's feet (Eph. 1:22). Satan has been defeated but God allows him to roar and thrash. As we have been redeemed by the Lamb's blood we need not fear his wrath (Rev. 12:11).

Satan's doom was pronounced in the Garden of Eden (Ge. 3:15) as God proclaimed that the seed of the woman, Messiah would bruise the serpent's head. In the crucifixion and resurrection Satan has been thoroughly defeated and decapitated but like the snake in the story he does not know it and so he continues to thrash mankind. At Christ's second coming Satan's thrashing will cease as he's cast into the bottomless pit for 1,000 years (Rev. 20:1-3) and into the Lake of fire where he's "tormented day and night forever" (Rev. 20:10).

Chapter 12 begins with assurance to Israel that during her time of distress Archangel Michael, the guardian of Israel will stand up and deliver Israel. This is the Great Tribulation described by Christ in Matthew 24:21 (Jer. 30:7, Isa. 26:20). This is the final 3 1/2 years set aside for Israel. Satan through Antichrist is virtually given a blank check to fulfill his evil desires for Israel and the whole world. Two-thirds of Israel will perish but one-third will be refined and delivered (Romans 11:5, Zech. 13:8-9; 14:3-4).

The one-third that makes it through the tribulation is the, "all Israel" that will be saved in Romans 11:25-26.

In verse 2 we have the only place in the Old Testament that "everlasting life" is used and the first clear reference to the resurrection of both the righteous and the wicked (John 5:24-29, I Thess. 4:16, I Cor. 15, Rev. 20:3, 5-6). The multitude of the righteous are blessed with the calm, sweet slumber of rest (Rev. 14:13) in the dust of the earth and will rise to inherit everlasting life. The wicked will also rise to everlasting destruction (Ps. 9:5; 69:28, Rev.20:15). Revelation 20:4-6 teaches that there is a thousand-year gap between the resurrection of the righteous and the wicked. Those persecuted and martyred by Antiochus received great encouragement for faithful perseverance (JFB p. 454). Those who remain loyal to Yahweh and His Messiah and lead others to righteousness will, "shine as the stars forever" (v. 3).

Unlike the instructions given to Apostle John in Revelation 1:1-3, Daniel is instructed to seal the book till the end of time (v. 4). Perhaps the angel wanted to prevent any premature zeal for the fulfillment of this prophecy after the captivity.

Many will be "running back and forth and knowledge will increase." Sir Isaac Newton, a Jewish believer in Yeshua and probably the greatest scientist of all time stated that before the second coming of Christ people will travel up to 50 miles an hour. Voltaire, the outspoken French infidel said, "This proves how ridiculous Christianity is! This otherwise very intelligent scientist makes this ridiculous statement. If people moved at that speed their hearts would fail." What would both of them think if today they could see people travel 600 miles an hours on airplanes and astronauts travel 17,000 miles an hour in space.

The increase of knowledge has been phenomenal! Today's computers are obsolete tomorrow. It is said that if we had advanced in automobiles as well as we had advanced in computers we could buy a new Cadillac for $2.00 and it would get 100,000 miles per gallon. Knowledge has indeed increased and we are "running back and forth." Amos 8:12 declares that people will run to and fro seeking the Word of the Lord as the knowledge of God's purposes is increased (p. 455, JFB). Few cared for Daniel's prophecy when it was first given but many are becoming more interested in it as we get near its complete fulfillment.

In verses 5-6, Daniel sees 2 angels standing on each side of the river. One asked the supernatural being with Daniel the length of time for the wonders. "When will you destroy wickedness and establish righteousness?" (Author's paraphrase) He lifted both hands to Heaven and gave his answer. Lifting the right hand to Heaven solemnly assures the truth (Dt. 32:40, Rev. 10:5-6) while lifting both hands gives fuller assurance. The angel's answer is, "A time (one year), times (2 years), and a half time (1/2 year). The 3 1/2 times equal 3 1/2 years. In Revelation 11:2-3, the 2 witnesses prophesy in sackcloth for 1260 days, remain unburied for 3 1/2 days, and Jerusalem is trampled down for 42 months. The beast rules for 42 months (Rev. 13:5). In Revelation 12 the woman (Israel) gives birth to a man (Jesus Christ) who will rule the entire world with a rod of iron (Rev. 19:15, Ps. 2:9). She is nourished in the wilderness for 42 months, or 1260 days (vs. 6, 14). The severe famine on Israel during Elijah's time was 3 1/2 years (Lk. 4:25, James 5:17). Israel will be helpless and greatly humiliated as she is persecuted during the final 3 1/2 years of this age. This tribulation will bring Israel to repentance as she turns to Yeshua, her Messiah, King and Redeemer (Rom. 11:25b-29, Isa 59:20-21, Zech. 12:10-13:1, Mt. 23:39).

When Will Messiah Return?

Daniel 9:25-26 tells us when Messiah comes the first time but Christ very clearly tells the disciples that only our heavenly Father knows the time of His second coming (Mt. 24:36). After His resurrection, Christ spoke to the disciples for 40 days about the kingdom of God (Acts 1:3). The disciples ask, "Lord, are you going to restore the kingdom to Israel now?" Christ did not rebuke them for the question but simply answered, "Don't be concerned about the timing of Israel's restoration and My second coming. It will happen on the day determined by My Father." (v.7, author's paraphrase) He then told them that they will receive power from the Holy Spirit and be witnesses in Jerusalem, Judea, Samaria, and even the ends of the earth (v. 8).

The disciples gazed at Him as He was lifted up from the Mount of Olives into the clouds. Two men in white clothing asked them, "Why do you stand looking into the sky? This same Jesus who has been taken up from you into heaven will come in just the same way as you have watched Him go into heaven" (Acts 1:12). Prophet Zechariah (14:4) confirms that message as he declares that Messiah's feet will stand on the Mount of Olives and restore the kingdom to Israel in the glorious 1,000-year reign of Jesus Christ (Rev. 20:4-6).

In verse 8 Daniel asks about the outcome of these events and received the same instructions given by Christ to the disciples in Acts 1:7-8. He is told not to be consumed with prophecy but to, "go your way" and return to your regular responsibilities of everyday life and leave the timing of the future events in God's hands because the prophecies are sealed until the end time (v. 9). Many will be purified as they are clothed with fine white linen (Rev. 19:8; 19:14; 22:14). The wicked remain wicked (Rev. 22:11) because of their depraved hearts. The righteous will then understand the prophecies in Daniel and all the other prophecies as they see their fulfillment. The fulfillment will be obvious when the events occur (v. 10).

Many Thessalonians thought that Christ would come at any time and therefore stopped their regular daily work and just sat down and waited for the second coming. Paul strongly rebukes this irresponsible lifestyle in 2 Thessalonians 3:10. "If anyone is not willing to work, then he is not to eat either." (I Thess. 4:11, Pr. 12:11; 14:23; 13:18).

Despite the angel's instructions to Daniel and Christ's clear teaching on this subject, many have predicted the date of Christ's return. William Miller (1782-1849), a gifted Baptist preacher first predicted that Christ would return between March, 1842 and March 1843. Miller, like many other students of prophecy erroneously believed that Numbers 14:3-4 and Ezekiel 4:4-6 teach that a day equals a year in prophecy. He therefore concluded that the 2300 evenings and mornings of Daniel 8:14 equal 2300 years which should be added to 458 or 457 BC. Then the sanctuary (the earth) is cleansed with Christ's second coming. Despite the disappointment Miller and his followers continued the camp meetings. In New Hampshire on August 12, 1844 a brother announced that Christ would return on the 7th month of the current Jewish year. Excitement filled and thrilled the place as October 22, 1844 was proclaimed as the date for Christ's cleansing of the sanctuary (the earth) with His second coming.

In ten weeks the great day was at hand. In a Philadelphia store window the following sign was displayed, "This shop is closed in honor of the King of kings who will appear about the twentieth of October. Get ready, friends to crown Him Lord of all." A group of 200 people left the city as Lot had left Sodom before impending doom. Most of the Millerites gave up their occupations during the last days. Farmers left their crops in the fields, as they awaited the coming of Christ. October 22--He never came.

Hope seemed to spring eternal in the Millerite breast. Though they were no longer adjusting their timetable for the Lord's return, they did keep their hopes alive and set another date. But five years later Christ did not come to Miller but Miller went to Christ. His tombstone reads, "At the time appointed, the end shall be." (Swindoll, *Ultimate Book*, p.507).

Christopher Columbus predicted in his book, *Book of Prophecies* that Christ would return in 1656. "There is no doubt that the world must end in 155 years." (Swindoll, *Ultimate Book*, p. 506)

In the 1970s several predicted that He would return before 1988 because by then 40 years (a generation had passed since Israel became a nation (Mt. 24:34). In 1988 a famous NASA scientist gave us 88 reasons why Christ would come in 1988. In 1989 he gave us 89 reasons why Christ will come in 1989. Many predicted that in the year 2,000 there would be chaos because of computer malfunctions which would trigger the second coming. Herald Camping predicted Christ's return on May 21, 2011. I hope Sir Isaac Newton is right in his prediction that Christ would return before 2060 (Moore, front page).

We need to be ready for Christ's coming any day and also be ready to live regular lives in case He comes later than we think He should. A pastor asked a farmer, "What would you do if you knew Christ would come tonight. He answered, "I would chop some firewood, light the fire, eat supper, read the Bible, pray, and then go to bed." The pastor then said, "That's what you do every day!" The farmer replied, "Yes, you're right. I live every day ready for Christ's coming."

This is Christ's message to His disciples and to all of us believers today. Be filled with the Holy Spirit, share the gospel to the ends of the earth, be always ready for Christ's coming, but don't be preoccupied with its timing.

Leave the timing of Christ's second coming completely in our heavenly Father's hands (Acys 1:7-8).

In verse 11, the angel states that 1290 days will transpire after the daily sacrifice is abolished by Antichrist and then pronounces a blessing on all who wait for and attain 1335 days. As shown in chapter 9, the abomination of desolation takes place in the middle of the 70th 7-year period set aside for Israel. 1260 days complete that period and so we have an extra 30 and 45 days. Why were the 75 days added? Many nations mourn for 30 days after a leader or famous person dies and so the 30 days might have to do with Israel's deep mourning for her messiah she rejected and cruelly crucified (Zech. 12:10-11a).

> "I will pour on the house of David and on the inhabitants of Jerusalem, the Spirit of grace and of supplication, so that they will look on Me whom they have pierced: and they will mourn for Him as one mourns for an only son, and they will weep bitterly over Him like the bitter weeping over a firstborn. In that day there shall be great mourning in Jerusalem..."

When the nation of Israel at large repents of its rebellion and rejection and crucifixion of her messiah and welcomes Him (Luke 13:35) the event described here will take place. At the crucifixion John 19:37 declares a partial fulfillment of this prophecy. "And again another Scripture says, 'THEY SHALL LOOK ON HIM WHOM THEY HAVE PIERCED'" Israel indeed looked on Christ but was not mourning but rejoicing with the death of this "trouble-maker." The complete fulfillment is future.

The meaning of the additional 45 days is anyone's guess. Commentaries give no help. Like other difficult prophecies we will know the meaning only after its fulfillment (v. 10). A blessing awaits those who wait and attain the 1335 days.

The angel gives comforting assurance to Daniel in verse 13. Even though the affairs of the earth will continue for a good while in the future he need not be agitated by them as he would very quietly, calmly, and peacefully rest and sleep in the dust of the earth until the resurrection (Rev. 14:13). Then he would receive his allotted portion; his inheritance.

Who is the king of glory?

> Then he brought me back by the way of the gate of the sanctuary, which faces east and it was shut. The LORD said to me, "This gate shall be shut; it shall not be opened, and no man shall enter by it, for the LORD GOD of Israel has entered by it; therefore it shall be shut. (Ezekiel 44:1-2).

Prophet Ezekiel sees in this vision that Jerusalem's east gate is shut. Why? Because the LORD GOD (Jesus Christ) has passed through it and God would permit no one else to enter it.

The LORD GOD of Israel (Yeshua) passed through the eastern gate many times. On Palm Sunday Yeshua entered the eastern gate as the people honored Him with their exalted praise (Lk. 19:28-41).

In 1530 after conquering Jerusalem Suleiman and the Ottoman Turks closed the eastern gate with huge stones in order to stop Israel's messiah from entering. (Mike Evans, *The Temple*, p. 256-258) They placed a cemetery at the entrance because the Jewish Messiah as high priest would not defile Himself by walking through a graveyard .

The Arabic inscription on the gate translated into English means *Everlasting doors*. The phrase *Everlasting doors* is used only one time in Scripture: Psalm 24:7-9. This brings understanding to Ezekiel's prophecy. In their zeal and determination to stop Israel's messiah from entering Jerusalem through the east gate and frustrate God's purpose for Israel, they fulfill prophecy (Ps. 2; 21:1).

> Lift up your heads, O ye gates; and be lift up ye everlasting doors; and the king of glory shall come in. Who is the king of glory? The LORD strong and mighty, the LORD mighty in battle. Lift up your heads, O ye gates; even lift them up, ye everlasting doors and the King of gory shall come in. Who is the King of glory? The LORD of hosts, He is the King of glory. (Ps. 24:7-10 KJV).

At the 2nd coming Messiah will descend to the Mount of Olives (Zech. 14:4, Acts 1:9-12), descend to the Kidron valley, climb to the eastern gate and will have no problem entering as the sealed everlasting doors are opened for Him. He then sets up His kingdom and rules over the house of Israel and the whole world for 1,000 years (Lk. 1:33, Rev.11:15, 19:6).

Conclusion

The king of Prussia) asked his chaplain if he could prove the existence of God in one sentence. He answered, "I don't need a sentence but only one word to prove the existence of God: **ISRAEL**"

There is no logical explanation for the continued existence of the Jews and Israel. After the 66-70, 113-117, and 132-136 AD rebellions against Rome the Jews were scattered all over the world and remained so for over 1800 years. Roman Emperor Hadrian renamed the land Syria Palaestina (Palestine) after Israel's ancient enemy Philistines. He renamed Jerusalem Aelia Capitolina and forbade the Jews to enter Jerusalem except on Tesha b'Av (the day Babylon and Rome destroyed the temple). Emperor Constantine gave the city its old name again. Unlike the other ancient nations, the Jews never amalgamated with their host countries but maintained their ethnic distinctions, continued to use the ancient language of Hebrew, and observed the Sabbath and the feast days. Though continued to be discriminated against, made second class citizens, and forced to live in the ghettos of Europe, they grew and continued to look forward to returning to the land of Israel and its capital Jerusalem.

In the late 1800s Russian Jews paid premium prices for worthless swamp land in Palestine and started settling there. They dried out the swamps and made the land productive. After Hitler's Holocaust many survivors came to Palestine but the British and the Arabs diligently worked hard to stop them.

David Ben-Gurian (1886-1973), the first prime minister of Israel on May 14, 1948 declared the establishment of the State of Israel. President Truman boldly rejected the advice of Secretary of State George Marshall and immediately recognized the nation. He instructed the US ambassador to the UN to vote for the establishment of the nation of Israel. The surrounding Arab nations (Lebanon, Syria, Iraq, Jordan, and Egypt) outnumbering Israel 100-1 in population and 40-1 in military personnel immediately declared war on and attacked Israel but were defeated and humiliated as Israel gained more land.

The Arabs were again defeated in 1956 and greatly humiliated in the 1967 6-Day War. Egypt, Syria, and Jordan were determined to eliminate these "racist Zionist invaders" by washing Israel into the sea but in this defensive war Israel was forced to conquer the Sinai, the West Bank and the Golan Heights.

After being generously rearmed by the Soviet Union, Egypt and Syria again attacked Israel in 1973. Egyptian President Anwar Sadat, the chief architect of the Yom Kippur War and Syria were on the verge of destroying Israel. The situation was so desperate that Israeli Prime Minister Golda Meir and government officials considered suicide.

Prime Minister Meir called US President Richard Nixon at 3:00 AM and told him of the desperate situation and asked for many weapons. President Nixon gave her all she requested. He remembered his mother's message to him in earlier days. "Some day God will use you to save the Jewish people." Despite his difficulties with Watergate President Nixon boldly stood up to the Soviets. His quick bold and decisive action helped turn the tide and Israel got the upper hand. Israeli soldiers under General Ariel Sharon were on the verge of occupying Cairo when US Secretary of State Kissinger brokered the cease-fire. Humanly speaking President Nixon saved Israel from destruction.

European nations turned a blind eye to the war while the Muslim nations were on the verge of destroying Israel but as soon as Israel got the upper hand it was amazing how quickly these nations offered cease-fire resolutions in the UN. Today Muslims show their gratitude in Europe by raping their women, burning buildings, and killing many with suicide bombings.

Prime Minister Meir declared after the war, "We can forgive you for killing our sons but it'll be very difficult to forgive you for forcing us to kill your sons."

I was in Israel in early 1991 when Saddam Hussein sent 39 missiles into Israel. They did virtually no damage and 13 people were killed; 11 from gas mask problems and heart attacks and 2 from a direct hit (It took 3 missiles to kill one Israeli). One Israeli said that the events might help atheists become agnostics.

For the first time since the establishment of the nation of Israel unparalleled hostility was generously dumped on Israel through US President Obama. His determination to insult, humiliate, and destroy Israel was generously frustrated in 2010 when the Republicans took over the House and in 2014 the US Senate. In 2016 Donald Trump, longtime friend of Israel defeated Obama's desired successor. The Democrats are learning the solemn truth of Genesis 12:3. God told Abraham, "I will bless them who bless you and curse them who curse you."

On Wednesday, December 6, 2017 President Trump boldly and heroically fulfilled his campaign promise to recognize Jerusalem as the capital of Israel and began the process of moving the US embassy to Jerusalem. King David made Jerusalem Israel's capital over 3,000 years ago (I Chron. 11:4-9, 2Sam. 5:4-10). Prime Minister Menachem Begin declared all of Jerusalem to be Iarael's capital and US officials said, "We don't recognize Jerusalem as Israel's capital." Begin replied, "That's ok. We don't recognize your non-recognition." God Almighty has chosen Jerusalem and soon Jesus Christ will rule Israel and the world from Jerusalem (Zechariah 2, 12:6-14, 14, Mt. 5:35).

All the ancient languages including Latin have died and have remained dead but the ancient language of Hebrew has been revived and is used in everyday communication in modern Israel just as it was during the time of Christ and the prophets. If the Hebrew prophets were resurrected and spoke the same language used during their lives they would be understood by modern Israelis.

Prime Minister Ben-Gurian declared, "To be realistic in Israel you have to believe in miracles." Israel exists only because God has sovereignly determined that His purposes will be fulfilled in Israel whether Israel cooperates or not. God also promises that after the Jews return to the land of Israel they would never be scattered again (Amos 9:14-15, Ezekiel 36-39).

A pastor announced to his church and community that he would speak on the subject, "How to Rid the World of the Jews." Many Jews and Rabbis showed up and the pastor read the text, Jeremiah 31:35-37.

> Thus says the LORD, Who gives the sun for light by day and the fixed order of the moon and the stars for light by night.

Who stirs the sea so that the waters roar..."If the fixed order departs from before me...then the offspring of Israel also will cease from being a nation from me forever."

Thus says the LORD (Yahweh), "If the heavens above can be measured and the foundations of the earth searched below, then I will cast off all the offspring of Israel for all they have done." Declares the LORD.

While sailing with Napoleon his men recommended that all religion be declared as nonsense. Pointing to the stars Napoleon replied, "Sirs, you will first need to do something about this."

God guarantees the perpetual existence of the Jews and Israel. All who seek Israel's destruction face the same consequences as Haman (Esther 5-8) and Hitler. Hamas and Iran's determination to "wipe Israel off the map" will have the same success as Hitler, Haman and the Romans had in keeping Christ in the tomb.

As previously shown all the prophecies given in Daniel concerning Christ's first coming have been fully and literally fulfilled. Over 500 years before Christ's first coming Gabriel predicted the exact day when Messiah will be revealed in Israel (April 6, 32 AD), the destruction of Jerusalem and the temple, and the difficulties of the Jews. The 4 kingdoms of chapters 2 and 7 have come and gone and therefore we should be assured that the 5th kingdom will also come but unlike the first 4 it will never pass away but will last forever. We can trust Daniel and also the whole Bible! Jesus said, "Heaven and earth will pass away but my Words will not pass away" (Mt. 5:18; 24:35, Ps. 119:89).

EPILOGUE

HalleluYah! Salvation is in Christ Alone!
(Author's Personal Testimony)

A very painful emotional event happened to me on May 21, 2003. My beloved mother, Evelyn Arnall Williams died. Even though she was blessed with over 76 years of life and I had her for almost 55 years the separation was still very painful and seemed unbearable at that time.

I thank God that He graciously allowed me to be with her the last 110 days of her life. She assured me regularly that she had trusted Jesus Christ and His shed blood for her salvation and so I rejoice that she is safe in the arms of her beloved savior, the Lord Jesus Christ. She has received a much deserved rest (Rev, 14:13) and her death was precious to Yahweh, our heavenly Father (Ps. 116:15). She like all the righteous has a refuge in death (Pr. 14:32) and is happier now as her spirit has returned to our creator (Ecclesiastes 7:1; 12:7, Acts 7:59-60, 2 Corinthians 5:8-10, Philippians 1:20-23). Soon our Lord will breathe His spirit back into her dead body and she will have an eternal, perfect body that will never perish, be sick, nor ever be in pain again (Job 19:25-27, I Cor. 15, I Thess. 4:13-18, Dan. 12:2, Jn. 5:25-29; 11:11-26).

Ecclesiastes 7:1 declares that the day of death is better than the day of birth and so I rejoice and shout, "Glory! Halleluyah!" Mother, like Daniel (12:2) is resting and sleeping so very peacefully and comfortably in the arms of our beloved Savior, the Lord Jesus Christ and will rise from the grave at His 2nd coming (John 5:25, 14:3). It's therefore most comforting to know and understand that our separation though painful is temporary.

When she rises I will rise with her and we will be together forever: Never again to separate (I Cor.15:51-58)!

In his book, *What in the World Is Going On* (p. 103), Dr. Jeremiah gives this excellent description of death.

> The concept of death is emphasized in the wonderful word early Christians adopted for the burying places of their loved ones. It was the Greek word, *koimeterion*, meaning, "a rest house for strangers, and a sleeping place." It is the word from which we get our English word *cemetery*. In Paul's day, this word was used for inns or what we would call a hotel or motel. We check in at a Hilton Hotel or a Ramada Inn, expecting to spend the night in sleep before we wake up in the morning refreshed and raring to go. That is exactly the thought Paul expressed in words such as *koimao* and *koimeterion*. When Christians die it's as if they are slumbering peacefully in a place of rest, ready to be awakened at the return of the Lord. The words have great import, for they convey the Christian concept of death, not as a tragic finality but as a temporary sleep.

While visiting the cemetery of the Zion Hope Baptist Church in my former hometown of Tifton, Georgia, USA, I saw the engraving on 2 tombstones, *Just Sleeping: A* perfect description of my mother and all who have died in Christ.

Yes, death is a cold, cruel intruder that causes all mankind including us believers in Jesus Christ to grieve but not as the world grieves (Jn.16:20-22, 33) because death is not final but the gateway to eternal life in Heaven (Job 19:26, Jn. 5:28-29; 11:25; 14:1-3, Phil. 1:21, Rom. 14:8, ICor. 15:20-26, Rev. 21-22).

Karl Barth (1886-1968), one of the best 20th century theologians wrote *Church Dogmatics*, a 6,000,000-word, 8,000-page, 13-volume commentary on Christianity. When touring the US a student asked him, "What is the most profound theological truth that you have discovered?" He answered, "Jesus loves me this I know for the Bible tells me so."

Mother, though not a theologian, had this same insight as she taught me this most profound truth when I was 5 years old. She helped me memorize and learn the awesome truth found in John 3:16;

"For God so loved the world that He gave His only begotten Son, that whoever believes in Him should not perish but have everlasting life."

Here Christ proclaims the simple and yet awesome supernatural plan of salvation. All who trust Jesus Christ for salvation will never perish (John 10:28) but will live forever. When I was 9 years old the seed Mom placed into my heart bore fruit as I repented of my sins, confessed Jesus Christ as my personal savior, and was baptized into the Highland Park Baptist Church, Jacksonville, Fla. Though understanding little about salvation I did understand this simple truth as I received eternal life.

Worthy in Christ: The Blessings and Benefits of our Salvation

Dr. Fred Evers, pastor of Northside Baptist Church in Tifton, Ga. USA, told the following story. While the Bolsheviks were on the verge of conquering Russia, Czar Nicholas wanted to give a valuable trophy to a loyal subordinate. The surprised man said he wasn't worthy to receive it and initially refused it. The czar replied, "Whether you fell worthy or not is not the issue. I am worthy to give it to you so please take it."

No one is worthy to receive Christ's blessings but Christ is worthy to give them to us therefore let us freely receive Christ's blessings.

While living in Korea I regularly visited an orphanage. The children were so delightful as they eagerly welcomed me there. One time a year old girl full of joy in typical behavior very eagerly jumped into my arms as she greeted me. Her pants from the top to the bottom were filled with urine on both sides. I joyfully received her and held her as she joyfully wrapped her legs around me. We continually played together with no care in the world. About 20 minutes later I saw the orphanage director's wife and pointed out the problem. She was shocked and immediately ran to me and took the child to the bathroom, washed her and put clean clothes on her.

My love for the child did not increase after she was cleaned. I already loved her with all my love even in her less than ideal situation. But I rejoiced that our situation would be much healthier with her cleaned up.

David Jeremiah regularly stresses that, "God loves you the way you are but loves you too much to leave you the way you are." When we came to Christ we were in far worse shape spiritually than this girl (Isa. 51:1, Eph. 2:12-13). Our righteousness was as filthy rags (Isa. 64:6, Zec. 3:3-4). (These filthy rags are found in the bottom of an outhouse). Even though we were unworthy Christ in His love freely and joyfully received you and me and predestined us to be like Christ (Rom. 8:29-30).

Jesus stated that it's the Father's pleasure to joyfully give you and me the kingdom (Lk.12:32). All our sins are separated from God as far as east is from the west and buried in the deepest sea (Ps. 103:12, Micah 7:19). We feel sorry for the fish!

We are completely eternally secure in Christ and will never perish. No one can take me or you out of our Father's hand (John 10:28; 6:39). Apostle Peter declared (I Peter 1:4) that we have an inheritance that will never perish or fade but is reserved and kept secure in Heaven. Nothing can separate me or any believer from the love of Christ. I have been predestined to be glorified like Christ (Rom. 28:29-35) and sealed by the Holy Spirit for eternity (Eph.4:30). Since no one can break the Holy Spirit's seal I shout again, "Glory! Halleluyah!" for my eternal security in Christ!

After His ascension into Heaven, Jesus Christ, our great high priest entered the most holy place of the Heavenly Sanctuary (Greek, *hagia hagion*, the Holy of holies) and obtained our eternal redemption through His shed blood (Hebrews 9:6-14). There in the Heavenly Sanctuary He intercedes for me and all who have come to God (Heb. 7:25, 9:11-12, Rom. 8:34).

We believers have unlimited free access to our heavenly Father in the heavenly holy of holies through Christ's shed blood (Hebrews 10:19-20; 4:16, Ephesians 2:18). His blood provides forgiveness and continually purifies all of us from all sin (I John 1:7, Eph. 1:7; 2:13, Rev. 1:5, Heb. 9:22). I am justified, made righteous (Romans 5:9), and also have power to overcome Satan, the prince of darkness through Christ's shed blood (Rev. 12:11).

I have freely received what Jesus Christ, the holy, pure, spotless Lamb of God deserved because He freely received what I deserved (2 Cor. 5:21, Isaiah 53:4-6). He was cursed with the curse I deserved so that I can be blessed with the blessings He deserved. He died the death I deserved so I can live the life He deserved.

John D Rockefeller liked a sermon so much that he gave the pastor a $100.00 check. (In today's economy it would be about $2,000) Even though the check had Rockefeller's signature on the right bank with sufficient funds the teller informed him that she could not cash it. Why? Because it needed his endorsement. He quickly endorsed it and got the cash.

Yahweh, our heavenly Father has given you and me a check infinitely more valuable than Rockefeller's $100.00 check. Though undeserved and unworthy to receive it let us freely receive and endorse our Father's generous check to us and receive His generous benefits.

The Great Invitation

The theme throughout Daniel is the sovereignty of God. God can do anything He wants to do. Nothing is too hard for God (Dt. 32:39, Ps. 115:3; 135:6-7, Isa. 14:27; 40:15; 43:13; 46: 9-10, Jer. 32:17, Lk. 1:37). But there are some things that God cannot do because His character would be violated. God's holy sovereign power will never violate His holy sovereign character. God has the power to send another flood like the one sent in Genesis 6 but He cannot do that simply because He said He wouldn't (Gen. 9:11-16). He cannot lie (Titus 1:2, Heb 6:18).

He can't make square circles, round squares, or a rock so big that He can't move it. He can not violate His holy character and let sinners dwell in his presence. He therefore provided the sacrifice of His Son so that through His shed blood sin is washed away (Rev. 1:5) and holiness and purity are obtained. Those who accept Christ's sacrifice live forever but those who reject it perish in the lake of fire. (Jn. 3:16, I Peter 2:12, Rev. 20:15).

Moses earnestly pleads for Israel to reject death and choose life (Dt. 30:15-19). Christ earnestly pleads for all mankind to do the same and come to Him for rest (Mt. 11:28-29). God earnestly desires that every human choose life and live with Him forever (2 Peter 3:9, Mt. 18:14, ITim. 2:4, Ez. 18:23, 32).

In 1829 George Wilson and James Porter robbed a United States mail carrier in Pennsylvania and killed its guard. They were tried and convicted on 6 indictments including robbery and murder and sentenced to death by hanging. Influential friends of Wilson petitioned President Andrew Jackson to grant him a pardon. The request was granted on June 14, 1830 as the president declared, "I, Andrew Jackson, president of the United States of America do hereby pardon... George Wilson the crime for which he has been sentenced to suffer death."

Even though President Jackson issued him a pardon, Wilson in his pride and arrogance rejected the pardon. US Supreme Court Chief Justice John Marshall declared that,

> "A pardon is an act of grace proceeding from the power entrusted with the execution of the laws, which exempts the individual, on whom it is bestowed, from punishment the law inflicts for the crime he has committed.... A pardon is a deed, to the validity of which delivery is essential; and delivery is not completed without acceptance. It may then be rejected by the person to whom it is tendered: and if it is rejected we have discovered no power in a court to force it on him.... The pardon is a slip of paper, the value of which is determined by the acceptance of the person to be pardoned. If it is refused it is no pardon. George Wilson must be hanged." (www.yahoo. com search-George Wilson, pardon).

Wilson was therefore hanged: So needlessly hanged! If only he had humbled himself and graciously accepted the pardon he would have lived.

All mankind is condemned to death because of sin against God (Ps. 51:5, Rom. 3:23, ICor. 15:22) but the pardon takes effect only when it is freely received by the sinner. Those who receive Christ's pardon live forever (1Tim. 2:4 2Peter 3:9, Mt. 18:14, Eze. 18:23, 32; 33:11, Jn. 3:16) but those who reject it face spiritual death in the lake of fire (Rev. 20:15).

On May, 1978 Evangelist Billy Graham spoke to the inmates of the Federal Correction Institute in Memphis, Tennessee. He quoted a director of a mental institute in London, England who declared, "Everyone here could leave if they knew they were forgiven." The same is true for all mankind. God our heavenly Father freely offers forgiveness to all in Christ. Everyone who receives His offer is freely pardoned and set free (Jn. 8:32).

In his book, *Heaven,* (p.31-32) Randy Alcorn tells the story of a wedding that was given by a very wealthy man in Seattle, Washington,

USA. The top 2 floors of the Columbia Towers, the highest skyscraper in the northwest were rented and hors d'oeuves and exotic drinks were freely offered to the guests at this very lavish banquet. Professional singer Ruthanna Metzgar sang at the wedding and with her husband Roy, very eagerly looked forward to the exotic reception.

The maitre d' greeted her and asked for her name. After her answer the maitre d' searched for it and said, "I'm sorry but your name isn't here." Ruthanna responded, "There must be a mistake. I'm the singer. I sang for the wedding!" The gentleman replied, "It doesn't matter who you are or what you did. Without your name in the book you cannot attend the banquet." A waiter therefore escorted them to the elevator and pushed the ground floor button.

After driving a few miles her husband Roy asked his wife what happened. She tearfully answered, "When the invitation arrived, I was busy. I never bothered to RSVP (*Repondez Sil Vous Plait,* French, Please respond to the invitation.) Besides I was the singer. Surely I could go to the reception without returning the RSVP!"

Mrs. Metzgar wept not only because she missed the most exotic banquet ever offered to her but also for the severe shock and disappointment that would haunt those who will stand before Christ and learn that their names aren't written in the book of life (Rev. 20:15).

Our heavenly Father invites everyone to a future wedding banquet that's far more exotic than the one at the Columbia Towers (Rev.19:7-9) but only those whose names are written in the book of life will be allowed to enter (Rev. 21:27). All others perish in the lake of fire (Rev. 20:15).

In one of his crusades Evangelist Billy Graham shared a conversation he had with a Catholic monsignor. He asked him, "Have you been born again?" The monsignor did not answer the question but later told Evangelist Graham, "After you asked the question I went to my place, got on my knees and made sure that I have been born again." He thus made sure that his name was written in the book of life.

On Sunday, February 26, 2012 about 9,000 participated in the 34th edition of the Cowtown marathon in Fort Worth, Texas, USA. Scott Downard crossed the finish line first in 2 hours, 31 minutes and 40 seconds but was disqualified because he failed to register. Kolin Styles, the 2nd one to cross the finish line, (2 hr. 37 min. 53 sec.) was therefore declared the winner of the 26.2 mile race (Star-Telegraph, Ft. Worth, Texas, USA, Feb. 27, 2012).

Christ invites all mankind to register for their place in Heaven (Mt. 18:14, Jn. 3:16-17, I Tim. 2:4, 2Pe. 3:9, Rev. 22:17). Those who follow Scott Downard's irresponsible example will be disqualified (ICor. 9:24, Heb, 12:1) and face severe consequences (Jn. 3:18, Rev. 20:15).

In Revelation 3:20 Christ is knocking on the door of the heart and earnestly desires to enter in order to have fellowship. As a gentleman He will never force himself on anyone but enters only when He's welcomed and invited in. In Revelation 22:17 and 21:6 the Father, Son, and the Holy Spirit invite all to "drink of the fountain of life freely." Christ assures us in John 6:37 and 39 that all who come to Christ will never be rejected but will be freely, unconditionally, and eternally accepted.

Dear reader, have you come to Christ by accepting His pardon and gift of eternal abundant life? Have you sent your RSVP to Heaven? Have you registered for your race in this life? Have you endorsed God's generous check to you? Christ assures us that all who come to Him will be unconditionally warmly welcomed, find rest (Mt.11:28-30) and will never perish (Jn. 6:37; 10:28). If you haven't, please do so now and receive all the blessings described earlier. Always remember that your good works like singing at a wedding or in a choir, teaching Sunday School, preaching the gospel, faithfully supporting the church, giving generously to charities, doing missionary work, being a high official in any church, winning a marathon or any other good work is completely worthless in obtaining salvation (Eph. 2:8, Tit. 3:4-6).

Your name is written in the book of life and salvation is guaranteed only after you come to Christ, repent of your sins, and invite Him to come into your heart and life.

I therefore earnestly plead with you to send your RSVP to Heaven and be assured of your place in the eternal heavenly banquet (Rev. 19:7-9). Our heavenly Father will run to you, joyfully receive, save, and restore you just as the loving father did in the parable (Lk. 15:11-31). The angels rejoice as you repent (Lk 15:10) and your soul receives rest (Mt.11:28-30).

Erwin Lutzer, longtime pastor of the Moody Church in Chicago, Ill, USA, tells the story of a man who came into the church asking, "Can any one here lead me to Jesus?" Surprised Pastor Lutzer replied that he could and joyfully led the man to Christ as savior after sharing with him the plan of salvation. Pastor Lutzer then asked, "What made you come to this church to ask for salvation?" He answered, "About 4 years ago while hitch hiking a truck driver picked me up and shared the gospel with me but I rejected it as nonsense. My conscience has continued to bother me and now my soul is troubled and I know I need Christ."

Bill Bright, founder of Campus Crusade for Christ says that successful witnessing is, "Sharing the gospel of Christ in the power of the Holy Spirit and leaving the results to God." God will always honor our sharing His Word (Isaiah 55:11).

Let us believers therefore continually rejoice and give thanks for our salvation (1Thess. 5:16-18) and remember our awesome responsibility to share this message with those who haven't received it (Mt 10:32). Jesus said, "Freely you have received, freely give" (Mt. 10:8). Freely accept and give His gracious and generous invitation in Revelation 22:17, 20-21.

> The Spirit and the bride say "come." And let the one who hears say "come." And let the one who is thirsty come, let the one who wishes take the water of life without cost. He who testifies to these things says, "Yes, I am coming quickly." Amen. Come Lord Jesus. The grace of the Lord Jesus be with you all. Amen.

Power in the Blood

As we study Scripture we can see that God has a rich sense of humor. Psalm 2 declares that God laughs as finite beings boldly oppose His will. Pilate stationed 16 elite professional soldiers outside the tomb of Christ to be absolutely sure that Christ stayed in the tomb. God and all the angels laughed with great celebration as Christ boldly defied death and came out of the tomb.

How utterly futile it was for Pharaoh to boldly reject the Almighty's will. This can be clearly seen in the 10 plagues given to Egypt as God delivers Israel from slavery. Yahweh with his rich sense of humor boldly insults the Egyptian gods in the plagues.

The symbol of authority in Egypt was the cobra. Yahweh through Moses shows the superiority of His power over Egypt when Moses' staff was turned into a snake and swallowed Pharaoh's magicians' snakes.

In the first plague the Nile was turned into blood. The Egyptians believed the Nile was the blood of their god and so Yahweh turns it into literal blood.

Egypt worshiped a large statue of a female frog as the god of fertility. We can smile as we see God's sense of humor in the proliferation of the frogs. The Egyptian god of fertility was definitely overworking itself. When Moses asked Pharaoh if he wanted the frogs removed Pharaoh answered, "Tomorrow" (Ex. 8:10) He wanted to spend 1 more night sleeping with the frogs.

The earth was worshiped as the father of the gods. Moses scatters the dust which turns into mosquitoes. The beetle (Swarms of flies) was revered as the symbol of life. The cow was sacred to Egypt and was never sacrificed. Moses boldly challenged the Egyptian deities as he spread ashes to heaven. (The Egyptians spread the ashes of the victims to Typhon). Hail destroyed their sacred livestock. The sun was warmly worshiped and so all of Egypt was insulted as the locusts blotted it out and then there was absolute darkness for 3 days.

After promising to let Israel go and reneging 9 times Pharaoh finally let Israel go after the 10th plague. In this final plague the Israelis were instructed to kill a lamb or goat and pour the blood into a container. The head of the family was then instructed to get a hyssop branch (like a paint brush) and paint the blood on the top and on both sides of the door. The blood will be the sign (Ex.12:13-22).

"For the LORD will pass through to smite the Egyptians and when He sees the blood on the lintel and the two doorposts He will pass over the door and will not allow the destroyer to come into your house to smite you." (Ex. 12:23).

When the death angel saw the blood applied to the sides and top of the door he passed by and the whole family was safe from death. The firstborn was killed in the dwellings where there was no blood on the top and sides of the door.

The message is clear and simple. The angel was not looking for good works like going to church, singing in the choir, being a good neighbor, or donating to charities. He only looked for blood. Where there was blood there was life. Where there was no blood there was death.

The instructions must be completely obeyed or there was death. If the lamb was slain and the blood put in the container but not applied to both sides and the top of the door there was death. Partial obedience is disobedience.

The death angel killed all the firstborn of Egypt but would pass over the dwellings that had blood applied to the top and the 2 sides of the door: A symbol of the cross.

We see blood throughout Scripture. After Adam and Eve sinned against God blood was shed as animal skins were prepared for their covering (Gen. 3:20). God accepted Abel's bloody offering but rejected Cain's bloodless sacrifice (Gen 4:3-7).

Throughout the New Testament we are taught that the blood of Christ alone cleanses us from all sin and justifies us. (Eph. 1:7, Rom. 5:9, IJn. 1:7-9). Hebrews 9:22 clearly states that, "without shedding of blood there is no forgiveness."

In Revelation 12:11 there is war in Heaven. They overcame Satan by the <u>blood</u> of the Lamb and the word of their testimony and loved not their lives even unto death.

Please notice and understand that they did NOT overcome Satan by their good works, generous giving to charities, regular church attendance, being good neighbors, paying tithes, praying 3 times a day, or any other action. We love, encourage, and applaud good works but realize they are totally worthless in diverting the death angel and saving us from destruction. We overcome Satan and escape death only through the shed blood of Christ. The death angel passed over the dwelling ONLY when he saw the blood.

The hyssop (brush) is our tongue. As we confess that the blood of Christ is applied to our lives we are saved from death and destruction and overcome Satan and therefore totally unafraid of death. "To live is Christ and to die is gain." (Phil. 1:21, Rom. 14:8).

We as Christian believers should continually do good works as they are commendable. God is pleased with our good works when they are done as a result and testimony of our love for Christ (Eph. 2:8-10) but never pleased if they are done to earn salvation.

For by grace we have been saved through faith and that not of yourselves. It is the gift of God; not as a result of works so that no one may boast. For we are His workmanship, created in Christ Jesus unto good works, which God prepared beforehand so that we would walk in them

The virgin birth of Christ

A new life begins after sexual intimacy as blood vessels appear in the woman's womb. The mother's blood NEVER mixes with the baby's blood. The placenta keeps the blood of the mother and baby totally separated. In rare occasions when the mother's blood mixes with the baby's blood there is serious injury or death.

Christ was made in the LIKENESS of sinful flesh (Rom. 8:3). His flesh was not sinful since He derived His blood and life solely from His Father Yahweh. Christ, our Messiah and savior is totally uncontaminated with Adam's blood. He is therefore the spotless "lamb of God who takes away the sins of the world" (Jn. 1:29, 36). Christ therefore was not in Adam as he sinned as we were (I Cor.15:22). This is why the virgin conception of Christ is absolutely necessary! If Christ derived His life from a human father His blood would be as contaminated with Adam's sin as the rest of us. If He were born with a sinful nature he would be totally unfit to be the sacrifice for our sins.

The importance of verbal confession of Christ can never be overstated! In Hebrew the word for *thing* and *word* is the same: *Davar*. Words have substance and therefore we should be very careful what we say. It's therefore so vitally important that we verbally and freely confess our faith in the blood of Christ. "Let the redeemed of the LORD **say** so. (Ps. 107:2). Psalm 91:2 states, "I will **say** of the LORD, He is my refuge, my fortress, My God: In Him I will trust." "Preserve me O God for I take refuge in you. I **said** to the LORD, 'You are my Lord. I have no good besides you.'" (Ps. 16:1-2).

Neurologists state that the verbal center of the brain controls all the other nerves of the body. We should therefore pray with King David (Ps.141:3) "Set a guard over my mouth O LORD. Keep watch over the door of my lips." "Let the words of my mouth and the meditation of my heart be acceptable in Your sight, O LORD, my rock and my redeemer" (Ps. 19:14). Christ declared, "For his mouth speaks from that which fills his heart" (Lk. 6:45). Solomon declared in Proverbs 18:21 that, "Death and life are in the power of the tongue..."

Our tongue is the hyssop (paint brush) that is used to apply the blood to our lives. We overcome Satan as we freely confess and testify that the blood cleanses us from our sins (I Jn. 1:7, 5:4-5) and gives deliverance from the fear of death. Understandably Satan hates the shed blood of Christ because he knows he's helpless and defeated as we confess that Christ's blood washes away our sins.

We are all totally helpless before Satan in our strength (Jn. 15:5, Ps. 28:26, Eze. 16:15) but Satan is helpless before the believer who is covered with Christ's shed blood. We are "more than conquerors" (Rom. 8:37) as we trust in Christ's blood. Let us therefore rejoice and praise God continually for the power of the blood of the Lamb of God, Yeshua Hamoshiakh in our lives. "Greater is He who is in you than he who is in the world" (I Jn. 4:4).

While teaching this truth at a university in Korea a student began to feel disoriented and dizzy. I opened the window and the door hoping she would feel better. She continued to feel disoriented and was fainting. I said, "I'm going to pray for you because you are under demonic attack." I knelt beside her and placed my right hand on her shoulder and prayed, "Heavenly Father please have mercy on this student and deliver her from this problem of fainting." I then boldly commanded the evil spirits in the holy name of Yeshua Hamoshiakh to come out of her and leave her alone and never return. She perked up and joyfully said, "Wow, I feel much better now. Thank you." I then counseled her to "continually confess that blood covers your life and make sure you are living a life that's pleasing to God our heavenly Father." She made an A+ in the course and I'm confident she is growing in her faith.

It is therefore so vitally important for all of us believers to joyfully confess our faith in the shed blood of Christ Jesus for our salvation and deliverance from sin.

BIBLIOGRAPHY

Alcorn, Randy, *Heaven*, Tyndale House Publishers, 2004.

Anderson, Sir Robert, *The Coming Prince*, (CP) Kregel Pub. Box 2607, Grand Rapids, Mich. 49501, USA, 1954,

Arbesman, Samuel, "Stumbling Toward Greatness", *The Wall Street Journal*, Friday-Sunday, June 14-16, 2013,

Barnes, Albert, *Barnes Notes on the Book of Daniel*, Baker Books, Box 6287 Grand Rapids, Mich. 49516, USA, Reprinted in 2005 from the original 1847 edition by Blackie and Son, London, England.

Boice, James Montgomery. *Daniel*, Baker Books, Box 6287, Grand Rapids, Mich. 49516, USA. 2004.

Boutflower, Charles, *In and Around the Book of Daniel*, Zondervan Pub. House, Grand Rapids, Mich. 49530, USA, 1963.

Collier's Encyclopedia, P.F. Collier, 866 3rd Ave. New York, N.Y.10022, USA

Crowley, Dale. *The Soon Coming of Our Lord*

Culver, Robert. *Wycliffe Bible Commentary* on Daniel

Dimont, Max. *Jews, God, and History*, Penguin Books, 375 Hudson St. New York, 10014, USA

Evans, Dr. Mike, *The Temple*, TimeWorthy Books, Phoenix, Az. 85046 USA, 2015

Finegan, Jack. *Handbook of Biblical Chronology*, Princeton University Press, Princeton, NJ, USA, 1964.

Graham, Dr. Billy, *Decision* magazine, January, 2009, "The Second Coming of Christ, Are You Ready?"

Graham, Franklin, *Rebel with a Cause*, Thomas Nelson Inc. 1995, Nashville, Tn. USA,

Halley, Henry H., *Halley's Bible Handbook*, Zondervan, 3900 Sparks Dr. S.E. Grand Rapids, Mich. 49546, USA

Herodotus, *The Histories,* translated by George Rawlinson, Knopf, New York, 1997.

Henry, John, *Cowtown's first finisher disqualified, runner-up wins*, Star-Telegram, Ft. Worth, Texas, USA, February 27, 2012.

Henry, Matthew. *Commentary on the Whole Bible,* Hendrickson Pub. Box 3473 Peabody, Mass. 01961, USA. 1991.

Holy Bible, King James Version, Thomas Nelson Publishers, Nashville, Tn. 1964.

Jamieson, Robert; **Fausset**, A.R.; **Brown,** David; *Jamieson- Fausset-Brown Bible Commentary* (JFB) Hendrickson Publishers, Box 3473, Peabody, Mass. 01961, USA, 2002.

Jeremiah, Dr. David, *Agents of Babylon.* Tyndale House Publishers, Inc. Carol Stream, Ill. USA.

Jeremiah, Dr. David. *Agents of the Apocalypse*, Tyndale House Publishers, Carol Stream, Illinois, USA, 2014.

Jeremiah, Dr. David, Radio broadcast. August 23, 2017

Jeremiah, Dr. David. *The Coming Economic Armageddon,* FaithWords, Hachette Book Group, 237 Park Ave. New York, NY, 10017, USA

Jeremiah, Dr. David. *The Handwriting on the Wall,* Word Publishing, Dallas, Tx. USA, 1992.

Jeremiah, Dr. David. *What in the World is going on?* Thomas Nelson, Nashville, Tn. USA. 2008.

Jewish World Review, *Ripley's Believe it or Not,* May 13. 2015.

Josephson, Elmer A. *God's Key to Health and Happiness,* Fleming H Revell Co. Old Tappan, N.J. USA

Josephus, Flavius *The Antiquities of the Jews,* 10.10.1 in *Josephus Complete Works* translated by William Whiston, Kregel, Grand Rapids, Mi. 49501 USA

Ju, Kwang-Jo. *More Than Conquerors,* Seoul, Korea

Keil & Delitzsch, *Commentary on the Old Testament,* Hendrickson PublishersMarketing, LLC, Box 3473, Peabody, Mass. 01961, USA.

Keil, C. F., *Biblical Commentary on the Book of Daniel,* Wm. B. Eerdmans Pub. Co. Grand Rapids, Mich. USA, 1959.

Kennedy, Geoffrey Anketell Studdert, *The Hardest Part*: Hodder and Stoughton, London 1919.

Knoxville News Sentinel, Knoxville, Tn. USA, February 12, 2016.

Kroll, Dr. Woodrow. *Back to the Bible* broadcast, February 21, 2006. Box 82808 Lincoln, Neb. 68501, USA.

Leupold, H. C. *Exposition of Daniel*, Baker Books, Grand Rapids, Mich. 49516, USA, 1949.

Lutzer, Erwin, *How to Say No to a Stubborn Habit*, Victor Books, Wheaton, Ill. USA, 1979, p. 26.

Maier, Paul L. Jo*sephus, The Essential Writings*, Kregel, Box 2607, Grand Rapids, Mich. 49501, USA. 1988.

McMillen, S.I., M.D. *None of These Diseases*, Fleming H. Revell Co. Old Tappen, N.J. 1980.

Merideth, Lee W. *1912 Facts about Titanic*, Rocklin Press, Box 64142, Sunnyvale, Ca. 94088, USA, 2003.

Milman, Henry H. *History of the Jews*, Vol.I and II, J. M. Dent Co. London, U.K.

Moore, Dr. Philip; *Messiah Conspiracy*, Ramshead Press, Atlanta, Ga. USA, 1996.

Moses and Muhammed, *Jewish World Review*; June 29, 2016.

National Geographic DVD, *Titanic: How It Really Sank*

New American Standard Bible, (NASB), The Lockman Foundation, Anaheim, Ca. 92816, USA, 1992.

New International Version Bible, (NIV) Zondervan, Grand Rapids. Mich. 49530, USA, 1985.

Olmstead, A. T. *History of the Persian Empire*, The University of Chicago Press, Chicago, Ill. USA. 1959.

Rubin, Dr. Jordan S. *The Maker's Diet*, Siloam A. Strang Co. 600 Rinehart Rd. Lake Mary, Fla. 32746 USA, 2005.

Russell, Rex MD *What the Bible Says About Healthy Living,* Regal Books, Gospel Light, Box 3875 Ventura, Ca. 93006, USA. 1996.

Settlefield, Barry, *The Christmas Star,* http.settlefield.org

Ruth, Peggy Joyce, *Psalm 91,* Charisma House, 600 Rinehart Rd. Lake Mary, Fla. 32746, USA.

Showers, Dr. Renald. *The Most High God,* The Friends of Israel Gospel Ministry, Inc. Bellmawr, N.J. 08099 USA. 1982.

Schultz, Samuel J. *The Old Testament Speaks,* Harper & Brothers Publishers, New York, 1960.

Stanley, Dr. Charles F. *Courageous Faith,* Howard Books, An imprint of Simon & Schuster, Inc. 1230 Avenue of the Americas, NewYork, N.Y. 10020. USA

Star-Telegraph, Ft. Worth, Texas, February 27, 2012.

Swindoll, Charles R. *Daniel, God's Man for the Moment,* vol I and II, IFL Publishing House, Box 251007, Plano, Texas 75025 USA.

Swindoll, Charles R. *Swindoll's Ultimate Book Of Illustrations &Quotes,* Thomas Nelson Pub. Box 14100, Nashville, Tn. 37214. USA 1998.

Van Diest, John. *Unsolved Miracles,* Multnomah pub. Box 1720, Sisters, Ore. 97759, USA. 1997.

Velikovsky, Immanuel, *Worlds in Collision,* Dell Pub. Co., New York, 1965.

Walvoord, John F. *Daniel,* Moody Press, Chicago, Ill. USA, 1971.

Wood, Leon, *A Commentary On Daniel,* Zondervan, 1973. Grand Rapids, Mich. 49530 USA,

World Book Encyclopedia, (WBE) 1985 edition

Wycliffe Bible Commentary.

Young, Edward J. *The Prophecy of Daniel*, William B. Eerdmans Publishing House, Grand Rapids, Mi., USA, 1970.

ABOUT THE AUTHOR

Douglas Williams was born in 1948 and born-again and baptized into a local Baptist Church in 1957. He graduated from Toccoa Falls Bible College, Toccoa, Ga. USA in 1971 with a B.A. in Theology. He did postgraduate studies and worked with Campus Crusade for Christ at Abraham Baldwin Agricultural College in Tifton, Ga., USA.

He participated in the ministry of the Narkis St. Baptist Church in Jerusalem, Israel from 1987-1991 and has traveled to 34 nations outside the US. He taught English in Mongolia, Thailand, and South Korea. He served as adjunct English professor at Seoul Jangsin University in Gwangju, Gyeonggido, South Korea from 2004-2014 where he taught English and Bible. He preached messages at the Well of Life Presbyterian Church out side Seoul for 4 years. He has participated in prison ministries in Thailand and Philippines and ministered in orphanages in Thailand and South Korea. His purpose in life is to make Yeshua Hamoshiakh (Jesus Christ), our savior and soon coming king known all over the world.

TEST ON DANIEL

1. Daniel is the _____ of prophecy.
   a. wishbone b. skeleton, foundation c. grace d. All are correct

2. The theme of Daniel is
   a. God's protection of Daniel's 3 friends through difficult situations
   b. the integrity of Daniel c. sovereignty of God d. All

3. Which of the following is true?
   a. Daniel and his 3 friends refused to eat the Babylonian food because it included pork.
   b. The 4 men rejected the Babylonian food because it had been offered to idols.
   c. The 4 men rejected the food because it contradicted the diet of Leviticus 11. d . All of the above.

4. Why were Daniel and his friends in Babylon?
   a. They wanted to see the world.
   b. They wanted to witness God's Sovereignty
   c. They were forced to go
   d. All of the above.

5. Why did Babylon conquer Judah?
   a. Judah refused to heed the prophets' warnings
   b. Yahweh gave Judah to Babylon.
   c. Judah worshiped idols.
   d. All of the above.

6. Daniel's name was changed to
   a. Belteshazzar
   b. God is my helper
   c. God is my judge
   d. All of the above

7. Daniel means
   a. God is my judge, deliverer
   b. God is my strength
   c. God is my helper
   d. All of the above

8. Hananiah means
   a. Yahweh's favored one.
   b. Yahweh is my grace
   c. All
   d. None

9. Hananiah's name was changed to
   a. Yahweh's favored one
   b. Shadrach
   c. Meshach
   d. Abednego

10. Azariah means
    a. Yahweh is my strength
    b. Yahweh is my victory
    c. Yahweh is my helper
    d. All of the above

11. Azariah's name was changed to
    a. Yahweh is my helper
    b. Abednego
    c. Mishach
    d. Shadrach

12. Misheal means;
    a. One like Yahweh
    b. One like God.
    c. Strong one
    d. God is my strength
    e. All of the above

13. The 3 men refused to bow before the king's image because
    a. they wanted to be different
    b. they enjoyed attention
    c. they were determined to be obedient to Yahweh's command
    d. they trusted their own strength

14. The 3 men were thrown into the fiery furnace and lived because
    a. they had a great positive attitude
    b. Yahweh protected them from harm
    c. the men trusted their own strength
    d. All of the above

15. In chapter 2
    a. Daniel had a dream and interpreted it for the king.
    b. The king told Daniel the dream and asked Daniel to interpret it.
    c. The king had a dream and forgot it.
    d. The king interpreted the dream for Daniel.

16. When God showed Daniel the dream and interpretation Daniel
    a. was so excited that he immediately told the king
    b. thanked God for the answer with his 3 friends
    c. bowed before the king and gave the answer
    d. All of the above

17. Which of the following is true?
    a. Iron is stronger and more valuable than silver.
    b. Silver is less valuable than gold but more valuable then bronze
    c. Iron is the strongest and therefore the most valuable metal.
    d. Gold is more valuable and therefore stronger than silver.

18. Which of the following is NOT true?
    a. Gold is the most valuable metal
    b. Silver is more valuable than bronze and less valuable than gold.
    c. Iron is the strongest metal.
    d. All of the above e. None of the above

19. King Nebuchadnezzar spent _____ living with the wild animals because he _____.
    a. was humble,
    b. 70 years
    c. 7 weeks.
    d. liked the animals
    e. was proud
    f. enjoyed fresh air
    g. 7 years

20. After living with the animals Nebuchadnezzar became
    a. proud
    b. humble
    c. angry
    d. All

21. King Belshazzar saw the handwriting on the wall and he
    a. humbled himself
    b. was unconcerned
    c. rejected Daniel's help
    d. was scared but did not humble himself
    e. All are correct

22. What did the writing mean?
    a. Babylon will soon be conquered
    b. Babylon is morally corrupt
    c. Babylon will be conquered by the Medes and Persians
    d. All of the above.

23. Why was Belshazzar so arrogant?
    a. He thought it was impossible for Persia to conquer Babylon
    b. He had a 20-year supply of food and plenty of water from the Euphrates
    c. It was impossible for the Persians to climb over the walls and get in
    d. All of the above.

24. How did Persia conquer Babylon?
    a. They climbed over the walls
    b. They diverted the river and marched under the city
    c. They burned the gates down
    d. All of the above.

25. Daniel was in the Lion's den because
    a. he refused to stop praying to God
    b. rejected Babylonian food
    c. refused to bow to idols
    d. All of the above

26. King Darius was_____ that Daniel was in the Lion's den
    a. happy
    b. sad
    c. totally unconcerned
    d. All are correct

27. Which of the following is NOT true?
    a. Daniel was angry for being in the Lion's den
    b. The accusers received what they planned for Daniel
    c, The accusers wanted Daniel dead.
    d. All of the above

28. Why did the satraps want Daniel dead?
    a. Daniel had perfect integrity
    b. Daniel demanded integrity from the satraps
    c. Daniel stopped their stealing from the king
    d. All of the above.

29. Why did the lions not eat Daniel?
    a. They were full with no with appetite
    b. Daniel did not taste good.
    c. The angel of the LORD closed their mouths
    d. All are correct

30. The head of the great image that Nebuchadnezzar dreamed about was made of _____. It represents _____ which had _____ without God.

31. The shoulders and arms were made of _____ representing the 2nd kingdom _____ which had _____without God.

32. The thighs were made of _____ representing the 3rd kingdom of _____ which had _____ without God.

33. The legs were made of _____, representing the 4th kingdom of _____ which had _____ without God.

34. The feet were made of _____ representing the _____ of the 4th kingdom.

35. The rock cut out without hands represents _____ which has _____ without _____.

36. In Daniel's vision of the 4 beasts the winged lion represents _____

37. The bear represents _____

38. The leopard represents _____

39. The very hideous 4th beast represents _____
    a) Rome b) Babylon c) Persia d) Greece e) religion f) power g) wisdom
    h) law j) everything k) Satan m) deterioration p) gold
    n) Christ's kingdom r) bronze s) silver t) iron w) iron & clay

40. The little horn in chapter 7 is
    a. Antichrist b. 11th horn c, beast of Revelation 13 d. All

41. He
    a. plucks 3 horns and dominates the rest
    b. declares war on the saints
    c. boldly speaks against the most high.
    d. All

42. How long does he persecute the saints?
    a. 3.5 years
    b. 7 years
    c. 35 years
    d. we don't know

43. Who is the antichrist?
    a. Adolf Hitler
    b. Josef Stalin
    c. Mao
    d. all above
    e. none above

44. Who is the Ancient of days?
    a. Moses
    b. Elijah
    c. Yahweh
    d. All

45. Who is the Son of Man?
    a. John the Baptist
    b. Jesus Christ
    c. Elijah
    d. All are correct

46. Daniel 8 to the end is written in _____ because _____
    a. Daniel loves the language
    b. it's the holy language in the temple
    c. the message is directed to Israel
    d. Aramaic e. Hebrew f. Greek

47. The goat with the horn between its eyes represents
    a. Alexander
    b. the Greek conqueror
    c. intelligent, powerful ruler
    d. All

48. Alexander, the _____ conqueror, died when he was almost _____ years old.
    a. 33
    b. 39
    c. 23
    d. 43
    e. Russian f. Greek
    g. Persian

49. After Alexander's death his empire
    a. was divided among his 4 generals
    b. continued for hundreds of years
    c. was conquered by Xerxes
    d. ceased to exist

50. Why were barnyard animals used in chapter 8 to represent the 2nd and 3rd kingdoms that conquered Israel?
    a. Unlike the 1st and 4th kingdom they were kind to Israel
    b. They were relatively harmless conquerors
    c. They were kind to those they conquered.
    d. All of the above

51. Which barnyard animal represented Persia?
    a. ram
    b. goat
    c. deer
    d. bear

52. Which barnyard animal represented Greece?
    a. ram
    b. goat
    c. leopard
    d. All are correct

53. Which barnyard animal represents Rome?
    a. ram
    b. cat
    c. dog
    d. None

54. Which barnyard animal represents Babylon?
    a. winged lion
    b. cat
    c. goat
    d None

55. When did Antiochus desecrate the temple?
    a. 70 AD
    b. 168 BC
    c. 165 BC
    d. 32 BC

56. When was the temple cleansed, restored, rectified?
    a. 168 BC
    b. 165 BC
    c. 445 BC
    d. 458 BC

57. The little horn of chapter 8 is
    a. the same as the chapter 7 little horn
    b. Antiochus Epiphanes
    c. Antichrist
    d. All are correct

58. Why is Daniel 9:24-27 called the backbone of prophecy?
    a. It's the only prophecy that reveals when Messiah will come
    b. It's the only prophecy where Moshiakh (Messiah) is used
    c. Both are correct
    d. Neither is correct

59. What motivated Daniel to pray in chapter 9?
    a. He knew that the 70-year captivity was almost fulfilled
    b. He was confident that Yahweh would hear his intercession for Israel.
    c. He knew that Yahweh would fulfil his promise to free Judah after 70 years of captivity.
    d. All are correct

60. Which of the following is true?
    a. Since nothing negative is recorded in Daniel's life we know he lived a sinless life like Jesus Christ
    b. Daniel earnestly interceded for Israel
    c. Daniel repented of his idolatry.
    d. All are correct

61. After his prayer Daniel
    a. received the backbone of prophecy
    b. received an immediate response
    c. received the message from Gabriel
    d. All are correct

62. In Daniel 9:24 how much time was cut off for Israel?
    a. 490 days
    b. 70 years
    c. 483 years
    d. 490 years

63. How many days are in a biblical prophetic year?
    a. 365
    b. 366
    c. 360
    d. 365.25

64. The time was cut off, set aside, determined for
    a. Israel
    b. the church
    c. kingdom of God
    d. All

65. When did the Jews receive permission to rebuild Jerusalem?
    a. 445 BC
    b. 458 BC
    c. 70 AD
    d. 586 BC

66. How much time is there between the command (authorization) to rebuild Jerusalem and the revealing of Messiah?
    a. 490 years
    b. 483 years
    c. 70 years
    d. 490 days

67. Why is Daniel 9:24-27 a very unique prophecy?
    a. It reveals when Messiah will come and rule the world
    b. It reveals when Antichrist will come.
    c. It tells us when Messiah will be revealed to Israel
    d. It reveals when the temple will be rebuilt e. All

68. When was the 70th 7-year period fulfilled?
    a. 32 AD
    b. 34 AD
    c. 70 AD
    d. 39 AD
    e. None

69. What happened in 70 AD?
    a. The Romans destroyed Jerusalem
    b. Titus became emperor
    c. The coming Prince destroyed Jerusalem
    d. All are correct

70. When was Messiah cut off; crucified?
    a. 32 AD
    b. 32 BC
    c. 30 AD
    d. 70 AD
    e. None

71. When will Jesus come again?
    a. We don't know
    b. When the Father chooses
    c. In the future
    d. All

72. How many Jews were killed in the destruction of Jerusalem?
    a. Very few
    b. 1,100,000
    c. 110,000
    d We don't know

73. When will the abomination of desolation take place?
    a. In the middle of the 70th 7-year period
    b. Just before Christ returns
    c. The beginning of the 70th week.

74. What is the abomination of desolation of Daniel 9:27?
    a. Rome's massacre of the Jews in 70 AD.
    b. Israel's rejection of her messiah.
    c. Antichrist's demand to be worshiped as God
    d. All are correct.

75. Which of the following is true?
    a. There's a 70-year gap between the 69th and 70th week of Daniel
    b. There's a 2,000-year gap between the 69th and 70th week of Daniel.
    c. There is no gap between the 69th and 70th week.
    d. The 70th week was completed in 34 AD.

76. In Matthew 24:15 what did Christ warn Israel about concerning Daniel's prophecy?
    a. The abomination of desolation spoken of by Daniel the prophet.
    b. Antiochus Epiphanes
    c. Both are correct

77. In chapter 10 Daniel prayed and
    a. the answer came immediately
    b. the answer came 3 weeks later
    c. Daniel received no answer
    d. the answer came 2 weeks later

78. Why was the answer delayed?
    a. God was too busy with other things
    b. The demonic prince of Persia tried to stop the angel.
    c. Daniel did not fast long enough d. All are correct

79. Which of the following is correct?
    a. Daniel did not write chapter 11 because it was impossible for him to know the detailed history in advance.
    b. Daniel did write 11 as the Holy Spirit inspired him to do so.
    c. Daniel 11 is a fraud and should not be taken seriously.

80. The abomination of desolation of 11:31 is
    a. the same as 9:27
    b. the desolation of the temple by Antiochus Epiphanes in 168 BC
    c. what Christ referred to in Matthew 25:15
    d. All are correct

81. Judas Maccabeus
    a. was a brave leader of guerrilla warfare against Antiochus.
    b. betrayed Christ
    c. became king of Israel.
    d. All are correct

82. Why do many Jewish and Christian theologians believe there is a gap of time between 11:35 and 36?
   a. There are many gaps in Scripture
   b. The prophecies in 1-35 have been fulfilled. The prophecies of 36 to 45 have not.
   c. Verses 36-45 will be fulfilled in the future.
   d. All are correct.

83. What's the significance of "everlasting life" in 12:2?
   a. It's the only time it is used in the Old Testament
   b. It's the 1st clear reference to the resurrection of both the righteous and the wicked.
   c. The righteous sleep peacefully in the dust of the earth.
   d. All are correct.

84. Who is Michael?
   a. Guard of Israel
   b. Archangel
   c. Name means one like God
   d. All

85. Why are 1290 days and 1335 days given in chapter 12?
   a. We do not know.
   b. We will learn after their fulfillment
   c. The extra 30 days are given possibly for a 30-day mourning period after Israel grieves her killing Messiah.
   d. All are correct

86. When was Christ born?
   a) Christmas Day, 1 AD
   b) Christmas Day, 3 BC
   c) Probably late September, 3 BC
   d) Christmas Eve, 1AD

87. Which of the following is correct?
    a) The wise men welcomed Christ at His birth.
    b) Only 3 wise men brought Christ 3 gifts.
    c) Herod was glad to worship the child.
    d) All are correct
    e) None is correct

88. Why was Herod upset after seeing the wise men?
    a. He thought he was the king of the Jews.
    b. His army was not in town to protect him.
    c. He knew the wise men was fierce fighters to be respected
    d. All are correct

89. Which of the following is correct?
    a. We know there were 3 wise men who visited Christ because they brought 3 gifts.
    b. Gold meant they were from Babylon
    c. They brought gold because it signified Christ as king.
    d. All are correct.

90. What's the significance of frankincense?
    a) Frankincense is a herb used in worship services
    b) It signifies Christ as High Priest
    c) It's a valuable herb from the Far East.
    d) All are correct

91. What's the significance of myrrh?
    a) It's an herb used to anoint dead people
    b) It's good for health.
    c) It helps you lose weight
    d) All

92. Why did Joseph take his family to Egypt?
    a) Joseph and Mary were bored with life in Bethlehem
    b) They loved international travel.
    c) Joseph was warned by an angel to flee there.
    d) All are correct

93. How long did they stay in Egypt?
    a. About 7 years
    b) About 7 weeks
    c) Till Herod's death

94. Why is the blood of Christ so important?
    a. It is one way in addition to many other ways to receive salvation.
    b. It is God's only way to receive salvation.
    c. Blood is not important as long as you live a good life.
    d. All of the above.

95. Why should we be careful about what we say?
    a. It's not important to be careful about our words.
    b. The Bible tells us to watch what we say.
    c. Words aren't important.
    d. All of the above.

Korean translation of *Digest of Daniel*40
By 이 득 주 (David Lee)

다니엘서 개관 (다니엘 요약)

이 득 주 편역(編譯)

다니엘서 개관 (다니엘 요약)
다니엘서의 배경 및 개요

요한복음 1:1-3과 골로새서 1:16-20은 예수님의 삶이 2000년 전에 유대 베들레헴에서 시작한 것이 아니라 영원 전부터 성부 하나님과 성령님과 함께 계셨음을 분명하게 보여주고 있다. 성자 예수님은 바로 영원 전부터 천지창조에 동참하고 계신 것이다. 인류 최초의 남자와 여자가 창조된 후 완벽한 낙원에 거했으나 불행히도 인간은 의식적으로, 고의로, 그리고 자의적으로 창조주의 뜻에 거역하는 (딤전2:14) 죄를 지음으로써 온 인류의 죽음을 초래하게 되었다 (고전 15:22). 그러나 야훼 하나님은 하와에게 인류의 구원자, 곧 구세주에 대한 약속을 주신다 (창 3:15).

그럼에도 인간은 너무나 패역하여 하나님이 홍수로 세상을 멸하셨다. 노아는 하나님의 은혜를 입어 그의 가족과 함께 구원을 받았다. 약 400년 후에 하나님은 아브라함을 가나안 땅으로 부르셨고 거기서 그를 통해 '큰 민족' (이스라엘)을 이루며 그 민족을 통해 인류가 복을 누리게 하겠노라(Gen. 12:1-3)고 약속하셨다. 아브라함의 손자인 야곱은 열 두 아들을 두었고 그의 총아인 요셉은 애굽의 통치자가 되었다. 그의 가족은 애굽에서 요셉과 합류하지만 이후 노예 민족로 전락하였다. 모세는 이스라엘 백성을 이끌고 출애굽한 후 그들에게 주님을 섬기도록 간청하였지만 그들은 하나님께 대적하였다 (신 1:26; 9:23-24). 히브리 선지자들은 그들의 죄에 대한 결과에 대해 준엄하게 예언하였지만 그들은 이를 무시하였고 하나님과 선지자들을 대적하였다. BC 8세기의 나지(Nazis)라 할 수 있는 앗수르는 북 이스라엘, 바벨론은 남 유다를 각각 정복하게 되었다.

느부갓네살은 BC 605년, 597년, 586년에 남 유다를 침공하였다. 다니엘, 하나니야, 미사엘, 아자리야와 많은 유대인들이 바벨론으로 끌려갔고 그곳에서 거세됨으로써 그들의 남성성을 상실하였다. 그러나 아이러니컬하게도 이 네 명의 히브리 청년들은 그들의 뜻과 무관하게 환관이 되었음에도 다니엘서를 통해 이스라엘의 '유일하고도 진정한 남성'들로 묘사되고 있다. 그들은 엄청난 억압에도 굴하지 않고 철저하게 우상을 배격하였고 의와 거룩을 위해 당당히 맞섰다.

1장

느부갓네살 왕은 네 명의 청년들이 히브리인의 정체성과 고대 히브리의 풍습 대신에 고대 바벨론의 풍습을 받아들이기를 원했으며 또한 강요했다. 이를위해 느부갓네살은 그들에게 이교도들의 이름을 지어 주었다. '다니엘'(하나님은 심판자요 구원자)은 '벨트사살'로, '하나니야'(야훼의 총아, 하나님은 나의 은혜)는 '사드락'으로, '미사엘'(하나님과 같은 자)은 '메삭'으로, '아지리아'(야훼는 나를 도우시는 자)는 '아벳느고'로 각각 불리었다. 네 명의 청년은 피와 기름이 곁들여진 바벨론 최상급의 고기(돈육)을 제공받았으나 그들은 '하나님이 금하신' 그 음식을 입에 대지 않았다. (레11:1-47; 3:17; 7:22-27; 17:10-14; 19:26; 신 12:16; 사 65:3-4; 66:15-17; 잠 23:1-3; 출 34:14) 그 대신 그 히브리 청년들은 열흘 동안 시험 삼아 채소와 곡식만 제공받았는데 오히려 다른 청년들보다 훨씬 더 건강해졌다. 이후 그들은 성경적인 식단을 계속할 수 있도록 허락을 받게 되었다.

2장

하나님은 느부갓네살에게 매우 흉흉한 꿈을 주셨지만 왕은 이를 곧 잊어버렸다. 그래서 그는 현인(賢人)들, 즉 모든 바벨론 박사들을 소집하여 자신의 꿈을 해석할 뿐만 아니라 그 꿈 자체를 기억할 수 있도록해 줄 것을 요구하였다. 느부갓네살은 현인들이 초자연적인 힘을 통해 자신의 꿈을 해석할 수 있다면 마땅히 자신의 꿈 이야기 자체도 쉽사리 기억나게 해 줄 수 있어야한다는 논리로 자신의 괴이한 요구를 정당화했다. 박사들은 이 요구에 이의를 제기하였지만 왕은 자신의 요구가 존중되지 않을 경우 그들을 죽이겠다고 협박하였다. 마침 동일한 요구를 받은 다니엘은 그의 세 친구와 함께 기도할 수 있도록 3일을 요구하였고 이를 허락받게 되었다. 하나님은 그들의 기도에 응답하셔서 느부갓네살의 꿈과 해석을 보여주셨다. 다니엘과 세 친구는 하나님의 계시에 대해 즉시 감사드리며 주를 찬양한 후 아리옥에게 이 소식을 알렸다. 다니엘은 만왕의 왕이신 주님께 규칙적으로 경배하였고 느부갓네살 왕 앞에서 담대하게 그의 꿈 이야기와 자신의 해몽을 전달하였다. 이에 느부갓네살 왕이 엎드려 다니엘에게 절하였다 (46).

느부갓네살 왕의 꿈에 나타난 거대한 동상은 세계 역사에 대한 예지이다. 금으로 된 머리는 바벨론 제국을 나타낸다. 은으로 된 어깨와 가슴은 바사 제국을 나타내다. 동으로 된 흉부와 허벅지는 알렉산더의 헬라 제국을 나타낸다. 철로 된 다리는 로마 제국을 나타낸다. 쇠와 진흙이 섞인 발은 로마제국의 타락을 나타낸다. 또한 '손대지 아니한 돌'이 나와 그 동상을 겨 같이 부순 후 바람에 불려 간 곳이 없게 한 것(Rev. 11:15; 19:6, 11-21)은 그리스도의 지상 천년 통치를 상징한다.

금, 은 동, 철로 이행하는 과정에서 나타나는 각 금속의 특성은 그 가치는 점점 떨어지고 힘은 증가한다는 것이다. 바벨론은 하나님이 없는 '종교'를 갖고 있었으며 바사는 하나님이 없는 '법'을 갖고 있었다. 헬라는 하나님이 없는 '지혜'를 갖고 있었으며 로마는 하나님이 없는 '힘'을 갖고 있었다. 그러나 결국에는 하나님이 존재하고 사탄이 존재하지 않는 다섯 번째 왕국인 '인간의 손을 대지 않은 돌'이 모든 것을 갖게 될 것이다 (Rev. 20:1-6).

3장

느부갓네살은 꿈을 꾼지 약 18년 후에 바벨론이 여전히 강성해지는 것을 보고 자신의 제국이 은이나 동이나 철의 왕국에 의해 지배되지 않고 영원할 것이라고 생각하였다. 결국 그는 온통 금으로 된 동상을 만들어 사람들로 그 앞에게 절하고 경배하도록 강요하였다. 하나냐, 미사엘, 아사리야는 이를 거절하였고 이로 인해 평소보다 일곱 배나 뜨겁게 달구어진 풀무속으로 던져졌다. 세 명의 히브리인을 던져버린 느부갓네살의 부하들은 나중에 불속에서 죽게 되지만 세 명의 용감한 히브리 청년들은 성자 하나님께서 그들과 함께 하심으로 불에 타지 않고 살아나게 되었고 더욱 창성해졌다. 풀무 불이 태운 것은 그들을 묶은 밧줄 뿐이었다. 이를 목격한 느부갓네살왕은 또 다른 죽음의

칙령을 선포하게 된다. 이번엔 사드락과 메삭과 아벳느고의 하나님께 경솔히 말하는 자들에 대한 죽음의 선고였다 (29).

4장

4장의 저자는 느부갓네살이다. 그는 모든 시대 모든 열방과 모든 민족들에 대한 하나님의 절대 주권을 그 자신의 신학으로 선언하게 된다. 그는 또 다른 꿈을 꾸게 되는데 그의 사기꾼 박사들과 술객들은 여전히 그 꿈을 해몽하지 못한다. 그러나 다니엘은 다시 한 번 그의 꿈을 해석해 준다.

나무 한 그루가 무성하게 자라지만 돌연 뿌리만 남긴 채 베임을 당한다. 그리고는 짐승의 심장이 인간의 심장을 7년간 대신하게된다.

다니엘의 해몽은 다음과 같다. 무성한 나무는 느부갓네살이다(잠 16:18; 29:23; 8:13; 11:2; 벧전 5:5b-6; 눅 18:14). 그는 나무처럼 곧 베임을 받아 수치를 당할 것이며 7년동안 짐승과 더불어 짐승처럼 살 것이다. 다니엘은 그에게 임할 심판이 경감될 수 있도록 죄를 회개하라고 경고한다. 그러나 다니엘의 요구는 무시되었고 극도로 교만해진 왕은 정신을 잃어버리고 예언대로 7년동안 짐승들과 함께 짐승처럼 살게 된다. 마침내 일곱 해가 지나 그는 제 정신을 차리게 되고 성경에서 가장 위대한 신학적 진리를 선포하게 된다(4:2-3; 34-37).

5장

벨사살 왕은, 부친 느부갓네살처럼 교만하고 자랑하기를 좋아하지만 부친과 달리 하나님 앞에서 자신을 낮추지 못했다. 그는 선왕에게 무슨 일이 잘 일어났는지 알고 있었지만 여전히 대담하게 야훼 이스라엘의 하나님을 모욕하였다. 그는 사람들에게 예루살렘 성전의 제기(祭器)로 술을 마신 후 광란의 난교(亂交) 파티를 벌이도록 하는 등 온갖 추태를 서슴지 않았다. 결국 그는 갈라디아서 6장 7절의 말씀, 즉 "스스로 속이지 말라 하나님은 업신여김을 받지 아니하시나니 사람이 무엇으로 심든지 그대로 거두리라"의 진리를 자신의 삶을 통해 뼈저리게 배우게 되었다.

갑자기 한 손이 나타나 벽에 글을 쓰자 그의 분위기가 180도로 바뀌게 되었다. 벨삿살은 얼굴이 창백해지면서 두 무릎을 꿇었다. 바벨론의 현자들은 여느 때처럼 무력하였다. 곧 다니엘이 소환되었고 그는 즉시 왕에게 메시지를 전하였다.

'메네'(Mene)는 하나님이 바벨론 제국의 시대를 세어서 그것을 끝나게 하셨음을 의미한다. '데겔'(Tekel)은 벨사살 왕이 도덕의 저울에 달려 부족함이 드러났음을 의미한다. 한 마디로 그는 도덕적으로 너무나 결함이 많은 왕이었다. '베레스'(Peres)는 바벨론이 나뉘어서 메대와 바사에게 바쳐졌음을 의미한다.

유브라데 강 줄기를 돌려놓은 후, 다리우스와 그의 군대는 조용히 성벽 안으로 잠입하였고 곧 성안으로 무혈 진입하게 되었다. 메대와 바사가 바벨론을 정복하면서 벨삿살은 죽음을 맞이한다.

6장

다리오왕은 다니엘이 나무랄데 없으며, 거의 완벽한 성품을 지닌 사람임을 파악했다. 그는 또한 120명의 방백(지방 총독)들이 기본적으로 진실성이 결여된 인물들임도 알았다. 결국 왕은 다니엘을 방독들을 다스리는 세 총리 중 1명으로 임명하였다. 다니엘은 방백의 요건이 진실성인만큼 일부 비양심적인 방백들이 왕의 세입을 도적질 하는 일을 원천적으로 불가능하게까지는 아니드라도, 적어도 상당히 어렵게 만들었다. 자연히 방백들은 다니엘을 증오하였고 그를 제거하고 싶어했지만 여의치 못했다.

그들이 다니엘의 흠을 찾을 수 있었던 유일한 단서는 그의 '낯선 종교'였다. 그들은 왕의 허영심을 자극하였고 그는 손쉽게 그들의 함정에 걸려들었다. 방백들의 부추김으로 왕은 한 달 동안 신으로 선포되었고 이 기간 동안 왕 외에 어느 누구에게든 무엇을 구하는 일체의 행위를 '불법'으로 선포하였으며 결국 변개치 못할 금령에 어인을 찍게 되었다(15; 에8:8).

다니엘은 왕의 금령에도 전혀 요동치 않았다. 그는 사자 굴에 던져질지언정 단 하루라도 하나님과 자신과의 풍성하고 부드럽고 친근한 관계를 유지하는 것이 하나님 없이 사는 것보다 훨씬 중요한 것임을 알았다. 그는 조용히 그러나 대담하게 '여전한 방식으로' 평소 그가 해오던 일을 계속하였다 (시 55:17-18).

다리오왕은 자신이 비양심적이고 부패하고 한심한 방백들의 덫에 걸려 다니엘을 죽여야 하는 상황에 처하게 되었음을 깨닫고 마음이 무너졌지만 불행히도 그는 스스로 자신의 법령을 변개할 수 없는 입장이 되었다.

왕이 밤새 뜬눈으로 뒤척이는 동안 다니엘은 사자굴 속에서도 편히 잘 수 있었다. 다리오 왕은 아침에 다니엘의 목소리를 듣고 뛸 듯이 기뻤다. 이제 굶주린 사자들의 먹이는 다니엘이 아니라 그를 고발했던 자들과 그들의 가족이 되었고 덕분에 사자들은 오랜만에 포식을 하게 되었다. 다리오왕은 느부갓네살이 3장에서 그랬던 것처럼 백성들에게 죽음의 경고를 통해 다니엘의 하나님(26)을 경외하도록 선포함으로써 자신의 신학을 재확인하게 되었다(26-27).

3장부터 6장까지의 교훈은 분명하다. 예수 그리스도와 함께 타는 풀무에 던져지는 것이 왕의 명령을 수행하는 고관대작들 중의 하나가 되는 것 보다 훨씬 낫다는 것이다. 또한 주의 천사들과 함께 사자 굴에서 자는 것이 거짓 고발자나 또는 그의 가족이 되는 것보다 낫다는 것이다. 하나님의 뜻은 모든 그리스도인들에게 그것이 타는 풀무든 사자 굴이든 항상 가장 안전한 장소를 제공한다.

7장

다니엘서의 첫 여섯 장은 거의 역사서인 반면 나머지 여섯 장은 예언서로만 구성되어있다. 이러한 관점은 다니엘서 2장의 예언을 보다 세밀하게 이해할 수 있도록 도와준다. 하나님의 관점에서 2장의 "인간의 손으로 빚은 크고 광채 나는 신상(神像)"은 단지 들짐승(눅 16:15)에 불과한 것이다. 하늘의 네 바람이 바다로 불어오자 거기서 네 짐승이 나온다. 여기서 바다는 이방 세계, 즉 인간의 세계를 대표한다 (사 17:12-13; 계 17:1, 15). 날개 달린 사자는 바벨론의 황금 제국을, 곰은 바사의 은(銀)제국을 상징한다.

머리 넷 달린 표범같은 짐승은 헬라의 동(銅) 제국을 상징한다. 네 개의 머리는 알렉산더의 급작스런 죽음 이후 네 개로 분할된 제국을 나타낸다. 형언할 수 없을 만큼 흉측한 네 번째 짐승은 철(鐵)의 로마 제국을 나타낸다. 열개의 뿔은 2장에 나오는 열개의 발톱처럼 그리스도의 재림 직전에 실현될 로마제국의 분리를 상징한다.

작은 뿔(적그리스도, 계시록 13장의 짐승)은 열개의 뿔에서 나와 세개의 뿔(제국들)을 뿌리 뽑고 나머지 일곱개를 지배한다. 또한 그것은 하나님을 능멸하고 시간과 율법을 바꾸려하며 하나님의 백성을 3년 반 동안 핍박한다 (7:25; 계 13:5-6). 9절에서는 옛적부터 항상 계신이가 통치를 시작한다. 성경에서 야훼 하나님이 이렇게 묘사되는 유일한 부분이 바로 이 절이다. 하나님은 영이시다 (요 4:24) 그러나 다니엘은 영원히 거하시는 '지존 무상'하신 (사 57:15) 분의 이러한 육체적 현현(顯現)앞에 압도될 뿐이다.

그는 이 세상의 제국을 인자(人子)이신 예수그리스께(고전 15:25; 마 24:30; 25:31; 26:64; 시 2:5-12; 눅 1:32-33; 계 11:15; 19:11-21) 넘긴다. 세상 죄를 지고 가는 연약하고 동정심 많은 어린 양(요 1:29, 사 53:7)은 전능하신 하나님의 극렬한 진노의 포도주 틀을 밟는(계 19:15) 포효하는 유다의 사자이기도 하다.

다니엘서의 비전은 존귀한 사자로 시작하여 형언할 수 없이 흉악한 짐승으로 끝난다. 동상은 금으로 시작하여 흙으로 끝난다. 하나님은 인간이 더욱 개선되기보다 쇠퇴하고 있음을 보여주고 있다(딤후 3:13). 미래에 대한 유일한 희망은 그가 세상 왕국의 형상을 부수어 바람에 날리어 영원히 사라질 고운 가루로 만들어 버리듯이 인간의 업적이 아니라 그리스도의 재림(사 48:22)일 뿐이다.

이 비전으로 다니엘은 중심에 근심하였고(15) 낯빛이 변하였지만 (28) 하나님은 그에게 새 힘을 주시어 더 많은 계시를 받게 하셨다 (사 40:29-31).

8장

다니엘서는 1장 1절부터 2장 3절까지 히브리어로 기록되어있다. 2장 4절부터 7장 28절까지는 이방 세계의 국제어라 할 수 있는 아람어로 기록되어있는데 그 이유는 이 부분의 메시지가 주로 이방세계를 위한 것이기 때문이다. 8장부터 마지막장까지의 메시지는 이스라엘을 향한 것이기에 다시 히브리어로 기록되어 있다. 이 예언은 2장과 7장에 나오는 둘째와 셋째 왕국에 대해 다루고 있다. 바사를 상징하는 은곰 왕국은 수양으로 표현되고 있다. 헬라를 상징하는 동 표범은 염소로 묘사되고 있다.

수양은 2개의 뿔을 갖고 있다. 한 뿔은 나중에 나와서 다른 하나보다 더 길게 자라난다. 긴 뿔은 메대바사 시대에 메대를 장악했던 바사를 나타낸다. 양쪽 눈 사이에 뿔이 난 염소는 서방에서 출현하여 맹렬하게 수양을 공격한다. 양쪽 눈은 지성을, 뿔은 힘을 상징한다. 염소는 전 시대에 걸쳐 가장 지적인 정복자였던 알렉산더를 상징한다. 그의 3만 5천 병사들은 여러 차례의 중대한 전투에서 바사의 30만 대군을 손쉽게 물리쳤다. 지면에 발이 닿지 않는 염소의 발은 곧 알렉산더의 엄청난 정복 속도를 말한다. 그는 3년만에 바사를, 그리고 8년만에 인도에 이르는 전 영역을 정복했다. 그러나 염소의 뿔은 곧 사라지고 4개의 다른 뿔이 나타난다. 이는 알렉산더의 요절(夭折)과 그의 제국을 분할 통치하는 4명의 장군을 의미한다. 그는 문란한 성생활을 즐겼고 스스로 하나님처럼 예배받기 원했으며 결국 삼십삼세의 나이에 취중 사망하였다.

7장에 등장하는 사나운 짐승들과 달리 8장의 바사와 헬라(그리스)는 상대적으로 그다지 해롭지 않은 가축들로 묘사되고 있다. 무엇 때문일까? 이 두 제국은 이스라엘을 제외한 다른 정복국가들에게는 공포의 대상이었지만 유독 이스라엘에게는 별로 직접적인 해를 끼치지 않았으며 심지어 어떤 면에서는 친절하기까지 했다. 바사는 이스라엘이 고토(故土)로 귀환하여 성전과 예루살렘을 재건하도록 허락했다. 알렉산더는 하나님을 대신하는 대제사장을 예루살렘에서 만났을 때 그에게 예를 갖추어 절하였다. 그는 또한 제단에 제물을 바쳤으며 제사장이 그에게 바사와의 일전과 관련한 다니엘의 예언을 전해주었을 때 용기백배하기도 했다. 알렉산더는 그의 제국 내에 거하는 유대인을 보호해 주기로 약속하기도 했다.

바벨론과 로마는 여러 가지 명백한 이유로 무해한 가축과는 거리가 먼 존재로 묘사되고 있다. 그들은 이스라엘을 가장한 혹독하게 다루었다. 그들은 성전과 도시를 파괴했으며 유대인에게 망명 생활을 하게 하였다. (대하 36:17-21; 눅19:43-44; 21:20-24). AD

70년에는 1,100,000명 이상의 유대인들이 로마군에 의해 무참히 학살되었다.

두 번째 작은 뿔

8장에 나오는 두 번째 작은 뿔은 7장의 작은 뿔과는 다르다. 7장의 작은 뿔은 네 번째 제국(로마)의 통치기간 중에 10개의 다른 뿔 가운데 나타나 3개의 뿔을 뽑아버리고 나머지 7개의 뿔을 다스렸다. 8장의 작은 뿔은 원래의 4개 뿔과 함께 자라나 다른 것을 대체하지는 않았다. 이 작은 뿔은 23절에 나오는 시리아의 셀류코스 왕조의 8대 왕인인 안디오코스 4세 에피파네스를 나타낸다. 그는 자신이 곧 "현현하시는 하나님"임을 자처함으로써 명백한 적그리스도(단 7:25; 12:11, 계13)의 효시가 되었다. 그도 처음에는 유대인과 우호적인 관계를 가졌지만 다른 경쟁자를 물리치고 선출된 메넬라우스를 유다의 대제사장으로 임명했던 BC 171년 이후부터 이스라엘을 핍박하기 시작했다. 적법한 대제사장이었던 오니아스 3세는 분노하였지만 안디오커스의 고위 관리에 의해 피살되었고 이로 인해 유대인의 분노는 극에 달했다. 결국 유대인의 분노 밖으로 표출되었고 이에 안디오커스는 적극적인 탄압으로 대응하였다. 이 상황은 그가 BC. 164년 그의 임종까지 계속되었다.

13절에서 '한 거룩한 자'(천사)가 다른 천사에게 묻는다. "작은 뿔로 인해 성소가 더럽혀진 일 때문에 도대체 언제까지 예물 드리는 일을 중단해야 하겠습니까?(필자 역). 이에 대해 다른 천사는 14절에서 '이천 삼백 주야(晝夜, 히. 에리브보케르)가 지난 후에야 성소가 정결하게 복원될 것이라고 답변하고 있다.

BC 168년 기실월 25일에 안디오커스는 예루살렘 성전을 철저히 유린했다. 그는 제단에 암퇘지를 바쳤고 성소 곳곳에 돼지 기름을 뿌린 후 제우스 동상을 제단에 세웠고 안식일과 할례를 금했으며 유대인들에게 돼지고기, 즉 '멸망하게 하는 가증한 것(단11:31)'을 먹도록 강요했다.

이스라엘은 매일 아침저녁으로 제물을 올리도록 가르침을 받았다(출29:38-42; 2, 대하2:4). 성경의 여러 곳에서 '지속적인, 정규적인'을 뜻하는 '타미드'(tamid)라는 히브리 단어가 '제사'(단8:11,

12, 13; 11:31; 12:11)를 뜻하는 단어와 별개로 사용되고 있다. 비록 히브리 성경에는 '타미드' 와 '제사'가 나란히 쓰이고 있지는 않지만 역자들은 원래의 의미를 살려 '타미드' 뒤에 '제사'란 단어를 합당하게 삽입하고 있다. 문맥에 따르면 8장 14절의 '아침 저녁'은 8:11, 12, 13: 11;31; 12:11에 나오는 '규칙적인'이란 단어와 동일한 의미의 형용사로 쓰이고 있으며 '제사'란 단어를 필요로 하고 있음을 강력하게 시사하고 있다. 결국 성전은 1150일 동안, 이천 삼백회의 '아침과 저녁 제사'를 놓친 셈이다.

BC 168년 기실월 25일에 일어난 성전 침탈사건 후 안디오커스는 그의 부하를 모딘(Modin)에게 보내어 유대 제사장 맛다디아 (Mattathias)로 하여금 그리스 신에게 제물을 마치도록 강요하였다. 그는 용감하게 이를 거절하였을 뿐 아니라 이 명령에 굴복한 지조없는 유대인들과 왕의 대신과 군인들을 살해하였다. 뒤이어 게릴라전이 시작되었고 그의 사후 그의 아들 유다 마카비우스 (Judas Maccabeus)가 유대를 승리로 이끌었다. 성전은 정화되었고 성전 침탈 이후 정확히 3년, 즉 BC 165년 기실월 25일에 원래의 목적대로 회복되었다. 안디오커스는 성전 침탈 약 두 달 전에 야훼의 제단을 철거하였는데 여기에 삼 년을 더하면 정확히 그동안 실종되었던 1150일 이천 삼백 주야의 제사일 수가 나오게 된다.

25절에서 천사는 작은 뿔이 '사람의 손으로 말미암지 아니하고 깨지리라'고 말하고 있다(25). 안디오커스는 창자에 충이 생겨 급속히 자라는 바람에 그의 살점이 떨어져 나가는 불치의 역병에 걸리게 되었다. 그의 고통은 극심하였고 악취가 심해 아무도 주변에 접근하지 못했다. 그의 고통은 오랫동안 그를 괴롭혔으며 마침내 그는 자신의 고통이 유대인과 예루살렘에게 가했던 그의 무자비한 처사에 대한 보응임을 깨닫게 되었다.

다니엘은 소진된 상태로 수일동안 앓았지만 하나님은 그에게 기력을 회복시키시어 그의 가장 중요한 예언이자 다니엘서 9장의 골격이 되는 예언을 받을 수 있도록 인도하셨다.

9장

이 장에서 다니엘은 사도 바울처럼 이스라엘을 위해 전심으로 중보하고 있다. 또한 가브리엘 천사는 야훼의 보좌로부터 다니엘 예언의 요체이자 골격인 24-27절의 예언을 갖고 찾아온다.

70주, 즉 7의 70 배수인 490일이 이스라엘과 유대 민족을 위해 따로 떼어진 채 설정되어 있다. (490일에 대한 여섯가지 이유에 대한 상세한 설명은 본서,『고결한 예언자, 다니엘』을 참조할 것.)

메시아 도래에 대한 카운트 다운의 시작점(terminus a quo)은 BC. 445년 니산월 1일(3월14일), 즉 아닥사스다 왕 제이십년(느 2:1, 8)이다. 이전에는 예루살렘 중건을 위한 어떠한 형태의 허락도 내려진 바 없었다. 그런데 에스라서에서 유대인은 예루살렘 성전을 재건하고 장식할 수 있는 유일한 권한을 부여 받았다. 따라서 에스라서에 나오는 여타 날짜 대신에 'BC. 445년 니산월 1일 (3월14일)'(느 2:1)을 70주 카운트 다운의 유일한 시작점으로 받아들여야 한다.

이 중요한 시간대의 예언은 크게 7주, 62주, 1주의 세 파트로 나뉜다. 예루살렘 성벽을 재건하는데는 52일이 소요되었지만 요새를 완전히 재건하는데는 7주(49년)가 소요되었다. 이후 62주(434년)만에 이스라엘의 메시아가 출현하였다. (합산하면 69주 또는 483년).

성경의 연도는 태양년(365.2422일)이나 태음년(354일)이 아니라 예언년(360일)에 기초하고 있다(계 12:6, 14; 11:2-3; 13:5; 단7:25; 12:7). 위의 구절에서 우리는 '때'의 분류가 3년 반, 42달, 또는 1260일에 해당함을 알 수 있다. 바벨론을 포함한 대부분의 고대 달력은 12개의 30일 월력으로 구성되어 있다.

아브라함은 이러한 달력으로 그의 가족을 지켰다. 483을 360일의 성경년일로 곱하면 173,880일이 나온다. 이 173,880일에 BC. 445년 니산월 1일(3월14일)이 더해지면 AD. 32년 니산월 10일(4월6일)이 나온다. 바로 이 날 (예수 그리스도께서 예루살렘에 입성하시던 종려주일) 예수님은 자신이 이스라엘의 메시아임을 선언하셨으며 백성들의 호산나 찬양(눅19:28-40)을 합당하게 받으셨다.

주님은 사람들이 다니엘의 483주의 예언이 성취되었던 바로 이 날 (42절)이 그들의 평화의 시기에 속한다는 사실을 전혀 인식하지 못하고 있음을 보시며 도시를 바라보며 눈물을 흘리셨다.

예수님은 이스라엘과 세상에 평화를 주기 위해 오셨지만 유감스럽게도 유대인들은 그의 평화 제의를 거절하였다. 평화의 왕이신 예수 그리스도가 거절되었기에 끔찍한 황폐함이 도래해야만 했다. 이스라엘이 예수 그리스도를 통한 하나님의 방문을 알아보는 것을 거절하였기 때문에 AD. 70년 로마의 끔찍한 이스라엘 파괴 (43-44절)가 불가피하게 되었다.

메시아가 이스라엘에 출현하신 이후 그는 거절과, 무소유, 그리고 잔혹한 죽음(26, 사53:8)을 차례로 겪어야 했다. 이후 세상의 왕으로 등극하는 미래의 시민(로마군사)이 도시와 성소를 파괴하게 된다. AD. 70년 타이투스(Titus) 치세 때 로마가 '돌 위에 돌 하나도 남기지 않고' 성전을 무너뜨리고(눅 19:43-44), 백십만 명의 유대인을 학살한 후 나머지는 노예로 팔아버린다. 밀만(Milman) 은 그의『유대사 2권』(History of the Jews, Vol. 2, p.77)에서 이 사건에 대해 다음과 같이 잘 요약하고 있다.

"이 유례없는 잔혹사에 피가 얼어붙으며 심장이 멎을 지경이다. 혹 절망적인 위로라도 찾는다면 이 사건이 역사가에 의해 과장되었길 바라는 것 뿐이다. 그러나 역사의 실체를 파헤친 사람들은 이나마의 여지도 용인하지 않는다. 이러한 잔혹사는 인간의 적나라한 야수성의 면모 그대로 받아들이는 수밖에 없다."

제 70번째주 (이스라엘을 위해 남겨진 마지막 7년)

장차 도래할 '한 왕'은 메시야 임금이 아니다. 하나님의 언약은 언제나 영원하시다 (스16:60; 37:26; 렘 32:40; 사 61:8). 그러므로 메시야가 이스라엘과 이 마지막 7년의 언약을 맺는다는 것 자체가 그분의 성품과 일치하지 않는다. 유대의 지도자들은 처음부터 그를 거절하였으므로 메시야와 이스라엘 사이에는 사실상 어떠한 합의도 없었다.

메시야 임금과 세상 임금은 전적으로 다르며 정반대이다. 메시야는 이스라엘과 세상을 위해 자기의 목숨까지 제물로 내어 주는 유다의 왕이시다 (롬 5:6-8; 요 10:10; 11:49-52; 사. 53:8). 이스라엘의 통치자인 메시야는 오직 초대받을 때에만 보좌에 오르실 것이다 (시 118:26). 반면 세상 임금은 자기의 이기적인 목적을 위해 이스라엘과 인류를 착취하고 파괴하고자 하는 로마의 왕이다(슥 11:16). 유대인들은 유대의 진정한 임금이신 예수 그리스도가 십자가형을 당해야 한다고 주장했으며 이 요청은 받아들여졌다. 그들은 또한 가이사를 그들의 왕으로 요구했으며 이 또한 받아들여졌다 (요 19:15-16). 불행히도 그들은 미래의 로마황제, 즉 적그리스도를 그들의 구원자로 환영할 것이며 그로 인해 더 많은 심각한 결과를 초래할 것이다.

적그리스도인 장차 올 '한 왕'(26)은 7장 25절에 나오는 '작은 뿔' 과 요한 계시록 13장에 나오는 '짐승'을 가리킨다. 예수 그리스도가 완벽하게 야훼 하나님 아버지(요 14:7-11, 31)를 가리키듯이 적그리스도는 철저하게 사단을 나타낸다. 예수님은 마태복음 24 장 4-5절('많은 사람이 내 이름으로')과 요한복음 5장 43절('다른 사람이 자기 이름으로')을 통하여 거짓 메시야에 대해 경고하였다. 유대인들은 하늘 아버지의 이름으로 오신 분을 거절한 대신 거짓 선지자들을 환영하였고 무엇보다도 장차 올 가장 큰 거짓 선지자, 곧 자기 이름으로 올 적그리스도, 장차 올 '한 왕'을 영접할 것이다. 그는 이스라엘과 '한 이레 동안의 언약'(70번째 주의 마지막 7년, 곧 490년 동안의 언약)을 정할 것이다. 그는 재건된 성전에서 제사와 예물을 허락하지만 3년 반 후에, 즉 7년 절반에는 이스라엘과 맺었던 언약을 파기하며 멸망의 가증한 것과 미운 물건을 세움으로써 그의 사단의 본성을 드러낼 것이다 (단 9:27; 12:1; 마 24:15-21). 바울은 적그리스도를 성전에 들어가 예배 받기를 요구할 '불법의 사람, 멸망의 아들'(살후 2:3-10, 계13:13)로 묘사하고 있다. 물론 경건한 유대인들은 두려워하여 그를 예배하기를 거부할 것이다. 이로 인해 그들은 마지막 70주(이스라엘에게 돌려진 490년)의 마지막 3년 반 동안 적그리스도의 분노를 사게 될 것이다(계12). 이것이 바로 '대환란' (마 24:21; 단 12:1)이요 '야곱의 환란의 때'(렘 30:7) 인 것이다. 다니엘서 12장 1절은 이에 대해 이스라엘에 도래할 최악의 대환란이 될 것이라고 예언하고 있다. 예수님은 다니엘의 메시지를 확증하시며 유대인들에게 대환란 기간 동안 살아갈

지침을 주고 계신다. 또한 예수님은 제자들에게 이 대환란이 끝난 직후 영광중에 돌아올 것이라 말씀하신다 (마 24:29-31). 이후 그리스도는 이스라엘이 그를 메시야요 왕으로 섬길(마 24:29-31; 슥 12:10-14) 새천년 동안, 그리고 이후 영원히 세상을 통치하실 것이다. 요한계시록 21장과 22장에서 이 영광된 새 왕국의 자세한 묘사를 볼 수 있다.

이천년의 간극

69번째주와 70번째주 사이에 분명히 이천년의 간극이 있는데 이 점 이상하게 보일 수 있다. 왜 그것은 다른 모든 주처럼 69번째 주 직후에 오지 않을까? 히브리 예언자들은 그리스도의 초림과 재림사이에 존재하는 간극을 이해하지 못했다. 여러 번에 걸쳐 선지자들은 그리스도의 초림과 재림 사건을 동시에 예언하고 있다 (시2, 사 9:6; 11:1-3; 35:4-6; 슥 9:9-10). 이사야 61:1-2이 가장 좋은 예이다.

"주 여호와의 신이 내게 임하셨으니 이는 여호와께서 내게 기름을 부으사 가난한 자에게 아름다운 소식을 전하게 하려 하심이라 나를 보내사 마음이 상한 자를 고치며 포로 된 자에게 자유를, 갇힌 자에게 놓임을 전파하며 여호와의 은혜의 해와 우리 하나님의 신원의 날을 전파하여 모든 슬픈 자를 위로하되"

누가복음 4:18-19에서 예수님은 이 구절을 인용하시다 2번째 절에서 돌연 멈추시고 다음과 같이 선언하신다. "이 글이 오늘날 너희 귀에 응하였느니라! (21)"왜 예수님은 모든 구절을 다 인용하시지 않았을까? 이유는 분명하다. 그는 초림 시에 보응의 날을 선포하기 위해 오시지 않았다. 이 일은 예수님의 재림 시에 있을 것이다 (나훔1:2-3; 살후1:8). 이 예언뿐 아니라 다른 예언들과 마찬가지로 다니엘서 9:24-27에도 간극 존재하는데 이는 놀랄 일이 못된다.

예수 그리스도와 그를 따르는 무리들을 위한 장차 올 영광에 대해서, 그리고 사단과 그의 모든 악한 추종자에게 올 심판에 관해서는 요한계시록 19장에 22장까지 상세히 묘사되어있다.

10 장

다니엘이 기도하며 금식하는 동안 천사가 즉시 답변을 갖고 그를 찾아온다. 그러나 그가 다니엘에게 오기까지는 3주가 소요되는데 이는 그가 영적전투를 치르기 위해 대천사 미가엘의 도움을 구해야하기 때문이다. 다니엘처럼 우리 모든 그리스도인들도 하늘 아버지의 사랑받는 자녀(엡 1:6)이지만 때로 응답이 지연될 수 있다. 그러나 결코 낙심하지 말고 오직 하나님만 바라보아야 한다 (시 27:14; 히 2:3; 갈 6:9; 창 25:21-26).

11 장

데이빗 캠벨(David Campbell)은 다니엘서 11:1-35에서 134 개의 세부적인 예언들이 성취되었다고 주장한다. 하나님은 전지(全知)하시다. 그는 처음부터 끝까지 모든 것을 알고 계시며 미래의 세부 사건까지 쉽게 계시하실 수 있다. 다니엘서 11장이 바로 이를 묘사하고 있는데 아쉽게도 다니엘서의 신빙성을 의심하는 사람들도 있다. 안타까운 일이다. 예수님도 다니엘서의 신빙성을 의심하지 않으셨으며 이 메시지를 사용하여 제자를 가르치기도 하였다 (마 24:15). 예수님이 인정하신 것을 우리도 인정해야하지 않겠는가?

12 장

이 장은 인류의 부활에 관한 가르침이 처음으로 묘사되어 있는 곳이다 (2). 대천사 미가엘은 이스라엘의 의로운 승리에 대해 확고한 태도를 취하고 있다. 8절에서 다니엘이 "이 모든 일의 결국이 어떠하겠삽나이까?"하고 묻자 주님은 "염려하지마라. 내 때에 내가 이룰 것이다. 내가 만사를 다스린다는 것을 알고 네 일상으로 돌아가 평강을 누리라"고 답변하신다 (필자 주).

사도행전 1장 6-7에서 예수님의 제자들이 동일한 질문을 했을 때 예수님도 이와 같이 대답하였다. "때와 기한은 아버지께서 자기의 권한에 두셨으니 너희의 알 바 아니요 오직 성령이 너희에게 임하시면 너희가 권능을 받고 예루살렘과 온 유대와 사마리아와 땅 끝까지 이르러 내 증인이 되리라 하시니라"(행1:6-8)

오늘날 우리가 동일한 질문을 할 때마다 하나님은 동일한 방식으로 대답하신다. 우리는 그리스도의 재림의 때에 몰두하기보다 지금 우리가 처해 있는 곳에서, 그리고 땅 끝까지 복음을 전하기만 하면 된다. 우리는 그리스도의 재림에 대비하여 매일의 삶을 살아야 하며 아울러 우리 생각에 곧 오셔야할 때임에도 오시지 않으실 경우를 대비하여 장래를 계획하며 살아야 한다.

그리스도의 초림과 관련한 다니엘의 모든 예언이 문자 그대로 성취된 만큼 아직 성취되지 않은 그리스도의 재림에 관한 그의 예언 또한 성취될 것이라 믿어야 한다. 예수 그리스도는 분명 이 땅에 재림하셔서 새천년동안, 그리고 이후 영원토록 의로운 통치를 수행하실 것이다. 그리스도를 구주로 영접하는 자는 영광과 행복으로 충만한 천국 공동체의 일부가 될 것이다.

여러분은 이미 그리스도께 나오셨습니까? 그렇지 않다면 지금 그 분께 나오십시오. 그러면 모든 죄를 사함 받고(시 103:12; 미가 7:19) 모든 지각에 뛰어난 하나님의 평강이 여러분의 마음에 임하실 겁니다 (빌 4:7; 요 14:27; 16:33). 여호와 하나님은 아들되신 예수 그리스도의 이름을 믿고 그 분을 찾는 모든 자를 기꺼이 받아들이시는 분이십니다 (벧후 3:9; 요 3:16; 6:37; 10:10; 마 11:28-30; 계 22:17). 그 분께서는 우리가 회개하고 그 분을 향해 돌아설 때 탕자의 부친처럼 우리를 향해 달려 나오시며 기쁘게 맞이하실 겁니다(눅 15:20). 주님의 이 위대한 초청(마11:28-30)에 응하시어 진정한 안식과 영원한 평강을 누리시기 바랍니다.

역자(譯者) 소개

이 득 주

· 성균관대학교 문학박사 (영어영문학)
· 성균관대학교 강사 (교양영어, 영미희곡)
· 연세대학교 강사 (고급영어, TOEIC)
. 경희대학교 강사 (영어산문, 교양영어)

· 안양대학교 강사 (교양영어, 셰익스피어)
· 서울장신대 교양학부(영어) 조교수

....

· 현 김천대학교 국제어학원 교수부장
· 현 우리들 교회(휘문고) 주일설교 동시통역